POWER SEWING
STEP-BY-STEP

POWER SEWING
STEP-BY-STEP

SANDRA BETZINA

The Taunton Press

Cover photographer: Jack Deutsch

Publisher: Jim Childs
Acquisitions Editor: Jolynn Gower
Editor: Susan Huxley
Assistant Editor: Sarah Coe
Copy Editor: Elaine Burke
Art Director: Paula Schlosser
Cover and Interior Designer: Carol Singer
Layout Artists: Susan Fazekas, Amy Bernard-Russo
Photographers: Jack Deutsch, Scott Phillips, Judi Rutz
Indexer: Lynda Stannard

Taunton
BOOKS & VIDEOS
for fellow enthusiasts

Printed in Malaysia
10 9 8 7 6 5 4 3 2 1

The Taunton Press, Inc., 63 South Main Street, PO Box 5506, Newtown, CT 06470-5506
e-mail: tp@taunton.com

Distributed by Publishers Group West

Library of Congress Cataloging-in-Publication Data
Betzina, Sandra.
    Power sewing step-by-step / Sandra Betzina
        p.   cm.
    Includes index.
    ISBN 1-56158-363-4
    1. Dressmaking. 2. Tailoring (Women's). I. Title: Power sewing. II. Title.
TT515.B48   2000
646.4'04—dc21   00-023431

TO MY DEAR FRIEND HELEN SNELL,
WHO HAS LOVED AND ENCOURAGED ME
IN ALL ASPECTS OF MY LIFE.
ALSO TO MY EDITORS, SUSAN HUXLEY
AND ELAINE BURKE, WHOSE ATTENTION
TO DETAIL HAS MADE THIS BOOK WHAT IT IS.

ACKNOWLEDGMENTS

Special thanks to one of my favorite stores in the world: Stone Mountain and Daughter Fabrics in Berkeley, California. The owners gave me many of the beautiful fabrics used for the garments shown in the fashion and step-by-step photos in this book. This store is located at 2518 Shattuck Ave., Berkeley, CA 94704. Call (510) 845-6106 for information on the company's swatch service.

The Fusi-Knit, Sofbrush, and Fuse-A-Shade interfacings in the step-by-step photos were contributed by HTC, Inc. You can contact the company for a list of mail-order companies and chain stores that carry these interfacings. The Test-Fuse Kit featured on page 177 is available through HTC, Inc., 103 Eisenhower Parkway, Roseland, NJ 07068; phone: (973) 618-9380; Web site: www.htc-inc.net.

Vogue Patterns supplied most of the patterns shown throughout this book.

CONTENTS

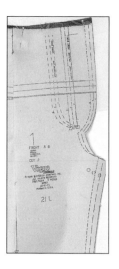

Chapter 3

PANTS 46

Chapter 6

JACKETS 164

Power Sewing Step-by-Step was written to guide you through many of the techniques you have watched on *Sew Perfect* (my show on HGTV), read in my syndicated sewing column, or seen demonstrated in my seminars. From grainline changes and walking ease to mastering all of the possible zipper applications, this includes the best of my *Power Sewing* books as well as many, many new techniques, all in a photographed format. The step-by-step photographs will give you a realistic picture of the sewing process and make it easier for you to duplicate these techniques at home.

I am continually inspired by techniques I see in ready-to-wear, and I love the challenge of figuring out "how they do that." You will find many of these techniques here, including inserting a zipper opening in a pocket; adding an elasticized back waistband; choosing inter-

facing and knowing where to put it; making fast, professional hems; creating innovative pockets; trimming a neckline with tiny bias binding; as well as a slick, professional method for joining the bias ends on a neckline. I also explain the nuances of each technique, so you'll get professional, flawless results.

This book was a mammoth undertaking for both the publisher and me. However, knowing how much the end result will help you in your own sewing, it was all worth it.

Chapter 1

POWER SHOPPING

More often than not, the success of a garment is determined right in the fabric store. If your fabric and pattern aren't compatible or If you buy the wrong size pattern, no amount of meticulous sewing will improve the situation. Depressing as this may sound, there is a bright side: You have the power to change this scenario. Your decisions set the groundwork for a successful project. Without learning any new skills, you can dramatically improve the appearance and fit of your finished garments.

SHOPPING STEP-BY-STEP

You're in heaven, surrounded by all sorts of wonderful fabric and a vast array of pattern catalogs. You stroke almost every bolt in the store, sit in front of the books for more than an hour, finally make your purchases, and head home. Full of excitement, you cut out the fabric and begin assembly. Finally, it's time to try on the partially finished garment. You look in the mirror…what a letdown!

Like a few other "dogs," this one is destined to hang unfinished in your closet. Can it be saved? Probably not. Why remind yourself of the disappointment? Just get rid of it. To prevent future dogs, follow my Power Shopping procedure before you start a new project.

1 Before you begin a new project, consider your wardrobe gaps. Do you need a new coat, a dressy outfit, something for the country, or a simple dress to wear at home?

2 Make a list of the style details you want. If you're thinking about a dress, do you want a tailored version, a tunic shape, full sleeves, or a mandarin collar? Be as specific as possible.

3 You are now ready for a trip to the fabric store. Look through the books and try to find a pattern similar to the garment you visualized, or several patterns that you can combine for the look you want. Buy ⅛ yd. (0.1m) each of the fabrics you love. Now muster up all of your willpower and head for home with your fabric samples and pattern numbers.

4 What is an outfit without accessories? Look at the items you already own to see what coordinates with your fabric possibilities. Shoes, necklaces, scarves, and other garments in your closet may influence your fabric choice.

5 It's not time to go back to the fabric store just yet. Instead, go "snoop shopping" in ready-to-wear shops. Trying on styles that are similar to the garment you're thinking of making gives you a realistic picture of how your finished garment will look on you.

6 If you're particularly attracted to a certain designer, try on everything in the collection. But don't make the mistake of thinking that just because the designer's ready-to-wear garment fits you perfectly, a pattern by that designer will fit the same. A designer pattern is, indeed, a line-for-line copy, yet the pattern company's starting point is its own standard measurements—not the designer's.

7 After spending some time in store dressing rooms, go to a coffee shop and draw up a list or make sketches of the garment styles and details that looked good on you. Also sketch any changes you might like to make on your own garment.

TRICK of the TRADE

NEEDLES IN AN INFORMATION HAYSTACK

Needles come in different sizes and point shapes in order to work with the wide range of fabrics on the market. Why struggle with puckered seams, funky stitches, or breaking threads when switching to the correct needle easily solves these major problems?

All you need to do is figure out the package codes. Numbers designate needle size. Small numbers indicate fine needles and large numbers indicate thicker needles. If a needle is too thick for the fabric, it pierces a hole that causes the fabric to draw up. If the needle is too fine, top threads continually break as you sew. That's why chiffon is suited to a 65/9 needle and denim to a 100/16 needle.

To complicate matters further, types of needle points are designated by letters.

H is for wovens, H-S for knits, H-M for microfibers, the small-size H-J for buttonholes and the large-size H-J for denims and upholstery, SUK for 100 percent Lycra, N for topstitching, H-E for metallic or embroidery threads, NTW for leather, and H-Q for quilting. My book *Fabric Savvy* (The Taunton Press, Inc., 1999) goes into detail about needles, thread, presser feet, seam finishes, and hems for all of the different fabrics.

Needles in newer machines dull rapidly because these machines offer such a variety of stitch functions. Remember to change the needle often to obtain the best stitch quality. I like the idea of starting a new project with a new needle. Also change the needle when your stitch quality deteriorates or when the fabric starts snagging.

8 If you tend to choose fabric and patterns that are incompatible, carefully study the fabrics used for ready-to-wear styles. Note the weight that works, particularly for pants. Also review the fabric recommendations on the back of the pattern envelope. It isn't necessary to limit yourself to the fabrics listed, but choosing one with similar characteristics is certainly best.

9 Listen to your inner voice when choosing fabric. Heed any nagging feeling that a fabric might be too stiff. Full styles call for fabrics that drape well. Gather the fabric in your hand and hold it in front of your body. Does it hang gracefully or is it too bulky for the style of the pattern you've chosen?

10 Now consider the fabric color you want to use. Color goes a long way toward setting the mood for your garment. For evening, dramatic colors are festive. For outdoor activities, earthy tones may be more appropriate. At-home wear is more fun when you unleash your wild side.

11 To avoid making garments in an unflattering color, bring the bolt of fabric to a mirror in the store. Unwind a few yards of fabric, hold the length in front of you, and inspect the results. Is the color spectacular or just acceptable? Nothing less than spectacular should motivate you to take money out of your purse.

TIP Think twice about buying white, gray, or black fabric for a blouse or jacket. Most women need to be well rested to wear these colors close to their face.

12 Some large fabric prints look better on the kitchen table than on your body. If you find yourself choosing prints that are overwhelming, limit yourself to solids for a while or opt for a solid with a small, subtle print.

13 Now you're ready to buy a pattern for your project. After altering your pattern, make up a quickie pretest garment in scrap fabric. (See "Pretesting a Pattern" on p. 18.)

14 If the pretest looks frumpy or unflattering on you, throw out the pattern. A few hours and the cost of the pattern were wasted, but this is nothing compared to the time and money you would have put into the completed garment.

15 If limited time is an issue, refer to "Fit Insurance" below to ensure that the garment is at least wearable.

16 This last step is the payoff for all your conscientious shopping. The pattern has been altered and you know it's going to look great on you. So buy your fabric and start sewing!

TRICK of the TRADE

FIT INSURANCE

Pattern dimensions aren't always consistent—even within a brand. One of the things you can do to ensure success is to cut the garment pieces an additional 1 in. (2.5cm) beyond the side-seam cutting lines. This gives you "room to grow" as well as a bit of fabric you can let out if necessary. But don't widen all of the seam allowances—just the side seams. Think of the garments you could have saved!

Interfacing Favorites

BRAND NAME	CHARACTERISTICS	USES
Armo Weft	Heavyweight Fusible Weft-inserted	For use in very crisp, tailored jackets. Use on the bias for the jacket front and on the straight grain for collars and front facings. Use a lighter-weight interfacing on the side fronts.
Pellon	Medium weight Nonwoven Fusible	Pellon is perfect for strengthening patterns, so preserve your favorites. Fuse it to the back of your pattern pieces using a low heat setting and absolutely no steam. Work from the center of the pattern out, with the pattern on top.
Fusi-Knit French Fuse	Lightweight Fusible Tricot knit	These versatile knitted tricots are suitable for most fabrics that need minimal support. They're good under jacket fronts and side fronts to prevent garment "cave-in" between the armhole and shoulder, as well as on facings for other garments.
Organza	Lightweight Sew-in Woven	Strong but thin, this is the best interfacing for all types of silk. It's an ideal sew-in for fabrics that drape poorly with fusible interfacing. It also makes great underlining and press cloths.
SofKNIT	Lightweight Bias Fusible	Another favorite for fusing large jacket pieces. Because of its bias nature, it's capable of relaxing with the fabric. This makes it suitable for knits as well as for wovens with drape.
So-Sheer	Lightweight Tricot knit Fusible	Similar to French Fuse and Fusi-Knit, but lighter weight. Good for blouses in lightweight cottons and rayons.
Textured Weft	Fusible Weft-inserted	The darling of the ready-to-wear industry because it's ideal for the soft, tailored effect seen in designer garments. Use on fronts, facings, and collars.
Veri-Shape	Stiff Sew-in	Perfect for stand-up or mandarin collars, the straight grain prevents collar collapse. Cut on the bias for the facing of a long coat or anywhere you want extra support. Although sew-in, a must-have for your stash.
Whisper Weft	Medium weight Fusible Weft-inserted	A slightly stiff interfacing for crisp lapels and upper collars. Works best for lightweight wools, cottons, and linens.

INTERFACING IDEAS

Choosing the right interfacing can be confusing because there are so many different types available. Each one has properties that make it suitable for specific fabrics and applications.

All of the interfacings listed on the facing page, except organza and Veri-Shape, are fusible. After application, no hint of the resin—or the interfacing—should be visible on the garment surface. In some cases, fusible interfacing isn't suitable because it changes the hand of the fabric, making it boardlike.

Preshrink your interfacing as soon as you get home from the fabric store so the yardage is ready when you need it. Submerge the interfacing in a basin of hot water for 15 minutes. Squeeze out the excess moisture and dry it over a shower rod.

The chart on the facing page lists my favorite interfacings and how I prefer to use each one. Most of them are HTC Inc. products. If your local fabric store doesn't carry HTC, write to the company at the address listed under Acknowledgments at the front of this book.

PATTERN BRAND AWARENESS

Your body measurements can help you choose a particular pattern size, but it still may not be right for you. Every pattern company designs its garments around a particular body shape. Depending on the brand, the pattern you select could have narrower shoulders, a wider upper chest, a deeper back crotch curve, or other variations.

Before getting into a complete explanation of assessing pattern fit, let's talk frankly about a few of the differences I've noticed between pattern companies.

Chances are good that you've sewn with patterns from the "Big Four": Butterick, McCall's, Simplicity, and Vogue. Generally speaking, McCall's and Simplicity patterns run larger than Butterick and Vogue patterns.

The patterns from all of these companies are large through the upper chest (from the bottom of the armhole to the neckline). If you select a pattern size by matching the full-bust measurement, you'll end up with too much fabric in the upper-chest area. To avoid this unflattering, frumpy look, measure your upper chest by placing the tape measure around your body immediately below the arms. Pick out a pattern size with a bust measurement that matches your upper-chest measurement.

If your measurement falls between two sizes, choose the smaller size if your bust is small and the larger size if your bust is full. When you're ready to alter the pattern, compare your full-bust

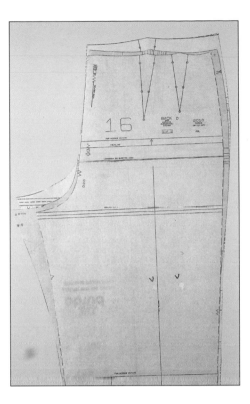

measurement to the bust measurement on the pattern and adjust as necessary. Now the pattern will fit nicely at the armholes, chest, and neckline.

Vogue has a new line of patterns called Today's Fit, which is based on a new sizing block that fits much better in all areas and is modeled on a realistic group of measurements. (See "New Pattern Sizing" on p. 11.) Choose Today's Fit patterns according to your full-bust and full-hip measurements, since they don't run large in the upper chest.

Today's Fit patterns are multisized, so you can transition from one size to another quite easily, and are available in three size groups (A to C, D to F, and G to J). (See "Today's Fit Sizing" on p. 11.) Check the left-hand corner of the pattern envelope to make sure you're buying the correct size group.

The size and drape of sleeve patterns vary. So when I work with expensive fabric, I test-fit the set-in sleeves of jacket patterns with scrap fabric, as shown at right.

New Look and Style patterns are both multisized and run true to measurement. Like Today's Fit, these patterns don't run large in the upper chest, so buy a pattern size that corresponds to your full-bust measurement rather than your high-bust measurement.

Style patterns don't have a lot of ease, so you may need a size larger than you usually use. They're multisized, so you can adapt the fit for different parts of your body. To be on the safe side, cut wider seam allowances so you can let out the seamlines if the fit is too close for comfort.

Garments made with New Look patterns are flattering on larger women or

anyone with substantial shoulders because their styling details are larger. Burda patterns, while often hard to find, offer a body-flattering European cut. Like New Look and Style, Burda's products also run true to measurement and are multisized.

Burda patterns have wide shoulders; downsize the width by cutting a Burda pattern a size smaller than your bust above the armhole. If you have very narrow shoulders, feel free to go two sizes smaller from the lower armhole to the neck on both the front and back. Burda patterns also run short in the crotch.

Seam and hem allowances aren't included in the older Burda patterns, which are printed on blue paper, but they are included in the New Burda patterns. Look for a star under the pattern number and beige pattern paper to identify New Burda patterns.

Stretch & Sew and Kwik-Sew patterns are based on realistic measurements. In addition, countless women find these patterns easy to fit. Both brands offer multisized patterns that run true to measurement.

Small, independent pattern companies abound. I've made at least one item from each of the companies listed on p. 226, and, trust me, they're all sized differently. I strongly suggest that you either measure the flat-pattern pieces or sew the garment in an inexpensive fabric first to test the fit. (See "Pretesting a Pattern" on p. 18.) If your fabric has a soft drape and the garment style is loose, a pretest isn't necessary.

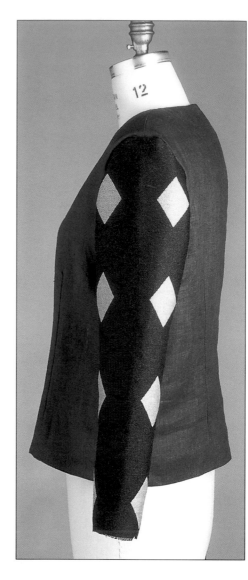

StyleMaker

NEW PATTERN SIZING

One major pattern company has finally decided to improve its sizing. I convinced Vogue to develop a collection called Today's Fit Patterns by Sandra Betzina. Using realistic body measurements in 10 sizes, Vogue created garments that run true to the numbers—including increased dimensions for the waist and tummy. I also asked Vogue to make the pattern sizing alphabetical, so buyers will know the fit they're getting is different from anything they've tried before (see "Today's Fit Sizing" below).

Today's Fit Patterns aren't based on standard measurements that are several decades behind the times. Research for the line started with 47 measurements from a recent University of Arizona study of 7,000 women. Based on these measurements, Vogue created an entirely new sizing block to fit the shape of today's woman, increasing the girth across the tummy, lowering the bust shaping, and varying the cup size from B to D.

Once a pattern company establishes the block, the pattern is graded (that is, a standard number of inches is added or subtracted) to make different sizes. I worked closely with a pattern grader to establish the fit for each size. Few people are equally small or large in every area of their body. For example, larger women need more fabric through the bust, but not in the upper chest and shoulders. In these sizes, I graded up (increased) areas such as the bust, waist, and hips, while "holding the grade" in the upper chest and shoulders. Other sizes needed an increased back width but a standard upper front chest.

When it was time to make the garments, I reduced the sleeve ease to create a smoother sleeve cap while increasing the upper-arm sleeve width. I also created better-fitting necklines and made an entirely new crotch shape to eliminate baggy seats in pants.

Finally, with finished garments in all sizes, I held forums where volunteers of all shapes and sizes tried on the garments. The patternmaker, the pattern grader, a dressmaker skilled in fit, and I were there to critique the results. Then the patterns were refined yet again.

Today's Fit patterns from Vogue run true to measurement, so you shouldn't be in for the usual fitting surprises. Choose pattern size according to your full-bust and full-hip measurements. The full-bust sizes range from 32 in. to 55 in. (81.3cm to 139.7cm), and the hip dimensions run from 34½ in. to 57 in. (87.7cm to 144.8cm). The patterns are multisized since few women are one size all over.

Today's Fit Sizing

	A	B	C	D	E	F	G	H	I	J
Bust	32 (81cm)	34 (86.5cm)	36 (91.5cm)	38 (96.5cm)	40½ (103cm)	43 (109cm)	46 (117cm)	49 (124.5cm)	52 (132cm)	55 (140cm)
Waist	26½ (67cm)	28½ (72cm)	30½ (77.5cm)	32½ (82.5cm)	35 (89cm)	37½ (95cm)	41½ (105cm)	44½ (113cm)	47½ (121cm)	50½ (128cm)
Hip	34½ (87.5cm)	36½ (92.5cm)	38½ (98cm)	40½ (103cm)	42½ (108cm)	45 (116cm)	48 (122cm)	51 (130cm)	54 (137cm)	57 (145cm)

Reprinted with permission from Vogue Patterns/Butterick Co., Inc.

MOVEMENT EASE AND DESIGN EASE

Pattern ease is confusing. It would be nice to offer a concise explanation and then present a basic set of numbers for the two general types, but this won't do the trick. The amount of ease added to a pattern varies by body area, plus every pattern company and designer has different preferences. No wonder a lack of understanding about ease messes up so many attempts to alter a pattern!

There are two types of ease: design ease, which is extra fabric that gives a garment a certain look, and movement ease, which is the amount of extra fabric that prevents a garment from clinging to you so tightly you can't move.

Both of the garments in the photos at right are the same size. The muslin is

Movement Ease

Bust	2½ in. (6.4cm)
Waist	1 in. (2.5cm)
Hip	2½ in. (6.4cm)
Front length from neck to waist	½ in. (1.3cm)
Back length from neck to waist	½ in. (1.3cm)
Upper arm	2 in. to 4 in. (5cm to 10.2cm) depending on garment fit and style
Thigh	2 in. (5cm)
Knee	2 in. (5cm)
Front crotch length	½ in. (1.3cm)
Back crotch length	¾ in. (1.9cm)

smaller because it only has movement ease. The coat, on the other hand, has lots of design ease to give the garment shape and personality.

A patternmaker starts by drafting to a set of standard body measurements (a block). Movement ease is added to areas where your body needs mobility. This allows you to swing your arms and legs, bend over, reach up, and perform the rest of your daily activities. If the pattern was sewn up now, the garment would fit snugly.

The last step is where the garment comes to life: The finished silhouette emerges as extra inches (design ease) are added to strategic locations. The hip measurement can be doubled to make a fabulous full skirt. Adding just a few inches along the leg makes a narrow, tapered pant; a few more and a fuller pant is born. Excess fabric under the arms becomes a dolman sleeve…there are so many possibilities!

At its simplest, altering means adjusting pattern pieces so that the finished garment fits your body. Both movement ease and design ease must be considered to do this successfully.

For example, let's pretend that the flat-pattern measurement for your garment is 38 in. (96.5cm) and your hip circumference is 35½ in. (90.2cm). If the pattern envelope describes the finished garment as fitted, you have enough movement ease. The difference between your body measurement and the flat-pattern measurement (2½ in. or 6.4cm) gives you the standard movement ease. But remember that you'll end up with a very snug fit.

So here's the formula for a very fitted garment: Body measurement + movement ease = flat-pattern measurement. Movement ease varies for different parts of the body. Standard movement ease is the bare minimum amount of extra fabric you need for a garment. Few people wear clothes that have movement ease only, but it's great to have this information when you're checking a pattern for fit (see the chart at left).

[TIP] Many patterns provide the flat-pattern measurements right on the pattern. If the bust, waist, and chest measurements aren't listed, you can figure these out on your own. (See "Movement Ease" on the facing page.)

Design ease serves a totally different function than movement ease. It's really a matter of personal taste: One designer may add 10 in. (25.4cm) at the bust and hip to create a big shirt, while another designer may add 25 in. (63.5cm) for a similar look.

How do you know the amount of ease that suits your body? Your best bet is to measure some of your favorite garments, or assess the flattering outfits you try on in a store. Here's your formula for a garment: Body measurement + movement ease + desired design ease = flat-pattern measurement.

The table at right is a very general guide based on the total amount of ease I like in a garment. The best sources for your design ease guidelines are in your closet. Measure your favorite garments for your personalized reference.

Sandra's Garment Ease

GARMENT	LOCATION	TOTAL EASE*
Dress	Bust	2 in. (5cm)
	Tummy or hip, less than 37 in. (94cm)	3 in. (7.6cm)
	Tummy or hip, more than 37 in. (94cm)	4 in. (10.2cm)
Overblouse	Bust	4 in. (10.2cm)
	Tummy or hip, less than 37 in. (94cm)	4 in. (10.2cm)
	Tummy or hip, 37 in. to 45 in. (94cm to 114.3cm)	6 in. (15.2cm)
	Tummy or hip, more than 45 in. (114.3cm)	8 in. (20.3cm)
Jacket	Bust	4 in. (10.2cm)
	Tummy or hip	5 in. to 6 in. (12.7cm to 15.2cm)
Coat	Bust	6 in. (15.2cm)
	Tummy or hip	8 in. to 9 in. (20.3cm to 22.9cm)
Pants or skirt, fitted	Tummy	1 in. (2.5cm)
	Hip	2½ in. (6.4cm)
Tailored pants or skirt, pleated	Tummy	2 in. (5cm)
	Hip	4 in. (10.2cm)
Bias-cut garments on less-than-perfect figures	Bust	3 in. (7.6cm)
	Tummy	4 in. (10.2cm)
	Hip	5 in. (12.7cm)

*Total ease is the amount you need to add to your measurement for a flattering fit.

Now you're ready to review the pattern. Does the style description on the back of the envelope indicate that the garment is close fitting, fitted, semi-fitted, loose fitting, or very loose fitting? These categories will narrow your selection. Patterns that include the total flat-pattern measurement for the bust and hip simplify things considerably.

Another resource is the ease chart found in the back of most pattern books, which tells you exactly how many inches of design ease there are in each fit category. (See "Misses' Ease Allowances" on p. 14.) Just compare the design ease on the pattern to your preferences, add or subtract your measurement and ease, then make the alteration on your flat pattern.

[TIP] Take care when purchasing patterns for "very loose fitting" garments. The fit overwhelms many figures. If you're under 5 ft. 6 in. tall, simply buy one size smaller and make pattern adjustments as if the pattern were in your size.

WALKING EASE

When I was learning to sew, my wrap skirt, long coat, and coatdress looked fabulous as long as I stood perfectly still. As soon as I began to walk, however, the garments separated at the center-front or side opening. The skirt unwrapped, the coat revealed the garments beneath, and the coatdress pulled apart immodestly.

Then I discovered walking ease. It eliminates the problems that occur with these types of garments, as well as with many others: a straight shirtwaist dress that strains at the lowest closures, a skirt with walking pleats, a side- or front-buttoning straight skirt that pulls apart below the last button, and all wrap garments.

Walking ease is added at the center-front opening or the side-front seamline. The following step-by-step instructions describe this process. "An Aside" on p. 16 explains walking ease additions for other garment openings.

Center-Front Ease Extensions

It's a good idea to make sure your pattern pieces have enough walking ease. Length and style have a lot to do with this. For example, when there's a waistline seam, a smaller amount of walking ease is required because the garment won't spread above the waist.

Walking ease for button and wrap styles is the same. Regardless of length, if the garment is full you don't need to add walking ease. There's already plenty of fabric to accommodate movement. And walking ease isn't needed unless the garment's hemline is below the crotch.

1 After making all other necessary pattern alterations, slash the front pattern piece vertically at center front from the bottom of the hem allowance to the neck seamline.

2 Still at center front, snip through the neck seam allowance to, but not through, the cutting line. You now have a small bit of pattern paper, or hinge, holding the garment's front extension to the main part of the pattern front.

[TIP] Plaid and striped fabrics are handled a bit differently because center front must remain on grain. For these fabrics, slash the front pattern piece near the side seam, from the bottom of the hem to within ⅛ in. (3mm) of the armhole cutting line. Spread the pattern piece at the hem, tapering to the original cutting line at the armhole.

Misses' Ease Allowances

Silhouette	BUST AREA			HIP AREA
	Dresses, blouses, shirts, tops, vests	Jackets	Coats	Skirts, pants, shorts, culottes
		Lined or unlined		
Close fitting	0–2⅞ in. (0–7.3cm)	Not applicable		0–1⅞ in. (0–4.8cm)
Fitted	3 in.–4 in. (7.5cm–10cm)	3¾ in.–4¼ in. (9.5cm–10.7cm)	5¼ in.–6¾ in. (13.3cm–17cm)	2 in.–3 in. (5cm–7.5cm)
Semifitted	4⅛ in.–5 in. (10.4cm–12.5cm)	4⅜ in.–5¾ in. (11.1cm–14.5cm)	6⅞ in.–8 in. (17.4cm–20.5cm)	3⅛ in.–4 in. (7.9cm–10cm)
Loose fitting	5⅛ in.–8 in. (13cm–20.5cm)	5⅞ in.–10 in. (15cm–25.5cm)	8⅛ in.–12 in. (20.7cm–30.5cm)	4⅛ in.–6 in. (10.4cm–15cm)
Very loose fitting	Over 8 in. (20.5cm)	Over 10 in. (25.5cm)	Over 12 in. (30.5cm)	Over 6 in. (15cm)

Reprinted with permission from Vogue Patterns/Butterick Co., Inc.

Recommended Walking Ease

GARMENT	GARMENT LENGTH	TOTAL WALKING EASE
Bathrobe	Knee	1¼ in. (3.2cm)
	Midcalf	2½ in. (6.4cm)
	Ankle	3 in. (7.6cm)
Coat	Midthigh	¾ in. (1.9cm)
	Knee	1¼ in. (3.2cm)
	Midcalf, no waist seam	2½ in. (6.4cm)
	Midcalf, with waist seam	1¼ in. (3.2cm)
	Ankle	3 in. (7.6cm)
Coatdress	Ankle	3 in. (7.6cm)
	Knee	¾ in. (1.9cm)
	Midcalf, no waist seam	2½ in. (6.4cm)
	Midcalf, with waist seam	1 in. (2.5cm)
Dress, without waist seam	Midthigh	¾ in. (1.9cm)
	Knee	1¼ in. (3.2cm)
	Midcalf	2½ in. (6.4cm)
	Ankle	3 in. (7.6cm)
Skirt, button and wrap styles	Knee	¾ in. (1.9cm)
	Midcalf	1 in. (2.5cm)
	Ankle	1½ in. (3.8cm)

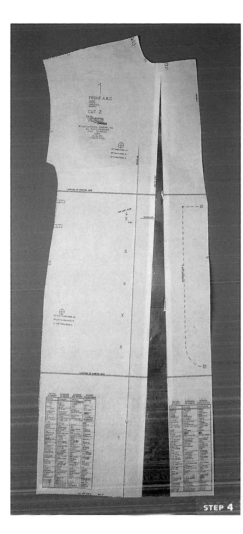

STEP 4

3 At the hemline, spread the front extension away from the main part of the pattern front. The greatest amount of spread (as indicated in "Recommended Walking Ease" at right) is at the hemline, tapering almost to nothing between the armhole and the neck seamline so that the pattern is flat.

4 Open the pattern along center front, then tape tissue into the spread to secure the alteration. The pattern-front grainline remains the same.

5 Cut out your garment pieces. During layout, only the front edge of the garment is off grain.

of the TRADE

AN ASIDE

On some garments, it's prudent to add the walking ease on the front sides rather than at center front. Otherwise, detailing, such as lapels, will be affected, and plaids or stripes won't be straight because the alteration throws the front extensions off grain.

In these situations, place all of the walking ease at the front side seam. Slash the pattern piece vertically, near the side seam and parallel to the grainline. Spread the pattern piece as desired, tapering to nothing at the armhole.

If a garment opens in the back, add all of the walking ease to the side seam on the back pattern piece. This keeps center back on grain, which prevents the seat from bagging. Another option is to cut a 2-in. (5cm) seam allowance at center back, tapering to a 1½-in. (3.8cm) wide addition from the top of the opening to the hem. This also keeps the skirt on grain. If a skirt has a pleat, you need to add ease at the side seam rather than at the pleat opening.

6 Using the pattern as a guide, cut a piece of fusible twill tape that's the same length as the front edge of the garment piece, and attach it to the wrong side of the fabric. This stabilizes the front so that joining it to a facing or applying trim won't stretch the edge.

7 Make the same alteration to the front lining pattern. Don't alter the back pattern.

FABRIC SHORTAGE SOLUTIONS

Even the most experienced sewer occasionally underestimates yardage or finds that a fabric shrinks more than expected. I used to panic when I didn't have enough fabric to cut out all of my pattern pieces, but not anymore. Now I consider it a design opportunity.

In all, there are three ways to solve your fabric shortage: Determine the pieced sections when you lay out the pattern pieces, make the garment from several fabrics, or divide the pattern pieces into smaller sections.

Layout Piecing

New seams aren't easy to position in some garments—a circle skirt, for example. In these cases, pick a spot where piecing isn't as noticeable. For example, an insert at center back of a skirt hem is very obvious, but an insert in the back near the side seam is lost in the fabric folds of the finished garment.

Place the pattern piece on your body and decide where a new seam would be most flattering. You may only need to piece on one side. Nevertheless, consider piecing on both sides so that the garment is balanced and the piecing looks intentional.

Whenever possible, try to make a pieced seam look like part of the garment's design by planning for a straight seamline and adding topstitching or other embellishments.

1 Pin the pattern piece on the yardage just as you would if you had enough fabric. Cut out the pattern piece, ignoring the missing chunk of fabric. Keep the pattern piece pinned to the cutout garment piece.

2 Find a scrap of fabric that's slightly larger than the missing section of the garment piece. Ensure that the grainline is the same as that of the garment piece it's joining.

3 Cut off any jagged edges and selvages on the scrap and the joining edge of the garment piece. Don't trim the scrap to fit. Depending on the way you want to "build" your garment piece, you can fix the problem right on the cutting table.

STEP 3

4 Along the area with the missing fabric, pull out the pins holding the pattern to the garment piece. With right sides together, pin the scrap to the garment piece along the piecing seamline. With the pattern still pinned (except for the pieced section), sew and press the new seamline.

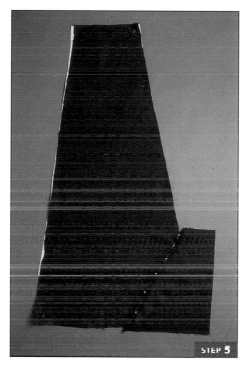

STEP 5

5 Insert the removed pins back into the pattern paper, garment piece, and joined scrap. Trim to match the shape of the pattern piece. Essentially, this no-draft method entails seaming a fabric scrap to the garment piece, then trimming it to the correct size and shape.

Fabric Combinations

Unless you're an avid quilter, combining fabric colors and patterns can be intimidating. Yet combining stripes, plaids, prints, and solids in a single garment is fun and lets you create a one-of-a-kind garment.

A successfully pieced garment is usually made from three to five fabrics. All should be compatible for visual continuity in the garment. Large prints aren't commonly used because they'll either dominate the garment or disappear when cut into small pieces. Small-scale designs, on the other hand, are effective.

Experiment with fabric placement on a small scale. Find a common element in each of the fabrics: a single color or motif that repeats in each fabric, or perhaps a star motif or paisley design that appears in several fabrics. Other options include using the same print in several colors or sticking to a monochromatic palette and varying the fabric textures.

1 Make several photocopies of the garment picture or illustration on the pattern envelope. Set one photocopy aside for reference while assembling the garment.

2 Pencil barely visible lines around the pattern-piece shapes on the finished garment image. For pleasing style

lines, consider splitting a pattern piece into smaller shapes that can be cut from coordinating fabrics. For now, just draw the style lines on the garment image.

3 Cut apart one of the photocopies along the style lines or garment lines to make pattern pieces for the pasteup. If you don't like the finished appearance, continue to revise the fabric placement using the remaining photocopies.

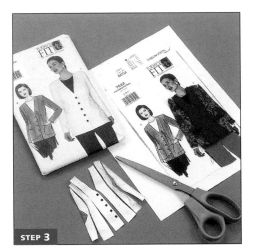
STEP 3

PRETESTING A PATTERN

Fabric that has been in your stash for more than three years is perfect for making a pretest garment using your altered pattern. After this length of time, this pretest is probably the only hope the material has for coming to life!

It's important that you make your pretest garment from a fabric similar to your fashion fabric, so choose one that has the same drape. Steer away from muslin. It doesn't drape like most garment fabrics, so a muslin pretest doesn't give a realistic idea of the finished garment's appearance. Knits on the sale table at a fabric store are perfect for pretesting a pattern you intend to sew up in a knit fashion fabric.

After altering the pattern—but before cutting out the fashion-fabric garment pieces—make up the garment in this inexpensive or expendable material. In less than an hour you'll know exactly how the finished garment will look on you.

You can now decide whether the pattern is worth making in a fashion fabric; if not, simply toss it in the trash. Getting rid of a $20 pattern and some old fabric is a lot less painful than spending an entire day on a disappointment.

1 Fold up all of the hems on your pattern pieces so that your pretest shows the finished garment length. Carefully cut the major garment pieces from the pretest fabric, transferring all marks and notches. Don't bother cutting out facings, collars, and pocket pieces.

StyleMaker

STEP 1

2 You also need to indicate center front, center back, darts, waist, buttons, buttonholes, pockets, and existing hemline. Machine-baste the pretest with a contrasting thread.

STEP 3

TRICK *of the* TRADE

KEEP YOUR OPTIONS OPEN

You have your fabric. The pattern is altered to fit. Now it's time to begin. Don't be too quick to commit to your seamlines—you may still want to do some last-minute tweaking. Every fabric behaves a little differently on the body.

When you cut out the garment, add an additional 1 in. (2.5cm) beyond the side-seam cutting line after adjusting for alterations. This gives you some leeway for fitting.

Now machine-baste the side seams together at 1⅝ in. (4.1cm), using a bobbin thread in a contrasting color. Try on the garment. No matter how well you altered the pattern, the fabric might influence the way the garment pieces hang on your body. Because the seams are wider and merely basted together, changes are easy to make.

At this point, it's also a good idea to scrutinize the garment's opening. If it buttons at center front, make sure that the center-front markings match exactly and check the button placement before stitching the buttonholes. If you can't match center fronts, you may need to let out the side seams a bit; otherwise, you won't be able to button up the garment.

3 Press the seam allowances and darts flat. Ignore all of the finishing. Pretesting a pattern is down and dirty sewing, so set aside any perfectionist tendencies.

4 Try on the pretest, pinning it together at the center-back or center-front opening. Stand back and critically assess the fit and style of the garment. (Try not to be influenced by the pretest fabric.)

• Inspect for wrinkles, which point to a fitting problem.

• Look at the shoulders. Try several shapes and thicknesses of shoulder pads to see whether any improve the garment's appearance.

• Check for enough ease at the bust and hips. If you're pretesting a coat or jacket, try on the pretest with garments underneath.

• Carefully assess the back fit to ensure that it's neither too narrow nor too wide.

• Are the hemline and the sleeve length attractive and comfortable? If you shortened the garment length, raise the pocket to maintain pleasing proportions. Don't move the pocket above the high hip or higher than 2 in. down from the waist.

• Are the darts, buttonholes, and pockets nicely positioned? I like a buttonhole between the breasts. If you shortened the jacket a lot, you may not need as many buttons.

• Scrutinize the openings. Make sure that center-front button and buttonhole marks match exactly.

• Is it worth making? Are you really excited about it, or are you indifferent? Unless the shape and style thrill you, don't waste time on this pattern. If, on the other hand, you love the design, note the changes you uncovered in the pretest and alter the pattern. Now you can sew without any doubts, knowing in your heart that the garment is a winner.

• Never feel guilty about tossing a pattern. Only 50 percent or so are worth making. A pattern that doesn't progress past a pretest doesn't count as a failure.

Chapter 2

VESTS

Don't you just love making vests? A vest is quick and easy and makes a great canvas for trying out new construction techniques or embellishment ideas. Slipped on over a top and a skirt or pants, it pulls together an outfit—and makes a wonderful substitute for a jacket. Whether you want a business, office casual, or weekend look, the right fabric can make your vest versatile enough to meet your needs.

Vests are wonderful garments for showcasing special material. And if the fabric is wide, the garment won't be too expensive since you only need one vest length.

Sandra's Closet

My wardrobe contains lots of vests. I like this type of garment because I can make each one unique. My passion for fabric—which you probably share—also gets free rein when I make a vest. A glorious silk print or textured, ruched yardage can take center stage.

The photos on the next few pages feature some of my favorite vests. I hope that the fabric combinations and instructions inspire you to embark on your own creative journey.

LITTLE BLACK VEST

Everyone needs a basic vest. Mine goes with many of the clothes in my wardrobe. I like to call it an anchoring piece because I can wear it with practically any top and skirt, then accessorize with black shoes or boots for a coordinated look.

I wear my black vest often because I need a professional yet casual image for seminars, interviews, and television shows. It's like a little jacket without being quite as formal.

I'll show you several vests here because the basic black vest can mean many things to many people. In fact, your basic vest doesn't even have to be black if your wardrobe is based on another color. What makes any basic vest a standout are interesting buttons, fabric, and trim.

A dashing piping and fabric combo, the vest on the facing page expresses a creative spirit while retaining a sophisticated air. The pattern comes from my book *No Time to Sew* (available from the author; see Resources on p. 226). The piping along the vest perimeter keeps the lining well hidden, and by sticking with an almost monochromatic palette I felt free to insert piping along the seamline. The labels on the vest come from old ties and discarded designer clothes, and are just plain fun.

Piping Choices

Outstanding piping enhances the look of a vest or jacket. A garment feature, like a shawl collar, becomes a focal point when the edges are piped. Interior trim is equally dynamic—and slimming—as long as you put some thought into the application. Since piping thickens an interior seam, choose a type that's very flexible and not too thick.

How I Made These Vests

You can make vests like mine using the step-by-step instructions in the following features:

Interfacing Decision (at right)
Armhole Gaposis Fix (see p. 28)
Piping Dreams (see p. 30)
At-a-Glance Bias-Binding Resource (see p. 41)

To avoid drawn-up piping seams, I strongly recommend hand-basting piping to the stitching line before machine-sewing the garment pieces together. This prevents the piping from shortening the seamline. The pattern at right is the Sandra Betzina vest from The Sewing Workshop.

Interfacing Decision

The dimensional, textured effect of the black fabric doesn't lend itself to fusible interfacing. The up-and-down pressing motion, which is necessary for a strong bond, flattens the fabric. A sew-in interfacing is the best option. In this situation, my favorite is Veri-Shape for a crisp vest and silk organza for a softer effect. Cut the interfacing pieces on the bias so that the finished garment molds attractively to your body.

PACIFIC RIM

In the vest at left, fabric is everything. Energy, elegance, and opulence combine in a vest that's suitable for the opera or dinner at a fancy restaurant. The powerful theme on the printed silk made it easy to select complementary fabrics and construction treatments. The garment shape, collar treatment, and edge binding were all inspired by the fabric. This vest was made using Vogue 7065 from Today's Fit by Sandra Betzina.

Inspiration

A student in one of my hands-on seminars found this fabric; it's the most beautiful I have ever owned. At the time of the discovery, I was developing my Vogue vest pattern and wanted to sew up a couple of garments to check the fit and construction details.

Having lived on the West Coast for so many years, my taste leans toward Eastern themes. I figured that the long

╠══╣
How I Made This Vest

You can make a vest like mine using the step-by-step instructions in the following features:

Interfacing Decision (see p. 23)
Armhole Gaposis Fix (see p. 28)
Lined Vest with Side Slits (see p. 36)
At-a-Glance Bias-Binding Resource (see p. 41)
On-the-Edge Binding (see p. 42)
╠══╣

vest surface would complement the fabric and prevent the large figures from overwhelming the garment.

The print also guided my fabric binding choice. I used a silk charmeuse that echoes several of the rich, dominant colors in the print. The safe choice would be a solid-color binding, but that would downplay the vitality of the main print. Besides, I prefer a flamboyant look.

Economics

An irresistible fabric is often quite expensive. To reduce the cost of the project, consider using another fabric for the back pattern piece. In this case, I used a simple, shiny black rayon. The garment needs body to hang well, so I interfaced the entire back with Fusi-Knit, adding texture by scrunching the damp yardage during fusing.

Interfacing and Underlining

My standard procedure is to interface the wrong side of the front and back vest pieces. This reduces wrinkling and helps maintain a better silhouette. A crisper vest also gives the effect of a sleeveless jacket. Choose an interfacing that's suitable for your fabric type. You

want the interfacing-backed fabric to
add body without being too stiff.

I underlined the fronts with prewashed cotton flannel to add body while
maintaining the vest's soft hand. The
interfacing, Fusi-Knit, is fused to the
underlining on the front because I didn't
want the silk to become too stiff.

Front-Collar Assembly

If you have a short neck or would like to
add a collar on a V-neck vest, I recommend this treatment. The fun part is the
easy application. Since this type of collar
is placed only on the garment front—
stopping at the shoulder seam on both
fronts—you don't have to shape it into
the entire neckline. Just interface the
upper and undercollar, sew the outer
edges together, and baste the pieces to
the shoulder and neckline. When you
attach the back and lining, the raw
edges of the collar are caught in the
seam allowances.

How I Made This Vest

*You can make a vest like mine using
the step-by-step instructions in the
following features:*

Piping Dreams (see p. 30)
Gold Medal Lining (see p. 34)
Lined Vest with Side Slits (see p. 36)

DRAGON'S FORTUNE

My garments are rarely a single color or
fabric. I love combining textures and
colors in a way that creates a dynamic
interaction between the elements.
Autumn colors—dark brown, gold, and
rust—go with my
out-of-the-bottle
red hair, so
I chose a
chocolate-
brown East-
ern silk bro-
cade for the
notched collar.

The dragon,
a symbol of
luck and
good

fortune in Chinese astrology, makes
an exciting allover motif for a cross-
cultural vest. I love this printed silk brocade fabric because its colors suggest
attractive options for the piping and the
collar. This garment was made using
Vogue 7065 from Today's Fit by Sandra
Betzina. Piping, also chosen for its
great color, completes the garment
by defining the center-front and
neckline edges.

Fabric Combinations

Frequently, students ask me for
advice on fabric combinations.
The trick is to rely partly on
instinct and partly on experience
Unless you aspire to the New
York City monochromatic-black
look, any time you put on separates—
pants or skirt plus a top, a jacket, or a
vest—you're successfully combining colors and textures. The trick is to apply
this knowledge to the garment.

Experiment rather than play it safe.
Colors don't have to be a perfect match.
Keep them in the same shade if you
combine fabrics in an outfit, or go for
total contrast with a collar that matches
the skirt or pants.

ANATOMY *of a Vest*

Whatever type of vest you're making, there are procedures that you're certain to follow. Construction details, such as bagging a lining or adding buttonhole windows, slightly vary the process, and sometimes it's easy to forget little details when you're trying something new from the Master Construction Methods in this chapter.

The step-by-step instructions that follow are a "cheat sheet" that summarizes the vest assembly process. With this game plan you'll spend less time worrying about assembly and more time enjoying the process.

1 **Before you cut out your vest,** decide on a flattering length and alter the pattern accordingly. Vest length is difficult to change once you get into the construction process.

2 **Make any other necessary pattern alterations.** Pay particular attention to the slope and width of the shoulder. If desired, you can compare your new vest pattern to one that you love, or pin-fit the pattern pieces.

3 **If your pattern includes pieces for a lining,** read "Better Lining Pattern" on p. 33. Now cut out your lining pieces. China silk, flannel, lightweight cotton, Ambiance rayon, and silk crepe de Chine all make great vest linings.

4 **Cut out the garment,** interfacing, and optional interlining or underlining pieces. To make your vest crisp enough to work as a jacket substitute, interface the wrong side of the entire front and back fashion-fabric pieces. Apply the interfacing out to the raw fabric edges so that the seam allowances are stabilized.

5 **Interface the collar and patch-pocket pieces.** To keep them from stretching, buttonholes often need extra interfacing. A patch of organza is ideal for this because it's lightweight, bulk-free, and strong. You can also use a fusible.

[TIP] **Cut and position the interfacing so that the grainline with the least stretch is placed in the same direction as the buttonhole.**

6 **Stabilize the neck and shoulders** with fusible or ¼-in. (2.5cm) wide twill tape, or strips of tightly woven selvage. Loose-weave fabrics especially need this treatment.

[TIP] **One of the common complaints about vests is gaping armholes. Most patterns exclude the fitting darts that prevent "gaposis" on the front armhole** for all but an A cup. If your back or shoulders are rounded, the back armhole will also have gaposis. Easing and stabilizing will eliminate gaping armholes and necklines. (See "Armhole Gaposis Fix" on p. 28.)

7 **Add pockets and a collar** if desired. Some types of buttonhole treatments, such as traditional bound buttonholes, need to be started now—before the vest and lining are joined. (On reversibles, I prefer the "Buttonhole Window" method described on p. 44, where the buttonhole is added after the vest is completed.)

8 **The assembly process** for completing your vest varies at this point. For several bagged-lining methods, and for vests with bias-bound edges, join the lining and garment pieces separately, then assemble the two parts. You don't need to join any garment pieces if you use the "Gold Medal Lining" on p. 34, the best bagged lining technique. For a vest with bias-bound edges, follow the instructions for "On-the-Edge Binding" on p. 42.

Master Construction Methods

Your decision to line and either bind the edges or bag the lining on a vest will help you decide which construction technique to use. This chapter features several methods for lining a vest.

The "Gold Medal Lining" technique on p. 34 allows you to alter the vest after it's assembled. Since this method isn't suitable for a vest with piping because the piping joints can't be continuous, I included instructions for a "Pull-Through Lining" technique as well (see p. 38).

By far the easiest and fastest construction method is basting together two vests—one in fashion fabric and one in lining—then covering the edges with bias binding. (See "On-the-Edge Binding" on p. 42.) Once you decide on an assembly method, it's time to think about the fun pocket and button details. This chapter contains some great ideas.

MINIMAL VEST SEAMS

Here's a simple process for making the front and back pattern pieces into a single unit. All you have to do to complete the vest is sew both shoulder seams and apply a binding. What could be easier?

This is a great way to avoid side seams, which break the print on a fabric. Or if the yardage costs a small fortune, you might be able to get away with a single vest length if there aren't any side seam allowances.

My only caution with this procedure is that the side seams on the pattern must be straight.

If you plan to line your vest, you can eliminate the

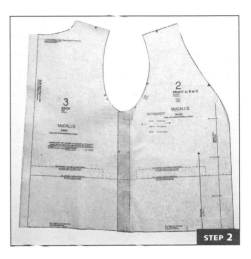

STEP 2

side seams only if you're finishing the edges with binding. Bagging a lining is impossible in this case because you can't pull the fronts through the shoulders.

1 Alter the front and back pattern pieces to fit.

2 Overlap the pattern pieces at the side seams, aligning the seamlines. Tape the pieces together.

3 Cut out the garment piece, placing center back on the folded edge of your doubled yardage.

StyleMaker

4 Join the vest shoulder seams. Cut another vest shape from the lining fabric and join the shoulder seams. Press all of the seam allowances open.

5 Join the lining to the garment around the perimeter and armholes, sewing ¾ in. (1.9cm) from the cut edge. Cut off the ⅝ in. (15mm) seam allowance and bind the edges according to the instructions in "On-the-Edge Binding" on p. 42.

ARMHOLE GAPOSIS FIX

Vests, jumpers, and sleeveless dresses tend to gape at the armholes unless they have darts. If your pattern doesn't have darts, you can eliminate the gaping with little more than straight stitching and twill tape. Essentially, you're giving shape to the front without making a dart.

All you need is an ease line at the lower half of the front armhole. (For a D cup or larger, you must ease the entire front armhole.) By reducing the circumference, you build a three-dimensional shape. Some fabrics ease better than others, so you can really contour the vest front.

Although the stitching encourages the finished garment to conform to your body curves, the armhole doesn't pucker. The amount that you draw in varies slightly according to your bust size and the amount the fabric is capable of easing. A rule of thumb is that you can ease in ⅛ in. (3mm) per inch (2.5cm).

If your back is rounded, use the same technique to shape the back armhole. Run the ease line from the shoulder to the underarm.

1 Set your machine for a long stitch length (3.5mm or 8 spi [stitches per inch]—or longer for a very firm fabric). There are three ways you can create the ease: pulling the bobbin thread on a line of straight stitching, crowding, or using fusible twill tape. (See "Easing Armholes" on the facing page.)

2 Position your easing ½ in. (1.3cm) from the raw edge on the lower half of the front armhole. (If your bust is full and you're trying to ease to the max, ease the entire front armhole.) The size of your bust determines the amount of the reduction. I rarely measure how much I'm easing; however, I've developed the guidelines on the facing page.

TRICK
of the TRADE
EASING ARMHOLES

You can use any of the following methods to add ease to an armhole to prevent gaping:

Crowding: Position the armhole wrong side up on the sewing machine. Sew at a 3.5mm (8 spi) stitch length, holding your finger on top of the fabric behind the presser foot. Let the fabric build up behind the foot, release your finger, then continue crowding the fabric behind the presser foot.

Pulling the bobbin thread: With the wrong side up, sew the armhole using a 3.5mm (8 spi) stitch length. Pull the bobbin thread to draw in the fabric as much as desired.

Applying fusible twill tape: Cut a length of twill tape to the finished armhole measurement. Trim off the amount that you want to reduce the armhole by according to "Armhole Gaposis Fix" on the facing page.

Pin the ends to the wrong side of the armhole, positioning the center of the tape ½ in. (1.3cm) from the raw fabric edge, or ⅞ in. (2.2cm) if you are adding binding. Fuse the ends to the garment piece. Distribute the excess fabric along the length of the tape. Fuse the rest of the tape along the armhole, letting the tape draw in the extra fabric at the armhole.

Sandra's Guidelines

FOR ARMHOLE EASING

Cup Size	Amount to Ease
A	⅛ in. (3mm)
B	¼ in. (6mm)
C	⅜ in. (1cm)
D	½ in. (1.3cm)
DD or larger	⅝ in. (15mm) or more*

*Ease the entire front armhole to reduce the measurement this much.

TIP When using binding around the edges, position the ease lines ¾ in. (1.9cm) from the cut edge since you'll be cutting off the seam allowances before applying the binding.

3 If you eased the armhole with stitching, it's best to stabilize the armhole. Easestitching may snap or stretch, so stabilize the wrong side of the armhole with a length of twill tape (or fabric selvage).

Style Maker

4 Place the twill tape on the wrong side of the armhole and straight-stitch on top of the ease line. Fusible twill tape eliminates the second line of stitching. Press the easestitching flat so that the area has contours but no obvious puckers at the ease line.

[TIP] **The firmly woven, ¼-in. (6mm) wide selvage from lining is a great alternative to stabilizing with twill tape.**

5 Switch to a regular stitch length (2.5mm or 10 spi). Easestitch the armholes on the lining pieces in the same manner. It isn't necessary to stabilize the lining stitching with twill tape.

PIPING DREAMS

Even the simplest garment shape looks sharp when you add piping or binding at the seams, edges, or pocket openings. Piping around the perimeter and arm-holes of a vest is a great way to frame the vest while keeping the lining hidden. It's an opportunity to draw attention to interesting design elements, such as an attractive collar.

With piping, you can introduce a new color for expanded clothing combinations. Piping in a contrasting color gives your garment a little pizzazz. It also

accents those vertical seamlines that make you look taller and slimmer. Introducing another color, texture, or print gives you another element to coordinate with other garments for a pulled-together look. If your garment lacks a seamline at the desired location for your piping, create one by splitting the pattern and adding seam allowances to both sides of the newly cut edges.

Creating Piping

Covering your own cording gives you unlimited options for a variety of piping effects. My favorite fabric choices for piping are stripes in wool jersey or cotton knit; I like the checkerboard effect created by cutting across stripes on a knit fabric (see the photo above). Moiré, rayon ottoman, silk charmeuse, and taffeta are great for a shiny look. For color, I choose handkerchief linen or silk crepe de Chine.

While bias-cut strips are always preferable for covering piping, crossgrain is better for knits because this direction has the greatest stretch.

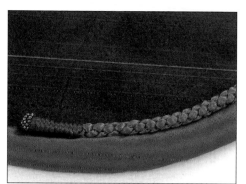

Off-grain strips work well on wovens if the fabric isn't rigid.

Solid-color knits cut on the crossgrain offer the flexibility of a bias-cut woven strip without using nearly as much fabric (see the vest at right). Satin lining strips cut on the bias give the piping a subtle sheen that looks gorgeous com-

bined with a flat-weave garment fabric, as in the top photo at left. Silk charmeuse and silk crepe de Chine strips, when cut slightly off grain, are almost as flexible as bias-cut woven fabric (see the center photo at left).

Inserting Piping

You can either add piping to the interior of a vest or march it along straight edges such as front openings, collars, and cuffs. If your garment doesn't have interior seams to pipe, make your own, as in the bottom photo at left.

It's very important that sewing be pleasurable, so I use efficient, top-quality construction techniques. I like to hand-baste the piping to the seamline of the garment before attaching the lining or facings. Some may think this is too labor-intensive. Believe me, the results are well worth the extra time. Besides, I never have to rip out the seamline and start over. My piping is exactly where I want it to be, and the piping hasn't shortened the seamline because I've built in some extra ease.

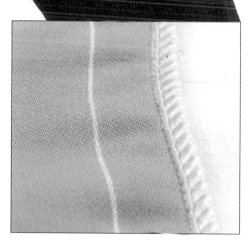

My step-by-step method isn't the fastest way to insert piping. Machine basting is quicker, but it often draws up the seamline, as shown in the photo above.

1 Join the garment pieces at the shoulders before applying the piping. Don't attach the lining or facings yet. Make or buy piping to apply to the desired seamline, including 4 in. (10.2cm) of extra length. (Even if your seamline is straight, you'll still need some extra length to build in ease for going around curves and angles.)

2 Trim the seam allowances on the covered piping so that the distance between the cut edge and the seamline that encloses the piping is ⅝ in. (15mm).

3 With right sides together, start pinning the piping to the garment piece. Position the piping's seam on the seam allowance right beside the garment seamline. Don't automatically place your piping on the garment piece with the raw edges even. It's more important that the piping be correctly positioned at the seamline.

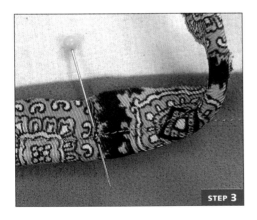
STEP 3

4 As you continue pinning, push slightly more piping into the seamline at the curves and corners. This way, the piping won't pull up the garment seamline or force the garment edge to cup.

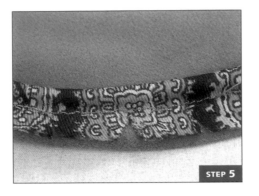
STEP 5

5 Use a running stitch to hand-baste the piping just outside the seamline. Don't machine-baste the piping in position. Machine stitching shortens the seam and the extra thread adds too much bulk.

6 Clip the piping seam allowances every ¼ in. (6mm) around curves and to within one thread of the seamline at all corners. Clipping into the seam allowances helps sharpen the corners.

7 Cut off the piping filler at the end of the seam allowance (not at the seamline). The seam allowance needs to be flat, so remove the "stuffing" inside the piping. Pull a bit of cording out of one end of the piping. Cut off ¾ in. (1.9cm) and let the cording slide back inside the piping.

STEP 7

STEP 8

8 Cut off the same amount of filler at the opposite end of the piping. This eliminates filler from the seam allowance. Although the piping looks completely corded on the finished garment, the seam allowance is flexible.

[TIP] At this stage, also cut filler out of the hem allowance. I prefer to stop the piping at the hemline by simply swinging the piping into the seam allowance, then trimming out the filler in the seam allowance.

9 To complete the piped seam, place the right side of the facing or lining against the right side of the garment with the piping sandwiched between the two layers. Pin the layers together with the garment side up so that you can see the line of basting.

10 Switch to a slightly longer machine stitch. (The longer straight stitch prevents the seam from shortening.) Install a zipper foot so that you can sew close to the piping.

11 To join the layers of fabric, piping, and lining, sew a slightly deeper seam allowance than you used for the hand stitching. Essentially, you end up machine-stitching closer to the piping.

STEP 11

12 When the stitching is complete, clip and grade all seams, turn the garment right side out, and press.

[TIP] **Press the garment well, but refrain from using a clapper on the piped seam. This prevents a seam allowance imprint from showing on the right side.**

BETTER LINING PATTERN

Do the points on your lined vest flip up? Throw out your lining pattern and make your own, advises industry sewing expert Kathleen Fasanella. She's made enough patterns through her company, Apparel Technical Services Inc., to know that an incorrect lining pattern causes construction problems and lousy results.

When a vest has two layers, the one closest to the body (the lining) follows your contours, arching over the bustline and shifting back to the chest underneath. So it stands to reason that the lining must be cut larger than the outer (fashion-fabric) layer, which merely skims the body.

Curled vest points mean that the lining and garment pieces were cut the same size, so the lining is too short to contour to your body. For perfect points, cut a lining that's longer than the garment pieces. Here's my simplified version of Kathleen's method for making a better lining pattern.

1 Set aside the pattern pieces for the vest lining. To make the new lining pattern pieces, trace the front and back vest pattern pieces.

2 Draw a horizontal line across the front and back lining pattern pieces, just under the waistline. Cut the pattern apart along the horizontal line. Spread the front and back lining pieces ½ in. (1.3cm) and insert a paper extension. Don't adjust the fashion-fabric vest pieces.

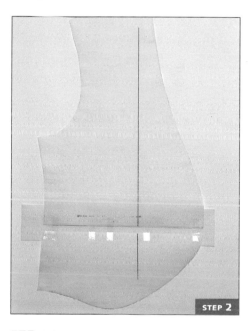

STEP 2

[TIP] **If the vest has princess styling, with front and side front pieces, lengthen the side front lining pattern pieces as well.**

3 Now cut out the garment and lining pieces from your fabrics. When joining the fashion-fabric vest and the lining pieces, place the lining against the feed dogs. This helps draw in the extra length to fit the raw edges of the garment pieces.

[TIP] **Cut the vest-front lining on the bias so that it molds better to your body.**

GOLD MEDAL LINING

Whatever vest-lining technique you normally use, I assure you that this one is faster, easier, and allows you to make alterations later if desired. It's a wonderful way to assemble a reversible or lined vest.

Vests always look better when they're crisp: They conform to the body and don't collapse around the upper chest. To achieve this effect, interface the entire wrong side of the vest pieces with a lightweight fusible like Fusi-Knit. Heavyweight fabric, like melton, doesn't need interfacing.

The Gold Medal Lining technique isn't suitable for a vest that has piping around the perimeter. The garment here shows what can go wrong: The piping joints don't match in a smooth line.

Most people are a bit surprised by this vest-assembly method because the matching fabric and lining pieces are joined first. Only after several steps does the garment really start to take on a vest shape, with two fronts joined to a back at shoulder and side seams. After the interfacing is fused to the wrong side of the garment pieces, the next step is to join the armhole, hem, and front-opening edges of the front garment and lining.

1 Cut out your garment, lining, and interfacing pieces. Unless your fashion fabric is quite firm, interface the entire wrong side of the front, back, and any side pieces. If necessary, join the side fronts to the fronts and the side backs to the back. Make your welt pockets, or add other embellishments as desired.

TIP Don't bother cutting the interfacing out of the seam allowances. The stitching helps secure the interfacing over the garment's lifetime.

2 Place one vest front and the matching lining piece with right sides together. Using ⅝-in. (15mm) seam allowances, sew all of the edges except the shoulder and side seam. Complete the other front in the same manner.

3 Clip the curves to the stitching, then press the seam allowances open and trim them to ¼ in. (6mm). Turn the vest fronts right side out through the open side seams. Press the fronts well, using a clapper for crisp edges.

4 At center back, sew 6 in. (15.2cm) of regular-length staystitching ½ in. (1.3cm) from the raw fabric edge of the back garment piece. This prevents the edge from stretching when you turn the vest right side out in a later step. Since lining fabric doesn't stretch as easily, don't bother staystitching it.

5 Place the vest back and matching lining piece right sides together with raw edges even. Sew the neck and armhole edges. Don't sew the shoulders or the side seams yet.

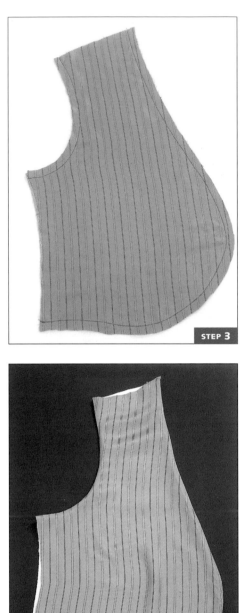

STEP 3

STEP 3

6 Sew the lining and garment piece together at the bottom of the vest, leaving a 6-in. (15.2cm) long opening in the center (at the staystitching). It's important to leave this opening at the center-back hem. In a later step you'll

STEP 6

pull the vest right side out through the opening, then hand-stitch it closed.

7 Clip the seam allowances at the curves. Open the seam allowances by pressing them against the garment, and trim them to ¼ in. (6mm).

8 Turn the fronts right side out. With the back still wrong side out, insert one front inside the back layers, between the back and lining pieces. The right side of the fashion-fabric vest front is facing the right side of the fashion-fabric vest back. The right sides of the lining are also together. When both fronts are inserted, the center-front edges face each other.

9 With the fronts sandwiched between the back and back lining, line up the raw edges at the shoulders. Make sure that the front shoulder fits snugly into the back. If necessary, deepen one of the seams for a snugger seam allowance. If the fit isn't tight, the neck seam won't be smooth when the vest is eventually turned right side out.

10 Sew the shoulders through all layers. In these photos, a sheer fabric is used for the back lining. This would look pretty odd in a finished garment, but it's a great way to show you exactly how the pieces go together.

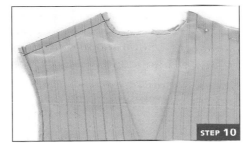

STEP 10

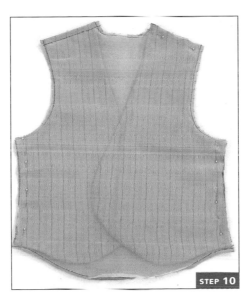

STEP 10

11 Join the side seams the same way that you attached the shoulders: With the fronts still inside the back, align the seam allowances at each side. Again, make sure the front fits snugly inside the back and back lining.

12 Sew the side seams through all four fabric layers at one side seam. This looks a bit strange, but

STEP 12

everything will be in the correct place—already joined—when you turn the vest right side out. Repeat this process at the remaining (opposite) side seam.

13 Turn the vest right side out by reaching in through the bottom opening at center back and pulling the front through the hole. Since the edges are already pressed, you're very close to finishing the entire vest.

14 Try on the garment, and don't hesitate to alter if necessary—it's simple. Just reach in through the back opening to take in or let out the side seams. You can also adjust the shoulder seams for sloping and square variations.

15 When satisfied with the fit, hand-sew the opening at the bottom of the vest back. Because the back opening was staystitched, no stretching has occurred and the back and lining are still exactly the same size.

LINED VEST
WITH SIDE SLITS

Long vests are perfect for a slimming effect. I wear this one with straight-leg pants and a simple top. It was made using Vogue 7065 from Today's Fit by Sandra Betzina.

While there are lots of different methods for lining a vest that has side slits, I prefer this one. Part of the attraction is that the method eliminates all facings. I've never liked the appearance of faced vests.

The first step is to join the fashion-fabric pieces, then make a separate "vest" from the lining pieces. Now the lining and fashion-fabric vest are machine-stitched together at the hem, the slits are finished, and the pieces are turned right side out. The finished hem ends up with a professional-looking take-up tuck at the top of the hem allowance.

1 Cut out and interface the vest's front and back fashion-fabric pieces.

2 Stabilize the neckline and armhole edges with fusible Stay Tape or a strip of tightly woven, ¼-in. (6mm) wide fabric selvage. (See "Armhole Gaposis Fix" on p. 28 and "Neckline Contouring" on p. 30.)

3 Sew and press down the darts in the fashion fabric.

4 Fold up the hem allowance on the front and back pattern pieces, then cut out the front and back lining. Note that the hem allowance on the lining is eliminated. This helps the lining stay hidden at the bottom of the finished vest.

5 Sew and press the darts in the lining, then set it aside.

6 With right sides together, sew the front and back garment pieces at the shoulders. Press the seam allowances open. Baste the side seams in contrasting thread from the underarm to the release point for the side slit.

7 Press up and pin the hem allowance on the fabric vest. Try on the garment, pinning in shoulder pads if they'll be inserted in the finished garment.

8 Adjust the side seams to fit, then sew them permanently from the underarm to the top of the side-slit opening. Switch to a short (3.5mm or

8 spi) stitch length for the last ½ in. (1.3cm) near the slit opening. This reinforces the seam at the stress point. Press the seam allowances open.

9 Using a regular stitch length (2.5mm or 10 spi), sew the front and back lining pieces together at the shoulders and side seams. Stitch with the right sides together and stop the side seamlines at the top of the slits.

10 Pin up the hem allowance. This makes it easier to attach the bottom of the lining in a later step.

STEP 10

TIP If the lining puckers as you stitch, try switching to a new needle. I prefer a 70/10 H-M or H-J needle for lining fabric.

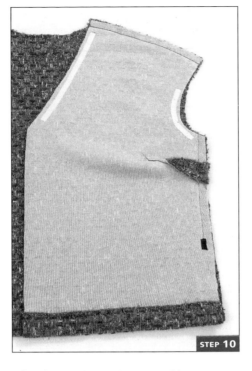

STEP 10

11 Hand-sew the pinned hem allowance to the wrong side of the garment ½ in. (1.3cm) from the raw edge of the hem. Start and finish the stitching 2 in. (5cm) away from the side slits. Stitching any farther makes it difficult to finish the slit. With the hem

STEP 11

allowance secured by hand stitching, it's easier to machine-sew the lining to the hem. Although the top ½ in. (1.3cm) of the hem allowance is left free, the machine-stitched seamline uses a mere ¼-in. (6mm) seam allowance.

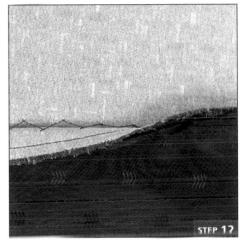

STEP 12

12 Place the vest and lining right sides together at the hem. Machine-sew the top of the hem allowance to the bottom of the lining using a ¼-in. (6mm) seam allowance. Press the seam allowances toward the lining. The remaining ¼ in. (6mm) of the top of the hem allowance folds down to create part of the hem take-up fold.

13 Turn the vest wrong side out at one of the slits. Pin the lining to the vest from the slit opening to the hem crease. Turn the hem allowance back on itself at the corner.

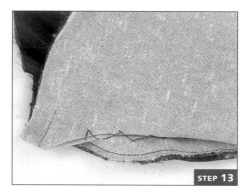

STEP 13

14 Sew with a ⅝-in. (15mm) seam allowance from slit opening to hem fold. Sew the remaining slit in the same manner.

STEP 14

TIP If the lining or fashion fabric is ¼ in. to ½ in. (6mm to 1.3cm) longer, sew the work with the longer side against the feed dogs. The mechanism will ease the longer sides to fit. If one side is a lot longer, you probably didn't end the side seams (the top of the slit) at the same place.

15 Turn the garment right side out. Use a point turner to make sharp corners. Press and pound the edges and seamlines flat.

PULL-THROUGH LINING

Of the three methods I like to use for lining a vest, this is my favorite for a piped vest. Since I often pipe my vests to keep the lining hidden at the edges, I use the Pull-Through Lining technique a lot; it gives me a smooth, continuous line of piping and is quite easy to execute. It can also be used for reversible vests that are made with two layers, but it doesn't allow alterations on the vest as with the Gold Medal Lining (see p. 34).

Machine-basting piping to garment pieces (shown at right in the top left photo on the facing page) is a mistake. Piping stretches. When the seam relaxes, the piping draws up the edge so that it's shorter and puckered. Hand-basting piping to the garment (shown at left in the top left photo on the opposite page) eliminates this problem.

When this pull-through technique is used with a bagged lining, the lining is partially attached to the vest, pulled right side out, then finished. In this case, the lining and garment pieces are sewn together at the armholes, front opening, neckline, and part of the bottom. The fronts are pulled right side out through the shoulder and back. Only then are the side seams sewn and the vest bottom closed.

1 Cut out your garment, lining, and interfacing pieces. Unless your fashion fabric is quite firm, interface the entire wrong side of the front, back, and any side pieces. If necessary, join the side fronts to the fronts and the side backs to the back.

2 Make your welt pockets, and add other embellishments to the fronts and back as desired, just as you would for any vest lining technique. Stabilize the bottom edge of the back vest for 6 in. (15.2cm) at center back.

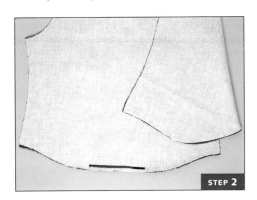

STEP 2

[TIP] **It isn't possible to adjust the vest's fit after starting the lining process, so make adjustments now. Pin or baste the vest pieces together at the shoulders and side seams, refine the fit, then proceed to Step 3.**

3 It's important to easestitch several spots on the garment pieces so that they conform to your body. First, do the lower half of the front armholes. (See "Armhole Gaposis Fix" on p. 28.) Easestitch the entire back armhole if your back is rounded. Also ease the front edge on a V neck so that it conforms to the shape of your upper chest.

4 Sew the front darts separately on the garment and lining pieces.

[TIP] **Cut through the center of the sewn darts and press them open. This helps eliminate bulk and shapes the darts to your body.**

5 With right sides together, sew the front and back shoulders of the fashion-fabric pieces. Press the seam allowances open. Join the front and back lining pieces in the same manner.

6 Hand-baste the piping to the front and back armholes and perimeter of the garment pieces. Place the piping on the right side of the fabric. Hand-baste close to the piping, right on the seamline.

7 Don't pull the piping taut. Keep in mind that the piping needs to be longer than the perimeter of the vest so that the finished edges don't curl. Some wonderful ideas for piping, and complete insertion instructions, are explained in "Piping Dreams" on p. 30.

8 Place the lining and fashion-fabric vest pieces, right sides together, on a table. Put the vest on top, wrong side up.

9 Pin the lining and vest together as they lie, joining the armholes, front opening, neck edge, and front bottom. Pins are positioned on the fashion-fabric side so that you can see your hand-basting.

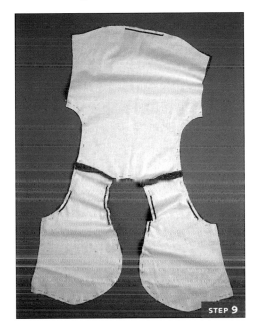

STEP 9

10 Switch to a zipper foot and sew the vest to the lining as pinned. Sew close to the piping, just inside the hand basting. Slightly lengthen your stitch to prevent the edges from drawing up.

11 Use one continuous seamline for the bottom, front opening, and neckline, starting and stopping at the midpoint at the bottom of the vest front. The side seams aren't joined yet, and the bottom back is still open. If you're using thick piping, remember to cut the piping filler out at the seamline.

12 Clip the armhole and neckline curves. Press the seam allowances open by pressing one back onto the garment. Trim and grade the seam allowances to a maximum width of ¼ in. (6mm).

13 Slide your hand between the fashion fabric and lining from the bottom of the back. Reach through one of the shoulders and grasp the bottom of the front. Since the side seams aren't joined, you can pull the fronts through the shoulders.

STEP 13

14 Pull the front through the back of the vest, and repeat for the remaining front. Now finish turning the entire vest right side out.

15 At both side seams, cross-pin the armhole seamlines together so that the seamlines won't shift when you seam in a later step.

16 With right sides together at the side seam, pin together the fashion-fabric front and back. Then pin together the lining front and back. Now you have a horseshoe shape that's sewn in one continuous seam. You're only stitching through two fabric layers at any time.

STEP 16

17 Press the seam allowances open. It's important to trim bulk out of the seamline, especially at the bottom of the armhole. Grade the seam allowances, and go one step further by snipping a V of fabric out at the underarm. Repeat for the remaining side seam.

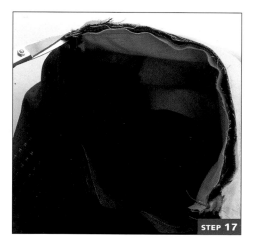

STEP 17

18 Fold the front's bottom edge and the lining so that they face each other. Tuck the bulk of the vest inside. With the fabric and lining right sides together, cross-pin the side seamlines. Now pin together the unstitched portion of the fronts and back.

19 At one side of the vest, sew the lining and front with the right sides together and the raw edges matching. Continue stitching across the bottom of the vest back, stopping 3 in. (7.6cm) from center back. Leave an opening at center back so that you can turn the vest right side out.

20 Join the remaining fabric front and back to the lining in the same manner. Press the seam allowances open and trim away fabric bulk at any curves and corners.

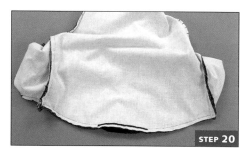

STEP 20

21 Turn the vest right side out through the bottom of center back. Fold in the seam allowances and hand-stitch the opening closed. Because the lower back of the vest was staystitched, no stretching has occurred and both sides of the opening are the same size. Press the vest.

TIP Hand-baste around the perimeter and armholes of the vest with long stitches. Press and pound all the edges flat. Remove the basting and admire your results.

AT-A-GLANCE BIAS-BINDING RESOURCE

Rather than using a self-fabric binding and following the same old application method, explore other options. Let your imagination go wild.

Choices, choices, choices! You can use wide, purchased bias tape, but you have a greater choice of colors and patterns if you make your own binding. Your one-of-a-kind vest can feature binding made from many types of fabric.

One of my favorite trims is crossgrain knit, which has as much stretch as bias and requires a fraction of the yardage. Since it's 60 in. (1.5m) wide, ¼ yd. (0.2m) is plenty for several garments. I frequently use wool jersey or cotton knit in plain colors and stripes.

The vests in the photo at left below feature bindings in faux leather, striped knit, and linen. I love faux leather because it stretches in all directions. Faux suede isn't suitable; it has no give, so you end up with ripples along the binding.

Binding application

1 Make the strips 2¼ in. (5.7cm) wide. First, cut a short strip of fabric to test the width. Press under ¼ in. (6mm) along one lengthwise edge.

2 Sew the strip onto the garment with a ⅜-in. to ½-in. (1cm to 1.3cm) seam allowance, with the binding next to the feed dog to prevent it from stretching.

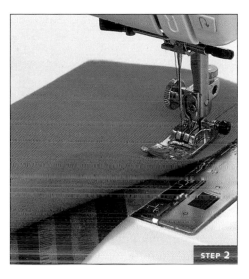

3 Consider a wider strip and a slightly different application method for very stretchy knit fabric strips. Cut the fabric strip 2¾ in. (7cm) wide and fold it in half

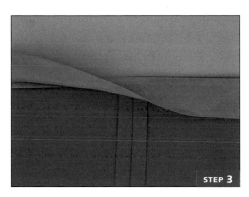

lengthwise. Treat the doubled fabric as a single layer when attaching it to the garment. Sew the two raw edges to the raw garment edge with a ⅜-in. (1cm) seam allowance. Now hand-stitch the pressed edge of the binding on the other side of the garment.

4 For narrower binding, sew the raw edges of the bias binding and garment at ⅜ in. (15mm) with the right sides together. Trim the seam allowances to ¼ in. (6mm). Now wrap the remaining pressed binding edge to the inside of the garment and hand-stitch it in position on top of the seamline. Sew by taking a small stitch, sliding the needle along the fold, then taking another stitch.

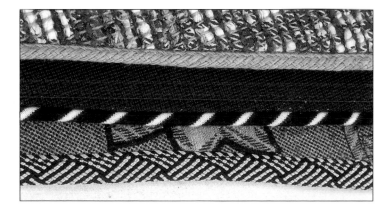

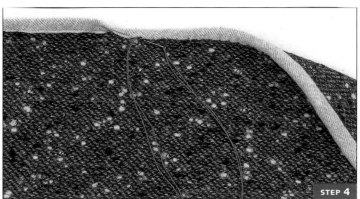

STEP 6

5 With raw edges even, place the right side of the (single-thickness) strip against the right side of the garment. Sew them together using a ⅝-in. (15mm) seam allowance. Trim the seam allowance to ¼ in. (6mm). Wrap the remaining edge of the strip to the wrong side of the garment.

6 Stitching in the well, or ditch, is the fastest application for crossgrain knit or synthetic fabric binding. The binding has an attractive, clean finish after the raw edge is trimmed. It's great if you're in a hurry and the vest isn't reversible. Don't press under an edge of the bias binding or fold it in half lengthwise.

The right side and using an edge-joining foot for accuracy, stitch in the well. If your seams ripple as you stitch, switch to a Teflon or even-feed foot.

7 From the wrong side of the garment, sew and trim the inside of the bias binding close to the stitching when using a binding made of knit or any other fabric that doesn't fray.

8 You can fold under the raw edge of the trim and hand-stitch the fold to the garment just past the seamline. A turned-under edge looks great on a reversible vest.

ON-THE-EDGE BINDING

A jacket or vest that's lined looks fabulous with edging around the neck, armholes, and front opening. The fabric strips add class and a lively touch to the edges and eliminate the need for facings. This is by far the simplest and fastest technique for making a vest.

This treatment is particularly effective on reversible or one-layer garments made from boiled wool, melton, or quilted fabric. Binding strips can be cut on the crossgrain of knit fabric or on the bias of wovens. My favorite vest bindings are faux leather, linen, striped cotton knit, and wool jersey.

1 Alter the pattern pieces to fit, including making the vest in a flattering length. It's very important to set the length now because it can't be done after you start the assembly process. Cut out and prepare the lining and garment pieces.

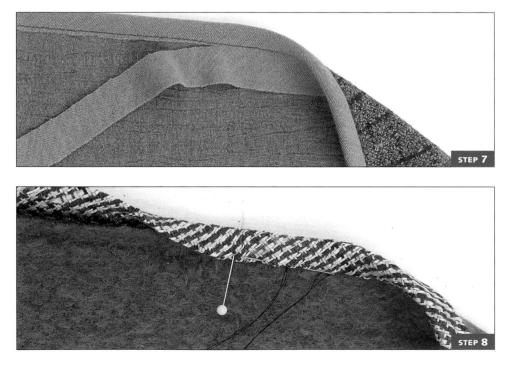

STEP 7

STEP 8

4 Slip the lining inside the vest with the wrong sides together and the raw edges even at the armholes and outside edges. Straight-stitch through both layers around the armholes and outside edges using ¾-in. (1.9cm) seam allowances.

5 Trim ⅝ in. (15mm) away from the seam allowances. This leaves a stitching line joining the vest and lining ⅛ in. (3mm) from the raw edges. Don't cut off the staystitching because it stabilizes the edges. Trimming the seam allowances won't reduce the front overlap of the finished garment (if your vest is designed for a closure). Any lost width is replaced by the bias binding.

[TIP] if you cut the lining larger to prevent your vest points from curling in, sew with the lining layer against the feed dogs. (See "Better Lining Pattern" on p. 33.) The machine's mechanism draws in the extra length to fit.

2 Stabilize the neck and armholes, placing the stitching ¾ in. (1.9cm) from the raw edges.

3 Join the shoulder and side seams of the garment pieces. Join the garment and lining pieces separately. Press all of the seam allowances open. Gaping armholes and necklines can be remedied with a few simple steps before you assemble the vest. (See "Armhole Gaposis Fix" on p. 28.)

STEP 5

TRICK
of the TRADE

FEED THE DOGS

When applying bias binding to an armhole, place the vest against the feed dogs. This makes the armhole slightly smaller so that the binding draws in at the armhole to fit your body shape.

On the other hand, apply neckline and front-opening binding with the vest on top. The feed dogs draw a little extra binding into the seamline, which prevents the edges of the finished garment from curling in.

6 Cut and apply your bias strips. Some interesting fabric suggestions and several application methods are shown and explained in "At-a-Glance Bias-Binding Resource" on p. 41.

BUTTONHOLE WINDOW

The buttonhole window is fast and easy to put in and always a success. I like it for many reasons, but mostly because it's strong and attractive on both sides— perfect for a reversible garment. You can make the windows any size you want, so this type of buttonhole works well for large buttons. I also recommend it if your sewing machine doesn't make reliable buttonholes or if your fabric is heavy and a good machine buttonhole is iffy.

Buttonhole windows look fabulous when the patch matches a binding made of cotton knit, faux leather, leather, or wool jersey. And even though felt and faux suede don't make great bindings, they're suitable for buttonhole patches. When selecting patch fabric, look for a material that will have a clean cut edge and won't ravel.

These instructions apply to a reversible vest, but this buttonhole window can go on any vest or jacket. The position of the buttonhole varies according to the garment style and the size of the button. Even if you transferred the buttonhole position marks from your pattern, try on your garment to see if you like the locations. I like a button at the bustline, the waist, and the tummy.

1 Cut out and assemble the garment pieces. Mark the buttonhole placement lines on the wrong side, 1 in. (2.5cm) from the finished edge of the garment. The following instructions explain how to make a single buttonhole. To ensure that your button-

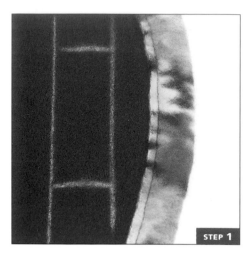

STEP 1

holes are identical, however, it's best to complete each step for all of the buttonholes before moving on to the next step.

2 Interface the wrong side at each buttonhole location with a ½-in. (1.3cm) wide strip of fusible interfacing that's 1 in. (2.5cm) longer than the buttonhole opening. Hand-baste all of the buttonhole locations through the fashion fabric and the interfacing. This way, you can see the buttonhole location on the right and wrong sides of the garment.

3 Buttonhole patches are cut larger than the button and buttonhole. Furthermore, several buttonholes start with one long strip. A strip lies flat as you move from one buttonhole to the next and requires no additional positioning. The patch isn't interfaced.

If your garment has only one button, cut a patch 2½ in. (6.4cm) wide and the length of the button diameter plus 1½ in. (3.8cm). For several openings, cut a patch that's 4 in. (10.2cm) longer than the distance from the top to the bottom buttonhole.

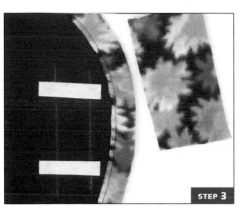

STEP 3

STEP 4

4 Center the right side of the buttonhole patch over the right side of the buttonhole openings. Pin the strip in place. Flip over the vest to expose the wrong side so that the buttonhole placement lines are visible.

The patch for your buttonholes starts out pinned to the right side, but ends up on the wrong side of the finished vest. Here, the patch is pinned in position and ready to be stitched from the wrong side, where you can see the buttonhole placement marking.

Stitching the patch in position from the wrong side ensures that each buttonhole is perfectly positioned on the garment. Pins on the right side hold the patch in position.

5 Using small straight stitches, sew about ⅛ in. (3mm) to one side of the buttonhole placement line. Just past the end of the placement line (about ⅛ in. [3mm]), pivot and sew six small stitches (about ¼ in. [6mm]) to the opposite side. It's difficult to sew just a few stitches with the foot pedal, so hand-walk the stitches by turning the machine's flywheel.

6 Sew a second line of stitching parallel to the first and an equal distance from the placement line. At the end of the second line, pivot and sew six stitches to complete the narrow stitched rectangle. Sew two stitches past the initial stitching. Don't backstitch.

7 Using small scissors, cut through the center of the stitched rectangle. Snip diagonally into the corners, to within three fabric threads of the stitching at the corners. Don't cut through the stitching.

STEP 8

[TIP] If your fabric is prone to raveling, dot fabric glue in the corners. Use a hair dryer to dry the glue before turning the patch.

8 If you've used a long patch for several buttonholes, cut through it midway between each buttonhole. Pull each patch to the wrong side through the center of the buttonhole opening.

9 From the right side of the vest, press the opening to reveal as much of the patch as you wish. I like about ⅛ in. (3mm) of the patch fabric to show on each side.

10 Using the edge of the presser foot as a guide and moving your needle to the far right, straight-stitch ½ in. (1.3cm) from all edges of the buttonhole opening. You can also use a quilter's bar. Trim the patch close to the stitching.

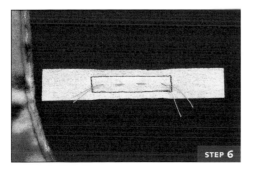

STEP 6

STEP 7

STEP 10

Chapter 3

PANTS

Purchasing or making a pair of flattering pants can be a real challenge. The trick is to find a pattern that's perfect for you.

My favorites are Vogue 7027 for a tailored pant, Vogue 7179 for a princess-seamed pant without a waistband, Vogue 7263 for a narrow pull-on pant, and Vogue 7281 for a full pull-on pant. All of these patterns have pockets and range from a 34½-in. (87.5cm) to a 57-in. (145cm) hip, based on the Today's Fit sizing block with a well-shaped crotch curve.

You can alter your pattern to fit your body, and you can make it up in a variety of fabrics and colors. In this chapter, I offer many alternative lining, underlining, and waistband treatments, as well as pocket details and a wide assortment of technical advice.

Sandra's Closet

While I was working on this book, I was simultaneously sorting through my wardrobe to come up with interesting pants I could show you. About halfway through the clothing hunt, it dawned on me that I have way too many clothes! I have a few items going back a decade. Every time I consider parting with something, I remember a student who needed to see an example of a technique that was on the finished garment. So I guess I'm stuck with at least a few of these treasures from yesteryear. It's hard to part with the clothes we make because we spend so much time on them. If you love to sew as much as I do, the garments represent wonderful memories.

On the next few pages, I showcase a few of my favorite pants. If you find a detail you like, turn to the accompanying step-by-step instructions for guidance.

How I Made These Pants

You can make a pair of pants like mine using the step-by-step instructions in the following features:

Painless Pants Fit (see p. 52)
Blocked Shaping (see p. 55)
Petersham Waist Facing (see p. 71)
Taming Pant Hems (see p. 84)

STYLISH SILK DUPIONI

Sleek and slim, the burgundy pants on the facing page are made from a medium-weight dupioni. I like using dressy fabrics for casual styles, so I couldn't resist this material. It made a great pair of versatile pants. I can wear them under a dressy jacket for the evening or with a casual sweater for daytime. The color also appealed to me because it complements a chiffon blouse that's already in my closet.

The entire wrong side of these pants is underlined with Fusi-Knit. The interfacing cuts down on silk dupioni's tendency to wrinkle. If you live in a hot climate, a cooler underlining alternative is silk organza.

A flat-front style is perfect for a waistband faced with petersham. This pattern had a waistband, but I eliminated it to give the pants a flat, streamlined look. To achieve the same effect, start with a pattern that doesn't have waist pleats. Vogue 7179 is perfect for this treatment. A smooth back is also essential, so you can rule out an elasticized back waist.

Selecting Fabric

Choose a fabric with body for very fitted pants. Wool gabardine, wool flannel, firm cotton, denim, and some Lycra blends are good choices. I'm in love with Lycra blends because these fabrics reduce wrinkles and help pants keep their shape. All of these fabrics take stress well and still retain shape. Be cautious about corduroy because it adds weight. You can use a weak fabric to make pants if you underline it to add body.

Lengthy Issue

Unless you're tall, be cautious about wide pant legs. If the fabric isn't drapey or color-matched with the top, wide pants make many women look shorter and wider. An alternative is to cut the pants two sizes smaller from the knee down to reduce the circumference. Most women wear their pants too short, which can make them look heavier. The style and length of pants have changed. For example, pants aren't hemmed longer at the heel anymore. Today, full-length pants cover much of the shoe and break in front.

To determine proper pant length, steal a technique from the alteration rooms of upscale designer departments. Without wearing shoes, slip into your pants. Fold up the hem so that the pant touches the floor at your heel. Cut off the pants at the fold. After the pants are stitched with a 1½-in. (3.8cm) hem allowance, they'll be just the right length. If you only wear flats, use a 2-in. (5cm) hem allowance. If you plan to wear the pants with high heels, use a 1-in. (2.5cm) hem allowance. The finished length for a very narrow pant is just under the ankle bone.

VERY VOGUE

A good pair of pants is comfortable and figure-flattering. The pants on p. 50 are part of an exciting new project I launched in 1999, when I created a line for Vogue designed to fit real women. (See "New Pattern Sizing" on p. 11.) I had a lot of fun conducting fit tests for the pants. So many women volunteered to try on the various sizes and assess the fit.

Each size isn't just a standard enlargement of the base pattern. In fact, the crotch has a great new shape. There's 4 in. (10.2cm) of additional ease over the tummy, to keep pleats from popping open. One of the best features of this pair is the waistband. It looks like a

TRICK
of the TRADE

GOING TO GREAT LENGTHS

To determine pant-length alterations, measure the side seam of a favorite pair of finished pants from the bottom of the waistband to the hem crease. Compare this measurement to the pant length listed on the back of the pattern envelope. The difference is the amount you need to alter your pants pattern.

Never lengthen or shorten more than 2 in. (5cm) in one place. To maintain the pant style, shorten above and below the knee rather than at the bottom of the pants.

classic tailored treatment, yet the back is elasticized. These pants were made from Vogue 7027, Today's Fit by Sandra Betzina, available for hip sizes 34½ in. to 57 in. (87.7cm to 144.8cm).

Today's Fit

Fitting pants used to be such a hassle. I've learned my way around many figure problems, but students were still telling me about their frustration with patterns that seem to fit no one. It's tough learning how to fit—and then alter—a pair of pants. I recently had the opportunity to improve this situation by redesigning a pants sloper for Vogue. I jumped at the

opportunity because it meant that I could design a pant with 4 in. (10.2cm) of extra fabric over the tummy and dramatically improve the crotch curve to eliminate a baggy seat. These are the two biggest problems students bring to me when I'm teaching fit classes.

People of all sizes are absolutely amazed at how few adjustments they have to make to the pattern I created, Vogue 7027. And if there are problems, the pattern instructions walk the reader through the alteration process.

How I Made These Pants

You can make a pair of pants like mine using the step-by-step instructions in the following features:

Blocked Shaping (see p. 55)
Pointed Tips about Darts (see p. 56)
Inseam Shaping (see p. 61)
Fly-Front Zipper (see p. 62)
Tailored Waistband with Elasticized Back (see p. 75)
No-Tear Lining (see p. 81)
Taming Pant Hems (see p. 84)

ANATOMY *of a Pair of Pants*

I always use my horseshoe method of pant assembly, so called because the crotch curve is sewn in a horseshoe shape, because it works with any style. The following instructions are suitable for pants that pull on, or that open with a zipper at center front, center back, or even in a pocket. You can combine this method with a variety of waist treatments, pockets, and hems. Once you use it to assemble a pair of pants, you'll use no other. Not only is it easy, but pants constructed this way are far more comfortable.

Many construction options are explained in this chapter, so the specifics of particular techniques aren't covered in detail here. Instead, I'll focus on the assembly method.

1 **Cut out the pant pieces** and the pant lining pieces (without the hem allowance). Sew the darts and pleats, sewing ½ in. (1.3cm) seams in the lining.

2 **Assemble the lining** with ½-in. (1.3cm) seam allowances. Press back the lining seam allowances at the zipper opening.

[TIP] Lining fabric has no give. By sewing slightly smaller seams and darts, the lining won't pull away at the zipper and stress at the darts.

3 **Run an ease line along the waist** of each garment piece. Stabilize the garment's waist with twill tape.

4 **If your plan includes a zipper opening** in a diagonal front pocket, insert it now.

5 **Whatever your zipper preference,** insert it now. But leave the 1 in. (2.5cm) area near the crotch point and inner leg unstitched. Apply the pockets.

6 **For a nice fit under the crotch in back,** ease the longer front inseam into the back inseam for 5 in. (12.7cm) below the crotch.

Sew the inseams with the front leg against the feed dogs so that the mechanism can draw in the excess length. You can stretch the back slightly to fit.

7 **Press the seam allowances open,** then baste the front and back pant pieces at the side seams.

8 **Turn one leg right side out.** Slip it into the remaining leg so that the right sides are together. With the raw edges even, the crotch has a horseshoe shape.

9 **Sew the crotch** in one continuous line of stitching. Crack the seam by pulling it taut. If any stitches break, sew along the seamline a second time.

10 **At the curved portion of the crotch,** lay down a piece of narrow twill tape and sew another line of stitching in the seam allowance, ⅛ in. (3mm) away from the previous stitching (a ½-in. or 1.3cm seam allowance).

11 **Trim the lower crotch curve** to ¼ in. (6mm). Serge or zigzag the lower crotch area and press the seam allowances flat. Press them open in the upper crotch curve.

12 **Turn the pants right side out.** Try them on and refine the fit. Because you've stabilized the waist with twill tape, you have an accurate basis on which to judge both fit and comfort.

13 **Permanently sew the side seams.** Then insert the lining, wrong sides together. Attach the waistband or waist facing.

14 **Hem the pants and the lining** separately, securing the lining to the top of the hem allowance with a swing tack. (See "Swing Tacks" on p. 98.)

Master Construction Methods

Who says that pants have to be boring? There are so many wonderful ways to underline, line, face a waistline or attach a waistband, add pockets—you have many choices.

This chapter includes a selection of techniques, details, and advice that I love and which my students get excited about. I'm also introducing a number of new ideas. There's an interesting way to underline a garment and finish the seams at the same time. (See "Wrinkle-Free Underlining" on p. 59.) How about a pocket insertion that allows you to create a continuous lapped seam from hem to waist? (See "Flat-Fell Inseam Pocket" on p. 78.) You may want to try hiding your zipper opening in a pocket. (See "Zipper in a Pocket" on p. 67.)

From copying a pair of finished pants for a dream fit (see "Painless Pants Fit" at right) to adding a Hong Kong finish to a hem allowance (see "West Coast Hong Kong Finish" on p. 86), this chapter covers a wide range of techniques. They're arranged in the order you would follow to assemble a pair of pants, so it's easy to find the topic you want.

StyleMaker

CLOSET CONSULTATION

Examining pants you wear and love can help with fabric selection. This is how I realized that my favorite pant fabrics are cotton twill, wool crepe, and medium-weight linen.

PAINLESS PANTS FIT

Making a pair of pants you love is easier than you think. One of my favorite methods is using a pair of well-fitting finished pants as the launching point. Compare the leg circumference, crotch shape, and crotch length to a commercial home-sewing pattern, and adjust your pattern to match. Now you have a starting point that's more likely to give you the pant fit you want.

Vogue 7027 and 7179 from Today's Fit by Sandra Betzina are great starting points for your dream pants. In other pant styles, look for patterns that have deep and long back crotches. For example, Burda pants patterns have a good crotch curve because they're designed for a European figure. Keep in mind that they tend to run short in the crotch.

1 When browsing pattern catalogs, look for features that are similar to those on your favorite pair of finished pants. For example, if your pants have pleats, don't choose a pattern with a flat front and darts.

STEP 4

2 Once you spot a suitable pattern, note the hem circumference listed in the catalog or on the back of the pattern envelope. It should be as close as possible to the measurement at the hem of your favorite ready-to-wear pants.

TIP **To taper legs, adjust both the inner and outer seams; otherwise, the legs on the finished pants will twist. Begin to taper below the fullest part of the hip on the outer leg and at the knee on the inner leg.**

3 Once at home with your pattern purchase, compare the crotch length to your favorite pants. Turn your pants wrong side out. Slide one leg inside the other so that the crotch curve is clearly visible.

4 Try on your favorite pants and critique the crotch length to determine the changes you need to make on your pattern. Trace the crotch shape onto a piece of pattern paper. Mark the waist seamline and the intersection of the inner leg seams. Measure the front and back crotch lengths from the waistline to the crotch point.

5 Compare the length and shape of the pants' front and back crotch to the front and back pattern pieces at the seamline. Don't be surprised if the front and back crotch lengths differ greatly. Some larger women have a crotch length 4 in. to 6 in. (10.2cm to 15.2cm) longer in the back than in the front because they wear their pants under their tummy in front.

6 Alter the pants pattern pieces to the same crotch length, adding a 1-in. (2.5cm) seam allowance at the top of the waist, inner leg, and side seams. This gives you some leeway for alterations.

7 Cut the garment pieces out of scrap fabric with a weight and drape similar to the fashion fabric you plan to use for your pants. Transfer all marks and seamlines to the garment pieces.

8 Assemble a pretest garment. Refine the fit, including the length. You may still need to adjust the fit slightly through the crotch because it's impossible to determine crotch length with total accuracy using pants you've worn.

TIP Before cutting out your garment pieces, reinforce the pattern by fusing a medium-weight interfacing to the back with a dry iron. Work from the center out with the pattern paper on top.

9 If necessary, adjust the pattern's crotch length either at the top of the inner leg seam or at the waistline at center front or center back. The fit of your pretest indicates where the reduction or addition is made.

a. A large tummy or higher front waistline needs extra fabric at center front along the waistline. On the pattern piece, taper the addition to nothing at the side seams.

b. A swayback or low back waistline looks better with a lifted center-back waistline, so cut down the pattern at center back, curving back to the original at the side seam.

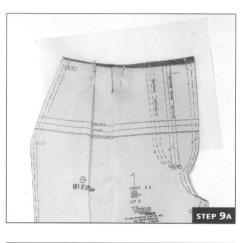

STEP 9A

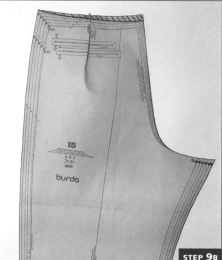

STEP 9B

c. Full or thin thighs require an inner leg adjustment on the front pattern piece. If your thighs are full, add to the front inner leg. If your legs are thin, subtract from the front inner leg.

d. If your bottom protrudes, add to the back inner leg. If your bottom is flat, subtract from the back inner leg.

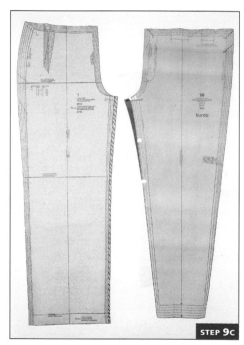

STEP 9C

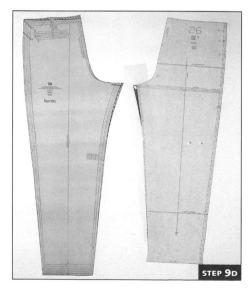

STEP 9D

TRICK of the TRADE

SMILES AND FROWNS

It may amuse you to think of pants smiling and frowning, but an ill-fitting pair does just that. When you wear the garment, horizontal wrinkles at the crotch and upper thighs curve up or down. They smile in the front if the pant legs are too tight through the thighs, and frown in the back if there isn't enough fabric for the seat or enough sitting room.

BLOCKED SHAPING

Pants designer Leonora Schulhoff taught me this shrink-and-stretch technique. It's a pants-pressing trick used by tailors to gain a close fit through the derriere without destroying the hang of the garment. Whenever fabric is pressed along a fold, it tends to stretch. So pressing a crease in pant legs after they're constructed causes the pants to hang improperly.

Silk shantung makes a beautiful pair of pants. To prevent excess wrinkling with this fabric, interface the entire back of the front and back garment pieces with Fusi-Knit before assembly. I shrink and stretch the center front and center back of the legs to perfect the hang without destroying the crotch shape.

1 Alter the pattern to fit and cut out the garment pieces. Clearly mark the front and back crease lines on the garment pieces. Now you're ready to shrink out fullness along the crease line and stretch the fabric along the seamlines.

2 Fold a pant-front garment piece along the marked crease line with the fabric's right side to the outside. Use a press-and-lift motion with your iron to set a soft crease, working from the hem to the waist.

[TIP] To help you set the crease, spray the fabric with a mixture of 3 Tbs. of white vinegar in 1 cup of water.

3 Shift your attention to the side seam. Hold the cut edges of the pants taut. Now start simultaneously stretching and ironing along the raw edge of the side seam.

TRICK
of the TRADE

MEET THE CREASE

To determine crease lines, fold the pant so that the inner and outer leg seams match from the knee to the bottom of the pant. The folds are the crease from the knee to the bottom of the pant. Above the knee, continue the crease line, on grain, to the waist. The waist pleat closest to center front lines up with the front crease line on well-designed patterns.

4 The crease-line fold wrinkles a bit during this process. Using an iron with plenty of steam, employ a press-and-lift motion to shrink out the fullness. If necessary, repeat this step until a distinct curve forms along the crease line.

5 Repeat this shaping on the remaining pattern pieces and assemble the pants.

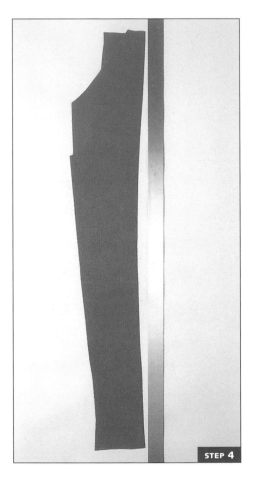

STEP 4

POINTED TIPS ABOUT DARTS

Darts are a good tool for shaping a garment to your body. They can take out fullness where you don't need it and transfer it to fuller areas of your body. For example, a dart can take out fullness at the waist and release fabric so that the pants aren't too tight through the hips.

Fabulous darts aren't elusive. In fact, if you're having problems, using my tips will dramatically improve your results.

• If you have a waist that's proportionally small in comparison to your hips, pants are more flattering when the fullness is taken out in darts rather than at the side seams. If the pant or skirt has four darts, consider doubling the number to eight, placing a dart on either side of the original dart placement.

• Consider increasing the width of the pleats and the darts if your waist is proportionally smaller than your hips. Sew every dart and pleat ¼ in. (6mm) outside the marked stitching line. If the pants have four front pleats and two back darts, you've decreased the waist by 3 in. (7.6cm) by simply sewing the shaping elements deeper.

• For a thicker waist or tummy, consider sewing narrower darts or eliminating them altogether. Instead, run an ease line at the waist. Stitch ⅜ in. (1cm) from the waist's raw edge of the garment pieces. This draws in the pants to fit

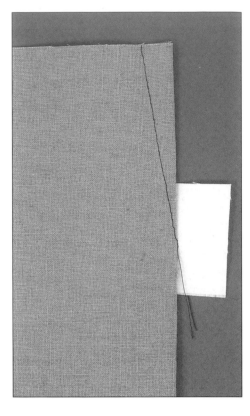

your waist while giving you a little extra fabric over the tummy and high hip. Stabilize the easing with twill tape and press over a tailor's ham to eliminate puckers.

• In some fabrics, such as faux suede and gabardine, a dimple often forms at the dart point because the material can't be shaped easily. Before stitching the dart, center a 2-in. (5cm) square of firm cotton or nonfusible interfacing on the dart point. Sew over the square as you sew the dart (see the photo above).

• Never backstitch at the beginning or end of a dart. This creates bulk and prevents the finished stitching from lying

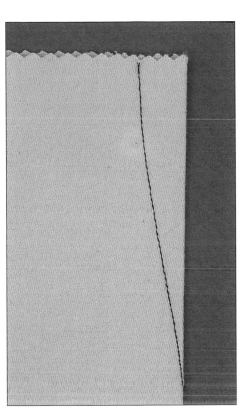

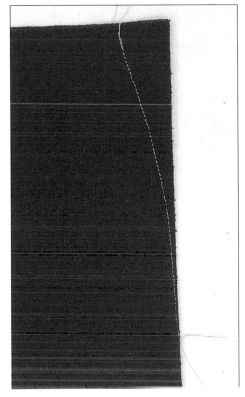

• Darts lie better when pressed over a tailor's ham, but this method isn't always appropriate. A molded front dart only draws attention to a tummy. In this case press the front darts flat, away from center front and center back.

• Darts in heavy fabric need to be cut open. If necessary, cut through the fold, stopping when the dart width is ¼ in. (6mm) wide (see the photo below).

• A fabric pouch under the front dart of pants and skirts means that your dart is either in the wrong location or not long enough. It's emphasizing a hollow rather than an outward curve. Shift the dart an inch or so (about 2.5cm) toward the side seams, where there's more fullness.

flat. Tying threads at the beginning and end of a dart takes too much time. Instead, make a machine knot. At the start of the dart, grasp the fabric 2 in. to 3 in. (5cm to 7.6cm) in front of the presser foot. Pull gently to prevent the fabric from moving under the presser foot. Hold the fabric for a split second—just long enough for the sewing machine to take one quick stitch on top of the first.

• As soon as you begin sewing a dart, think about ending it. In other words, angle the stitching so that you're sewing on no more than a few threads for the last ½ in. (1.3cm). Decrease the stitch

length for the last ½ in. (1.3cm) near the point so that knotting isn't necessary (see the photo at left above).

• Personalize your back dart with a curve that matches your body shape. Rather than having a straight line from start to point, let a back dart bow out—toward the fold—if you have a full high hip. To fit a curved spine, reverse the curve, making it concave (see the photo at right above).

• Don't use curved darts over a tummy; the shape will only emphasize the problem.

TRICK *of the* TRADE

PLEAT PERFECTION

To eliminate weakness at the bottom of a pleat, try this nifty trick on a pair of pants or a skirt. Start by folding the fabric to match the pleat marks. Sew the pleat from the waist to the end of the stitching line. Stop with the needle down and pivot the fabric clockwise so that the pleat fold is horizontal to you. Pivot it a bit more and sew across the pleat toward the fold, angling the stitching line up about ½ in. (1.3cm).

The stitching line extends across the bottom of the pleat to the fold, which strengthens the pleat. A stitching line that ends at the bottom of the pleat is more likely to pull out at the stress points. Sew all of the pleats in the same manner and press them toward center front.

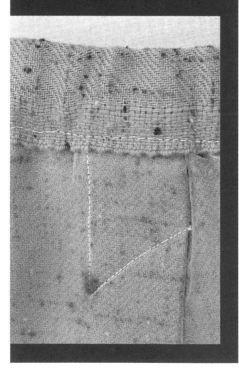

PROTRUDING TUMMY FIX

An overfitted garment molds to the tummy, thereby emphasizing its roundness. Wrinkles form under the waistband. A tummy also lifts up the front of the garment so that the hem is uneven.

Since you have to do something to prevent side seams from pulling forward and the front hemline from poking out on finished garments, use a subtle alteration. Try adding extra width at the high hip and height at the center-front waistline, tapering to nothing at the side seam. Then ease the excess width into a waistband that fits comfortably.

1 Try on a finished garment, pushing down the waist at center front until the hemline is even across the front or the front crotch on pants doesn't pull up. There's a good chance you'll need to add ½ in. (1.3cm) or more for the garment to hang properly.

STEP 1

2 If you've pushed the waist down even farther—1 in. (2.5cm) or more—it's quite all right; your waistline may hike up at center front to cover your tummy. Whatever the amount, this is the size of your alteration.

3 Tape a piece of pattern paper above the waist on the front pattern piece of your pant or skirt. Since the alteration returns to the original cutting lines at the side seams, no other pattern pieces need to be altered. Temporarily tape the darts and pleats closed.

4 Mark the alteration amount above the pattern's cutting line at center front. Using a French curve, draw a new cutting line that arcs from center front to the original cutting line at the side seam. Cut out the pattern piece.

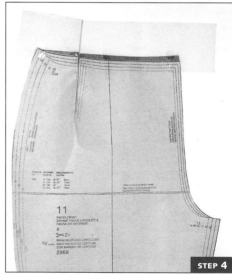

STEP 4

[TIP] To alter a pattern with side fronts, overlap the pattern pieces at the seamlines so that you can redraw the waist cutting edge all the way across the front waist.

5 Cut out your garment pieces, sew the waistline darts or pleats, add pockets, and join the side seams. If you need extra fabric to go around the tummy and high hip, a pattern addition at the side seam makes your garment larger than the waistband, so draw it in with ease. Don't dart out the added fabric.

6 Easing the front waist of the garment will draw in enough fabric for the adjusted waistline to fit into the unaltered waistband. Using a 3mm stitch length, sew two ease lines near (or on top of) each other ½ in. (1.3cm) from the waist cutting line. You can ease in ⅛ in. (3mm) per 1 in. (2.5cm) of fabric and still get a smooth seamline.

7 If the waist is still a bit large, take in a tiny amount at the side seam. To "lock" in the ease lines, sew a ¼-in. (6mm) wide length of twill tape on top of the easestitching.

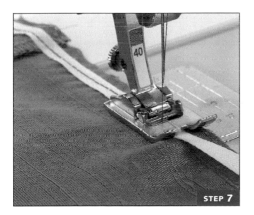

STEP 7

8 Shape and flatten the ease without stretching the waist by placing it over a tailor's ham, setting your iron for steam, and pressing the fabric above and below the stitching with a press-and-lift motion.

WRINKLE-FREE UNDERLINING

Have you ever wondered how the ladies who lunch never seem to look wrinkled, while the rest of us appear as if we dressed out of the laundry basket? What keeps their linen dresses and pants from wrinkling?

The secret lies in a garment's structure. Wrinkle-free clothes are often underlined in lightweight silk organza. Unlike other fabrics, organza has a resiliency that keeps it from crushing. When used as underlining, the organza pushes the fashion fabric back into shape. If you sit at a desk most of the day, your pants and skirts should be underlined in organza.

If you'd like your next pair of pants to look as if they cost $1,000, try this technique. The seams are beautifully finished and underlined. My good friend Margaret Islander, a fellow sewing expert who specializes in industry techniques, taught it to me.

1 Use a pattern you've pretested so that any alterations have already been made. You can't refine the fit of the pants with this technique.

2 Using 1-in. (2.5cm) seam allowances, cut out a pair of pants in fashion fabric and another pair in lightweight silk organza. This means cut ⅜ in. (1cm) beyond the cutting line. Don't include a hem allowance in the garment pieces cut in silk organza.

3 Sew the darts and pleats separately in each pair of pants. Press the darts and pleats toward center front and center back.

4 Place two matching pant pieces, one of organza and one of fashion fabric, right sides together. For this procedure you underline the left front, right front, left back, and right back separately. Pin the organza to the fashion fabric along

STEP 4

STEP 5

one long side with the pinheads on the organza side, since it's the stable layer.

5 Using the side of the presser foot as a guide for a ¼-in. (6mm) seam allowance, sew the organza to the fashion fabric on one long side only. This is the first step in finishing the seam allowances during the underlining process.

6 At your ironing board, open the sewn pieces. Press the seam allowances open. Refold the joined pieces so that the wrong sides are together. Press the seam flat with the seam along the edge of the pressed pieces.

7 Place the underlined piece on a table with the fashion fabric on the bottom and the organza side up. Place a row of pins down the length, in the middle of the pieces, from the waist to the hem.

8 Bring the long finished side toward the center. At the unseamed side, the organza will peek out. This will be trimmed off for turn of cloth.

9 Trim off the unattached long edge of the organza underlining so that it's even with the fashion fabric.

10 Remove the pins and flip the organza so that the right sides are together once again. Pin together the remaining sides of the organza and the fashion fabric, matching the cut edges of the inner leg and crotch curve. Sew them together. Leave the waist and hem open for turning. Turn right side out.

STEP 8

STEP 10

11 Press this second seam in the same manner as the first, following the instructions in Step 6. Finish all four pant pieces in the same manner, and continue constructing the pants.

12 At the crotch point, open up all four seams within the seam allowance. This gives the crotch seam flexibility since it's not trimmed down.

TRICK of the TRADE

ATTACH A MINI-LINING

A technique we can borrow from men's trousers is underlining a pant front from the waist to just below the knees. This stops knees from stretching and prevents wrinkling above the crotch, which are caused by sitting too much.

Using your pant front pattern piece, cut an underlining from lining fabric or a soft, stable cotton. Make the underlining the exact size of the front pattern piece, but stop 3 in. (7.6cm) below the knee. Serge the bottom edge. Complete the pant front and pant front underlining separately by sewing the darts and pleats and easing the waistline. Press the pleats and darts toward center front.

Place the fashion-fabric pant front wrong side up on a table. Put the underlining on top so that the wrong sides are facing. Hand-baste the pieces together around the edges. Continue constructing the pants while handling the basted underlining and fashion fabric as a single layer.

INSEAM SHAPING

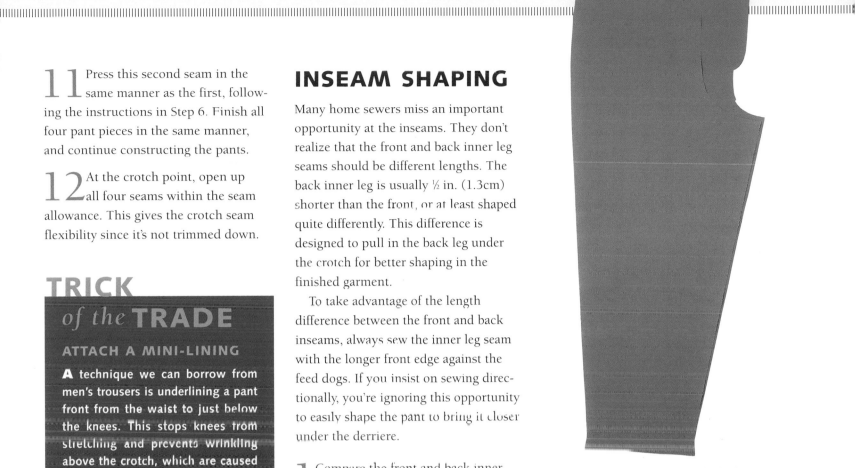

Many home sewers miss an important opportunity at the inseams. They don't realize that the front and back inner leg seams should be different lengths. The back inner leg is usually ½ in. (1.3cm) shorter than the front, or at least shaped quite differently. This difference is designed to pull in the back leg under the crotch for better shaping in the finished garment.

To take advantage of the length difference between the front and back inseams, always sew the inner leg seam with the longer front edge against the feed dogs. If you insist on sewing directionally, you're ignoring this opportunity to easily shape the pant to bring it closer under the derriere.

1 Compare the front and back inner leg seam lengths on your pattern pieces. If they're the same, eliminate some of the excess fabric under the seat by shortening the back inner leg seam.

2 Draw a horizontal line across the back pattern piece 2 in. (5cm) below the crotch point. Cut through the line, leaving a hinge of paper ⅛ in. (3mm) from the side seam. Overlap the cut edges at the inner leg to take out a total of ½ in. (1.3cm), tapering to nothing at the side seams.

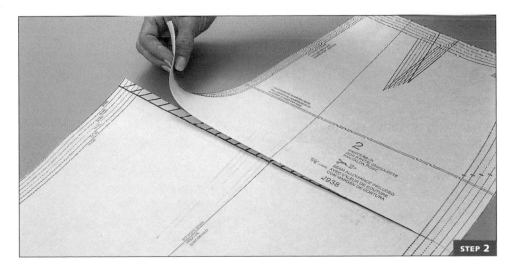

STEP 2

TRICK *of the* TRADE

SLEEK SIDES

No matter how much you diet or exercise, many cannot get rid of the hills and valleys between the tummy and hips or hips and upper thighs. Here's a nifty way to smooth out the silhouette on pants and skirts. Sew the seamline and press the seam allowances open. Cut a 1-in. (2.5cm) wide strip of medium-weight interfacing that's as long as the garment from waist to knee. Now fuse this strip to the open seam allowances.

3 With right sides together, match the raw edges of the inseam on the front and back garment pieces. Although the back inseam is shorter, match the crotch points. Also match the bottom of the leg.

4 For maximum shaping, seam the back and front leg so that all of the excess ease is distributed between the knee and the crotch. Pin the pieces together with a 1:1 ratio from the bottom of the leg to the knee.

STEP 5

5 Place the inseam on the sewing-machine bed with the back against the presser foot. The feed dogs ease the longer piece (the front inner leg) to the shorter one (the back inner leg).

6 Repeat Steps 3 through 5 for the remaining leg. You're stitching correctly if the remaining leg's inseam is sewn in the opposite direction (hem to crotch or crotch to hem).

TIP **Press up the hem allowance immediately after sewing the inner leg seam. It's much easier to press up a flat pant hem than to work with a cylinder.**

FLY-FRONT ZIPPER

One of the most obvious signs of a homemade pair of slacks is a narrow placket that's trying to pass for a fly front. Wider is better. Head off any problems by ensuring that the extension is 1⅜ in. wide and 8 in. long (3.5cm by 20.3cm). By the way, you can use these same dimensions to convert any zipper opening to a fly front. Just add the extension beyond the center-front cutting line.

Once you're ready to tackle the sewing part of the insertion, ignore the instructions that came with your pattern. Most are so complicated that you'll give up and switch to a lapped zipper insertion.

It's time to banish your fear of fly-front zipper insertions! You think they're difficult only because of the method you're trying to follow. Why not use this simplified Power Sewing version for top-notch results? This pair of

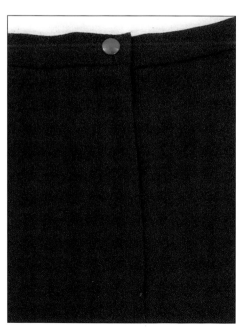

pants is finished with a waistband underlap that extends 1 in. (2.5cm) beyond the zipper closure. The effect is more polished than stopping the underlap flush with the opening.

1 On the wrong side of both front garment pieces, interface the entire fly extension from the seamline to the raw edge. Use a fusible knit tricot interfacing cut in the nonstretch direction.

2 Overlock or zigzag all of the raw edges on the pant front pieces. Sew any darts and pleats. Run an ease line around the waist and stabilize it with Stay Tape.

[TIP] Mark the center-front seamline—from waist to crotch—on the wrong side of the front garment pieces. The marked seamline will show you exactly where to place the interfacing and, in the next step, the machine basting.

3 Pin the pant front pieces with right sides together and raw edges even. Starting 1 in. (2.5cm) away from the inner leg crotch point, use regular-length straight stitching to seam the crotch curve. Stop 1 in. (2.5cm) above the bottom of the fly-front extension. Switch to a basting stitch length and sew the remainder of the seamline (to the waistline).

4 Make a few backstitches at the top of the basting to prevent the seam from opening during the zipper insertion. Make ¼-in. (6mm) deep clips through the seam allowances along the curved, crotch portion of the seamline. Press the seam allowance open on the fly extension.

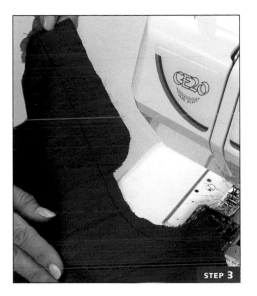
STEP 3

5 Place the pants wrong side up on a flat surface with the waist away from you. Fold the garment, right sides together, along the basted seamline so that the right and left fronts are to the left. Only the fly extension to the right of the seamline remains on the right (as viewed from the wrong side of the pants).

TRICK
of the TRADE

GO LONG

Although the standard zipper opening is 7 in. (17.8cm), use a zipper that's 9 in. (22.9cm) or longer. Now you can eliminate the space between the bottom of the waistband and the top of the teeth. The excess zipper isn't trimmed off until the waistband is applied. Since the zipper is well hidden behind the placket, an exact color match with the fashion fabric isn't necessary. What a great opportunity to use old zippers.

6 Position the closed zipper, face down, on top of the fly extension that's to the right. Butt the left edge of the zipper tape against the basted seamline.

7 Place the zipper stop 1 in. (2.5cm) above the bottom of the extension, where the basting begins. Let the excess zipper extend above the waist. Any excess zipper is trimmed off after you attach the waistband.

STEP 7

8 Using a zipper foot, sew the fly extension to the right side of the zipper tape, sewing on the tape nearest the cut edge of the fly.

[TIP] These instructions feature the fly overlap on the left front of the pants. If you prefer your fly on the right side, switch the overlap and underlap—and the right and left—references in these step-by-step instructions.

STEP 10

STEP 13

9 Flip the zipper over so that it's right side up. Pull the attached fly extension to the left, tucking it underneath the other fabric layers.

10 A narrow strip of fabric is visible between the zipper teeth and the seamline to the left. Sew through this strip, placing the stitching line to the left of the zipper teeth and ⅛ in. (3mm) from the seamline.

The new seamline flattens the fabric against the zipper tape. No stitching shows on the outside of the finished pants yet.

11 With right sides together, fold the right and left fronts to your right. Place them on a flat surface, wrong side up, with only the unattached fly extension to the left of the zipper.

12 Pull the left (unstitched) side of the zipper tape to your left as far as it will go and still lie flat (this is the trick to making this work). The left side of the zipper tape is now on top of the

wrong side of the unattached fly front, although it doesn't match the raw edge of the fly extension.

13 Sew close to the teeth, stitching only through the zipper tape and the fly front. No stitching shows on the outside of the finished pants yet.

14 Open the pant fronts and turn them over so that they're right side up. Flatten the zipper so that the teeth are on the table. Chalk-mark the topstitching line 1¼ in. (3.2cm) away from the center seam. Place a pin directly below the zipper's bottom stop.

[TIP] A fly-front template—whether purchased or made from a piece of adhesive-backed paper—is an ideal guide for perfectly shaped topstitching.

15 Starting at the bottom of the zipper opening (where the basting starts), topstitch along the guidelines from the right side of the garment and through all fabric layers. If you really

want to show off, use buttonhole twist and an N needle. Don't worry about catching the zipper tape in the seam because it was already anchored in place in a previous step.

16 Use the pin as a reference point to ensure that you don't snap a needle by stitching on the zipper stop when you round the curve. Make a bar tack over the start of the seam, at the bottom of the opening where the stitching is horizontal.

17 Press the fly with a press-and-lift motion to avoid ripples. Remove the basting and admire your attractive fly front.

[TIP] Sew from the bottom of the zipper to the waistline to eliminate fabric ripples. Place your hands on either side of the placket as you sew, creating a nice flat path for your topstitching.

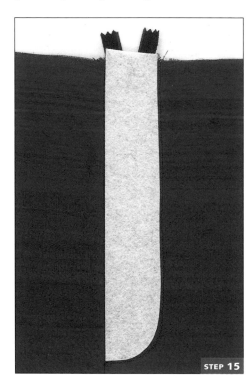

STEP 15

Style Maker

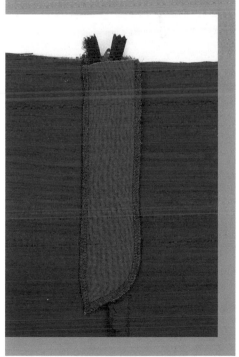

LAPPED ZIPPER

Whether you're choosing an opening for a pant or a skirt, consider a lapped application. A lapped zipper takes a bit more time to make than a centered zipper, yet it's often the best choice since the zipper is truly hidden in the finished garment. It's hard to beat a lapped zipper when it comes to hiding a closure in a dress, pants, or a skirt.

If you've avoided inserting a lapped zipper because the stitching line jogs at the top, here's a neat trick that solves this problem. Start with a zipper that's longer than the opening. You can cut it off after applying a facing or a waistband, thus eliminating the small gap or bulge between the top of the zipper and the finished edge of the garment.

1 With right sides together and raw edges even, join the garment pieces that have the zipper opening. Start at the bottom of the seam using a regular stitch length.

2 Switch to machine-basting stitches where the bottom of the zipper is indicated, and continue to the top of the zipper opening. Make a few backstitches at the top of the basting to prevent the seam from opening during the zipper insertion.

[TIP] Lightweight fabric needs additional support to eliminate ripples in a zipper and prevent the fabric from pouching out at the bottom of the zipper. Cut a ½-in. (1.3cm) strip of interfacing in the nonstretch direction, 1 in. (2.5cm) longer than the zipper opening. Fuse the strip to the wrong side of the seam allowances at the zipper opening. Place one long edge of the strip beside the basting.

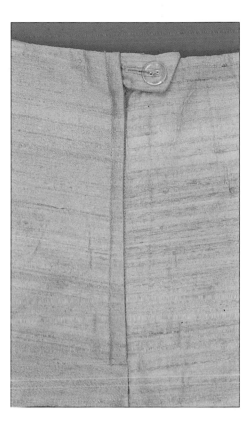

3 Hold the garment in front of you so that you're looking at the wrong side of the zipper opening, with the waist at the top. From this vantage point, the construction starts on the left side. Fold the garment pieces and right seam allowance away from the left seam allowance.

4 To avoid a gap between the waistband or facing and the top of the zipper, use a zipper that's at least 2 in. (5cm) longer than the opening in the garment.

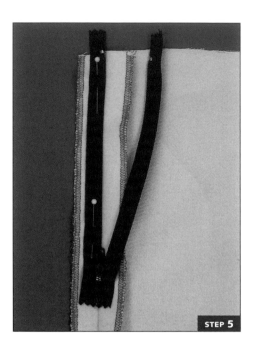

STEP 5

5 Open the zipper. Place it face down on the left seam allowance with the top of the zipper extending above the opening. Align the bottom zipper stop with the bottom of the basting. Line up the zipper teeth on the left side with the basted seam.

6 Sew the zipper tape to the left seam allowance. Start stitching 1 in. (2.5cm) above the bottom of the zipper stop. You can sew a straight line of stitching from bottom to top because you don't have to work around the zipper stop and the slider.

7 Close the zipper and turn it face up. Fold the joined garment pieces and seam allowances away from the zipper. There's now a small width of fabric between the zipper teeth and the basted zipper opening.

8 Pin the last 1 in. (2.5cm) of the zipper in place. Machine-stitch along the fabric fold, from the bottom of the zipper to the top, through all layers. No stitching shows on the right side of the finished garment.

9 Now sew through the main part of the garment for the first time. With the wrong side up, spread the garment flat. Let the zipper relax into its finished position, which is a little to one side of the basted seamline.

StyleMaker

THE EURO TREATMENT

I've noticed that expensive European ready-to-wear handles the lapped zipper in an interesting manner: It uses a very narrow (¼ in. to ⅜ in. [6mm to 1cm]) lap in the zipper. Experiment to see how narrow you can go and still cover the zipper tab. Sewing close to the zipper teeth narrows the width of the lap.

10 Pin the unattached side of the zipper tape to the garment and seam allowance. At the sewing machine, straight-stitch across the bottom of the zipper and up the pinned side. Follow the woven guideline on the zipper tape.

11 Remove the basting in the zipper opening. Press across the lapped zipper toward the fold using a sliding motion. Don't trim off the top of the zipper yet.

TIP Always press a zipper with a press-and-lift motion as you move toward the fold. Pressing up and down on a zipper creates ripples.

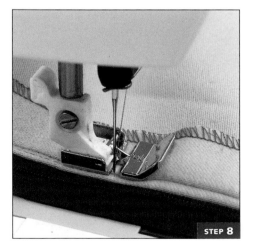

STEP 8

STEP 10

12 Open the zipper and attach the garment's waistband or facing. When sewing through the zipper area, hand-walk the stitches, turning the flywheel across the teeth; otherwise, the needle may break.

13 Trim the zipper even with the waistline.

STEP 12

TRICK
of the TRADE

REFINING THE APPLICATION

Zipper weight and flexibility need to match the fashion fabric. In other words, a lightweight fabric demands a lightweight zipper. Interfacing the seam allowances can beef up the fabric so that it can support a slightly heavier zipper. However, a stiff plastic zipper, which has a mind of its own, won't conform to the garment's shape. When strength is needed—in the fly front of tight-fitting pants, for example—a metal zipper is the best choice.

ZIPPER IN A POCKET

I've long admired ready-to-wear pants and skirts that open with a zipper concealed in a side pocket. Garments with this treatment have a clean, figure-flattering line. No front, back, or side-opening zippers are needed. Usually combined with a tailored waistband, they're easy to slip on and off.

When I first started playing around with methods to replicate this zipper insertion in my clothes, I thought the procedure would be complicated. Then it dawned on me that all I had to do was make a centered zipper in a patch of fabric, then cut the side-front pattern piece from the fabric patch. What could be easier? When I show students this procedure, they're surprised by its simplicity.

Start with a pant or skirt pattern that has slanted front pockets. The easiest way to place a zipper inside a pocket is to work slightly backward. Before cutting the pocket pieces from the pant fabric, insert a centered zipper between two rectangles of your fashion fabric.

1 Cut your waistband 3⅜ in. (8.6cm) wide and the length of your waist measurement plus 6 in. (15.2cm). Cut the waistband with one long edge on the selvage of the fashion fabric. Alternatively, serge or use a Hong Kong finish on a long edge. Cut all but the side fronts of the pattern pieces from the fashion fabric.

2 Cut one side front with the printed side of the pattern against the right side of the fabric. Don't cut the second side front (the one that will have the zipper) yet.

3 Cut two pieces of fashion fabric, each 6 in. by 14 in. (15.2cm by 35.6cm). With right sides together, machine-baste one long edge for 7 in. (17.8cm) or the length of the zipper. Switch to a regular stitch length for the remainder of the seam.

4 Press the seam allowances open. Insert a centered zipper on the basted seam.

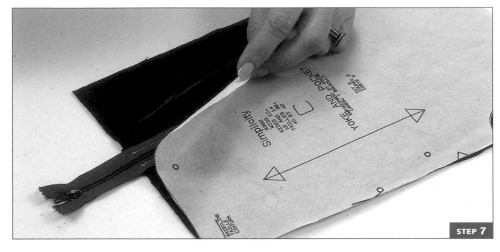

STEP 7

5 Place the pattern piece for the side front (not the pocket facing) on the wrong side of the zippered fabric patch. The pattern piece must be right side up so that the zipper ends up in the left pocket of the finished pants.

6 Position the pattern piece so that the zipper is 1 in. (2.5cm) away from the inside pocket edge of the side front. If you position the zipper too far away from the inside edge, the zipper will show in your finished garment.

7 Cut the garment shape from the zippered patch.

8 Assemble the pants. Attach your new, longer waistband so that one end is flush with the top of the left pocket (on the outside of the pants). The other end of the waistband is inside the garment so that the end is lined up with the inner edge of the pocket.

STEP 8

9 Cut off any excess waistband that isn't needed to go around the waist-line and the inside of the pocket.

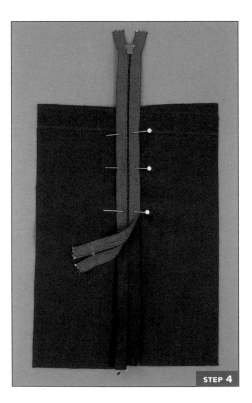

STEP 4

HIGH-RISE WAISTBAND

Want the illusion of longer legs? Then try a high-rise waist on your next pant or skirt. Rather than stopping at—or just above—the natural waistline, the garment extends an inch or so (about 2.5cm) higher. The pattern pieces are shaped through the waist for an attractive fit.

Although most patterns with high-rise waists don't tell you this, you have to stay the waistline and sew boning into the facing. This helps retain the pant shaping and prevents the extension above the waistline from wrinkling and rolling when you sit.

1 It's very important that a high-rise waistband fit properly. Alter your garment and facing pattern pieces. Now cut them from your fabric with 1-in. (2.5cm) seam allowances. Extra-wide seam allowances provide fitting insurance, just in case you want to let out the side seams during the test-fit.

TIP **If your high hip or tummy measurement is larger than your hip circumference, the pants are most flattering if they hang from the tummy rather than from the hip.**

2 Pin a length of twill tape to the waistline (as indicated on the pattern) on the wrong side of each front and back garment piece. Don't place the twill tape at the top of the pants because this isn't the waistline.

3 Sew the twill tape to the waistline. Since the pants extend past the waistline, your garment needs to be drawn in at the waist. This prevents the garment above the waistline from sliding down.

4 Baste together the pants and try them on. Pin-fit the pants at the side seams along the hips, waist, and midriff. Make identical adjustments on the facing pieces.

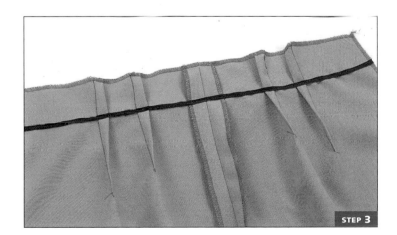

STEP 3

5 Insert the zipper and optional pockets.

6 Stabilize the facing with a light-weight interfacing such as Fusi-Knit. Join the pieces. Check that the facing is the same size as the pants. If not, take in or let out the side seam on the facing.

7 Clean-finish the bottom, raw edge of the facing with three-thread over-locking or a Hong Kong finish.

8 With right sides together and raw edges even, sew the top of the pants to the facing. Grade and trim the seam allowances to approximately ¼ in. (6mm). Reduce bulk by understitching the seam allowance to the facing ⅛ in. (3mm) away from the original seam.

9 On the facing, measure the center-front seamline from the waistline seam made in Step 8 to the edge of the facing. Cut a piece of ¼-in. (6mm) bon-ing ½ in. (1.3cm) shorter than the seam-line measurement. Cut two more pieces of boning, each ½ in. (1.3cm) shorter than the side seam.

[TIP] **Rigilene, a see-through poly-ester boning, is the most comfort-able. For less bulk, use the ¼-in. (6mm) width. A ½-in. (1.3cm) width also works.**

TRICK of the TRADE

BLUNT ADVICE

Boning has sharp ends that can poke both your skin and your fabric unless you do something about them. Use a lighted match to melt and slightly round the cut ends. Now cover them with ribbon or a fabric patch. The first time you wear a garment with boning, you'll be glad you padded the ends.

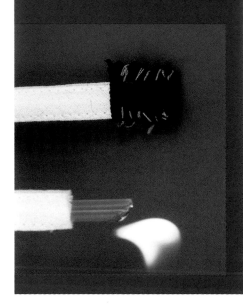

STEP 8

STEP 13

10 Place the first piece of boning at center front on the wrong side of the facing. The boning should curve in toward the body, which means the inward curve of the boning faces the wrong side of the facing.

11 If your pants open at center front, place the boning at center back. Position the boning between the seam allowance and the facing. Sand-wiched between the facing and the garment, the boning won't rub against your skin.

12 Slide one end of the boning under the seam allowances at the seamline that joins the facing to the pants. Hand- or machine-sew the boning to the seam allowances of the facing.

13 Place one piece of boning at each of the side seams, following Steps 9 through 12.

14 Fold the facing to the inside of the pants. Anchor the facing at center front and at the side seams with a ¼-in. (6mm) long swing tack.

15 Hand-baste the facing and garment seam allowances together at the top of the pants. Press and pound the top of the pants flat.

TRICK
of the TRADE

WAIST EASE

If your garments often ride up and have a fold under the front waistband, you need more fabric under the tummy. Increase the garment waistline and high hip on the pattern pieces ¼ in. (6mm) at each side for a total of 1 in. (2.5cm). This makes the garment larger than the waistband, so you need to ease the waistline on the garment pieces to fit.

Stabilize the ease by stitching over it with ¼-in. (6mm) wide twill tape. When finished, your garment releases fabric immediately below the waistband, where you need the extra fabric to accommodate a tummy or full, high hips. The effect is subtle—and you don't end up with fabric folds under the waistband. If you have a large tummy and a proportionally small waist, add even more at the side seam. You can successfully ease in ⅛ in. (3mm) per inch (2.5cm).

PETERSHAM WAIST FACING

In recent years, designers have revived a beautiful waist finish that was popular in the 1940s. Rather than attaching a waistband, they use a facing made of petersham ribbon to secure the top of pants or a skirt. It's a sleek and flattering look that eliminates the bulk of a waistband.

If you find waistbands uncomfortable, you'll love this treatment. When finished, the top of the pants or skirt sits at your natural waistline—fabulous for short-waisted women. What I like about this waist treatment is that it isn't bulky, it lies flat, and it molds to the shape of the body. Most important, it's very comfortable.

These stretch wool pants were made from Burda 3204. This waistband is suitable for pants and skirts that have darts or seams. It doesn't work with pleated pants.

TRICK
of the TRADE

DON'T ACCEPT SUBSTITUTES

The petersham facing is easy to make, but you must use the correct product. Petersham ribbon looks almost identical to grosgrain ribbon. It's important not to confuse the two because petersham has special characteristics necessary for this technique.

Both grosgrain and petersham have closely spaced horizontal ridges, but petersham has a flexible picot edge. The pliable edge is very important when making the facing because the ribbon must be shaped to fit the curve of your natural waistline. At the same time, you need to stretch the lower edge so that it fits smoothly over your tummy. Grosgrain, on the other hand, can't be shaped with an iron.

Couture sewers consider petersham a treasured sewing supply. It's available in a variety of widths, but my favorite is 1½ in. (3.8cm). The easiest way to find petersham is through mail-order suppliers. (See Resources on p. 226.)

Immerse the petersham in hot water, then take it—still wet—to the ironing board for shaping. Press the petersham dry while stretching one edge so that the ribbon curves. Don't worry if the unstretched edge ripples a bit.

TIP **It's important to work with wet petersham so that it's easier to shape while preshrinking.**

3 On the finished garment, the inner, shorter edge sits at the waist and the stretched edge is over the tummy. Since most of us have a tummy, stretch the one edge as much as possible. If you have a flat tummy and lack a full, high hip, you don't need quite as much shaping.

4 Set the petersham aside while preparing your garment.

5 Alter your pattern pieces, temporarily close the darts and tucks, and measure the circumference of the waistline—excluding all seam allowances. The waistline of the pattern needs to be 1½ in. to 2 in. (3.8cm to 5cm) larger than your natural waistline.

6 Also measure 3 in. (7.6cm) below the waistline. About 1½ in. to 2 in. (3.8cm to 5cm) of ease at the tummy is crucial for preventing pants and skirts from riding up on the body. Add whatever you need at the side seams.

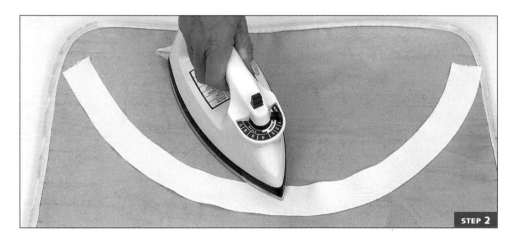

STEP 2

1 Cut a length of petersham to your waist measurement plus 4 in. (10.2cm). You'll need the extra length to finish the ends of the waistband.

2 It's very important to preshrink the petersham. Since it also has to be damp for shaping with an iron, you can combine these two processes to save time.

7 Cut out the garment pieces. Ease stitch the waist seamline of each garment piece to reduce the total circumference by about 1 in. (2.5cm)— approximately ¼ in. (6mm) per garment piece. The easestitching slightly draws in the garment waistline for a better fit and a quick fabric release to accommodate the tummy and high hip.

8 Stabilize the ease by sewing a ¼-in. (6mm) wide strip of twill tape on top of the ease line, on the wrong side of the fabric. Steam the waistline over a tailor's ham to eliminate the easing puckers below the seamline.

[TIP] You can stabilize the easing with a ¼-in. (6mm) wide strip of lining fabric selvage instead of twill tape, with the frayed edge of the selvage in the seam allowance.

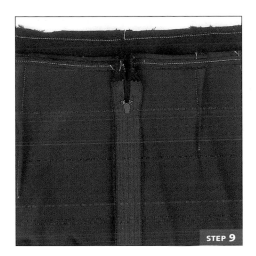
STEP 9

9 Whatever your preferred zipper treatment, insert the zipper with the teeth starting 1¾ in. (4.5cm) below the waistline so that you stay out of the way of the petersham. The petersham facing needs to fold completely inside the waist without interfering with the zipper. Later, a button tab closure finishes the opening at the waist.

10 Join the garment panels and try on the garment. Refine the fit by taking in or releasing the side seams so that the waist is comfortable. Trim the waist seam allowance ¼ in. (6mm) wide.

11 Open the zipper. Work with the garment right side up and start at the overlap side of the zipper.

12 Place the unstretched edge of the petersham on top of the casestitching with the wider (stretched) edge off the top of the garment (above the waist). On the overlap side of the zipper, extend the petersham ½ in. (1.3cm) beyond the zipper teeth.

13 Wrap the extension around the end, to the inside of the garment. This finishes off the end of the garment's waist. Temporarily secure the wrap with hand basting.

STEP 8

STEP 13

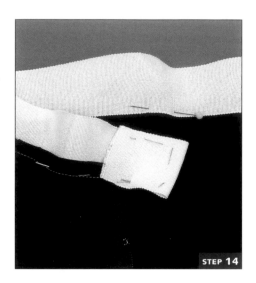

STEP 14

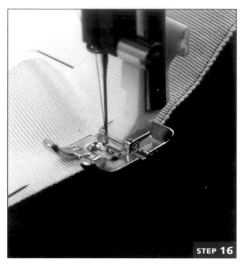

STEP 16

14 Continue placing the petersham around the waist. When you reach the opposite side of the zipper opening, wrap the excess petersham to the underside. Allow about 1 in. (2.5cm) for the underlap.

15 Cut off any excess petersham. Again, temporarily secure the wrap with hand basting.

16 Topstitch the petersham to the garment as close as possible to the edge of the petersham. You may even want to sew directly on top of the easestitching. Near the ends, your topstitching goes through both layers of the petersham.

17 A tab for the top of the zipper opening starts with a 3-in. (7.6cm) square of interfaced garment fabric. Fold it in half with right sides together and sew together a long and a short end.

18 Trim the seam allowances, turn the tab right side out, then press and pound it flat. Make a buttonhole ½ in. (1.3cm) from the end of the tab.

STEP 19

19 Slide the raw edge of the tab between the garment and the folded-down petersham on the overlap side of the zipper opening. Topstitch it in place—through all layers—from the right side of the garment, right on top of the stitching line for the zipper.

20 Fold the petersham inside the garment, enclosing the zipper tape and the top of the waistband. Pin it in place. Press the waist over a tailor's ham.

21 Anchor the petersham inside the garment by straight-stitching in the well of the vertical seams from the right side of the garment. Sewing a second time, at the top of the garment to hold the petersham in place, is optional.

STEP 21

22 Topstitch the opposite end of the petersham to the other side of the zipper. This secures it on the underside at the waist. Sew a matching button to the outside of the pants.

TAILORED WAISTBAND WITH ELASTICIZED BACK

Tailored waistbands can look great and still fit comfortably. The trick is to retain the traditional sew-on front waistband, while converting the back into an elasticized version. I love this technique because the waistband expands as you do and is therefore comfortable for long periods of time.

There's a good chance that a ready-to-wear garment with this waistband treatment caught your eye during a recent shopping spree. However, as I

discovered, instructions for duplicating the look are hard to find.

Start with a tailored pant or skirt pattern that has a traditional sew-on waistband and any style of zipper opening. Built for easy adjustments, the waistband consists of three pieces: one for the back and two for the front. If your weight changes, simply take in or let out the side seams.

1 Tape additional pattern paper to the sides of the back pattern pieces from hip to waist. Draw a straight line up the side of the back pant, starting at the widest part of the hips and extending to the top of the waist.

2 Also draw lines through the back darts so that you don't transfer the markings to your fabric. By eliminating back darts, you're giving the waistband more wearing ease.

[TIP] These instructions explain how to make a waistband with a center-front closure. You can easily adjust the procedure so that the zipper is at center back. Simply cut two shorter back waistbands, adding an extra 1 in. (2.5cm) for the underlap and overlap. The front waistband is cut to the length of the front waist seamline with seam allowances.

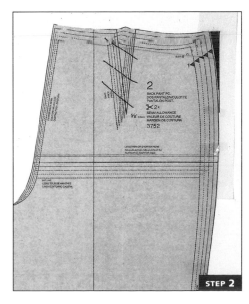

STEP 2

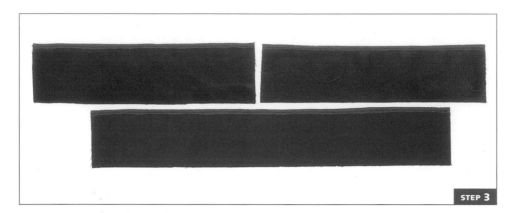

STEP 3

3 Cut a waistband to your waist measurement plus 6 in. (15.2cm) and 3⅜ in. (8.6cm) wide. This waistband will end up in three pieces, but you can use the length as you need it. If you can't cut one lengthwise edge of the waistband on the fabric selvage, finish it with a serged overlock stitch or a Hong Kong edge finish.

4 The back waistband doesn't need interfacing. The elastic you'll insert in a subsequent step provides all the necessary support.

5 Complete the darts, pleats, and zipper opening in your garment pieces. Don't sew the back darts or side seams. Easestitch the waist of each front garment piece at the seamline, drawing in the seamline about ¼ in. (6mm) for each front piece. The elastic will draw in the back.

6 With right sides together, sew the unfinished long side of the waistband to the pant back using as much length as you need. Cut off the excess and save it for the front waistband.

7 Cut a length of 1-in. (2.5cm) wide elastic equivalent to half of your waist circumference minus ¾ in. (1.9cm). For example, if your waist is 32 in. (81.3cm), cut the elastic to 15¼ in. (39cm).

8 Sandwich the elastic between the seam allowances and the waistband. Sew one long edge of the elastic to the seam allowances using a long, wide zigzag stitch and stretching the elastic to fit. This prevents the elastic from twisting inside the waistband.

STEP 8

9 Interface the leftover waistband length with Veri-Shape. Cut the waistband in half, one for each side of the front.

10 With right sides together and raw edges even at the waist, sew the front waistbands to the garment fronts. Let the excess waistband length extend beyond the center-front zipper opening.

11 Open the front and back waistbands to their full width. Machine-baste the front and back garment pieces and waistbands together at the side seams, then try on the garment to assess the fit.

12 Take in or let out the side seams until the waist fits comfortably. If desired, you can also lower or raise the waistband at this stage.

STEP 11

13 Once the fit is perfected, permanently sew the side seams. Clip through the seam allowances at the waistline side seams. Press the garment side seams open and press the waistband seam allowances toward the front.

14 To finish the ends of the waistband, fold one front waistband to the front of the garment. For several inches at center front, extend the finished but unattached long edge ⅜ in. (1cm) beyond the waist seamline.

15 To ensure that the waistband is perfectly aligned with the zipper opening, don't sew the waistband ends together by stitching straight up from the opening. Instead, sew across the ends of the waistband ⅛ in. (3mm) past the zipper opening to compensate for turn of cloth.

16 Secure the opposite side of the front waistband 1 in. (2.5cm) from the end of the zipper closure to provide an underlap. This gives you a bit more fabric for attaching the snap or button. Trim the seam allowances and turn the ends right side out.

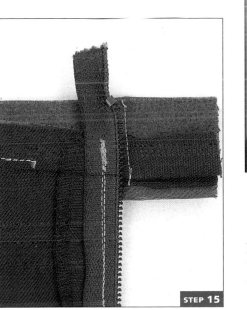
STEP 15

17 If you're lining the garment, slip the lining into the pant with wrong sides together, and baste at the waist before attaching the remaining side of the waistband. Fold the waistband to the wrong side of the garment. The elastic is now enclosed in the back waistband.

18 The loose edge of the waistband extends about ⅜ in. (1cm) beyond the waist seamline. When the waistband fits snugly around the elastic, pin the waistband in position.

TIP You may find it easier to attach the inside of the waistband to the seamline by using a curved surface. I like to place the waistband over a tailor's ham, right side up, then pin the waistband in position.

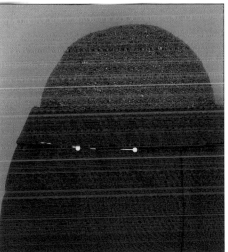

19 At the zipper teeth, take a ⅜-in. (1cm) deep clip through the pinned back waistband. Position the clip ¼ in. (6mm) outside the zipper teeth toward the waist circumference.

20 Fold under the inner waistband from the teeth to the end of the waistband and hand-sew it in position. The clip near the seam allowance makes it possible to do this without turning under the entire waistband.

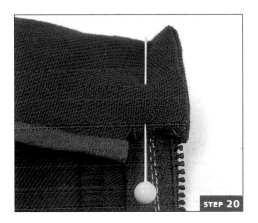
STEP 20

21 Secure the interior of the waistband by straight stitching in the waist seamline through all layers. Use an edge or edge-joining presser foot for accuracy when stitching in the seam line well.

22 Stop stitching before you reach the zipper teeth without breaking your threads. Turn the handwheel while guiding the stitching across the zipper teeth to prevent the needle from breaking. Close the top of the zipper opening with a snap or button.

STEP 22

FLAT-FELL IN-SEAM POCKET

The more years we spend in front of our sewing machines, the more we expect from ourselves. We see a new treatment on a finished garment and wonder how it's done. This is one of those situations.

I love flat-fell seams on pant legs, but I used to avoid this technique if the pants had in-seam pockets. I didn't want the flat-fell topstitching interrupted by the pocket. I've since developed a wonderful new method that solves this dilemma.

The stitching around this pocket is an illusion. The side seam looks as if a flat-fell treatment runs from waist to hem—uninterrupted by the in-seam pocket.

This is done by flat-felling the seam below the pocket, then topstitching the pocket opening and side seam above the pocket. This procedure should be the first thing you do because it's easier to execute before sewing the inseams. This finish is permanent, so use it with a pant pattern that you know fits well.

1 Cut out your garment pieces. Most of us make the pocket and pocket facing (the front of the pocket bag) from the fashion fabric. There are times, however, when it's a good idea to consider other options.

When you don't want a lot of bulk, use a lining or soft cotton for the facing. Organza is also a good choice, because it's strong yet fine. If your pant fabric is white, choose a peach- or skin-colored pocket facing so that the pocket bag doesn't show through the pant leg.

2 Sew the pocket to the back garment piece at the side-seam placement marks. Use ¼-in. (6mm) seam allowances. Press the seam allowances closed and toward the pocket.

3 Serge to finish the raw edges. Serging is less bulky, but use double-fold bias if you don't have a serger. Join the pocket facing to the front garment piece in the same manner, with right sides together.

4 Since the seam is flat-felled, the garment pieces are seamed with the wrong sides together. Place the right side of the front and back pant pieces wrong sides together and the raw edges even at the side seam and pocket.

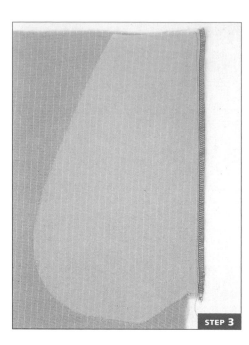
STEP 3

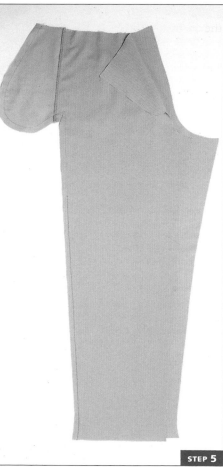
STEP 5

5 Starting at the bottom of the hem, sew up the side seam, around the outside edges of the pocket to the waist. Use one continuous line of stitching. Clip diagonally into the seam allowances at the inner corner at the bottom of the pocket.

6 Serge together the raw edges with a three-thread overlock stitch, or bind the seam allowances on the pocket bag. This is a wonderful way to give the pants a classy interior appearance and make the pockets sturdier.

7 Flat-fell the side seam below the pocket, pressing and wrapping the seam allowances to the front of the pants. At the bottom of the pocket, slip the end of the double-fold bias tape into the flat-fell seam before stitching.

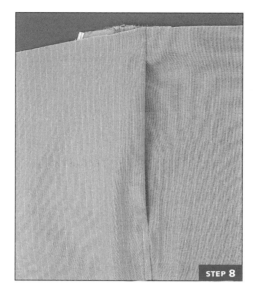
STEP 8

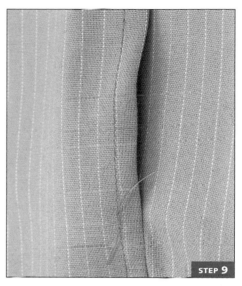
STEP 9

8 Tuck the pocket bag inside the pants. Press the pocket toward the front of the pants. Fold the pocket bulk out of the way.

9 Starting at the bottom of the pocket opening, sew to the top of the pocket and stitch the same distance from the pocket fold as the flat-fell stitching. The goal is to make the seam look like one continuous line of stitching. Use small stitches at the beginning of your seam to reinforce the opening without backstitching. Press the new stitching.

10 Pockets need to be sturdy enough to take a lot of strain. If you want yours to stay attractive as long as possible, reinforce stress points. Reinforce the pocket opening and hide the topstitching connection points with horizontal bar tacks at both locations. Use a narrow, short zigzag stitch (1mm wide and 0.7mm long).

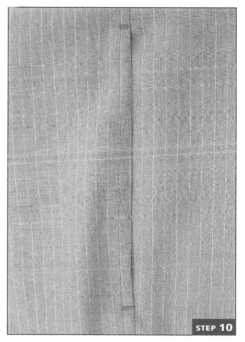
STEP 10

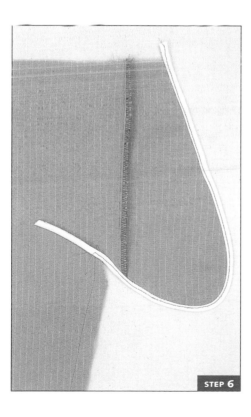
STEP 6

GAP-FREE HIP POCKET

You don't have to settle for pocket openings that gap. Just a few minutes of shaping and stabilizing make a dramatic difference in the way the pocket opening sits on your body. If your pants are properly fitted, this procedure ensures that the pocket openings will hug your hips rather than pull away or hang open.

Stabilizing is one of two measures that keep this continental pocket flat against the hip. The next step is shaping the garment pieces on a tailor's ham. These pants were made from Vogue 7027. By following these instructions, your pocket will be smooth and flat from waist to hem. The results are fabulous.

1 On the pattern, measure the length of the seamline that attaches the pocket facing to the pant front. Cut a piece of stabilizer (fusible Stay Tape, twill tape, or a strip of ¼-in. [6mm] wide selvage) to this length.

[TIP] Twill tape can be eliminated if you cut the pocket facing with the straight joining edge on the selvage.

2 Cut out the garment pieces. Sew the darts or pleats in the pant fronts and backs. Place the pocket facing onto the pant front at the pocket location.

3 With right sides together, pin the stabilizer to the seamline of the joining edge of the pocket facing and garment. This prevents the pocket opening from stretching out of shape when it's used.

4 With right sides together, sew the pocket facing to the pant front at the pocket opening. Make sure that you catch the stabilizer in the seamline. Trim the seam allowances to ¼ in. (6mm).

5 Press the seam allowances toward the pocket facing and understitch the seam allowances to the pocket facing ⅛ in. (3mm) from the seamline. Understitching the trimmed seam allowances to the pocket facing ensures that the seamline won't roll to the outside of the finished pants.

6 Fold the pocket facing to the wrong side of the pant front along the seamline. A crisp edge is important, so

STEP 3

press the edge flat using steam and a tailor's clapper.

7 With right sides together, sew the pocket piece to the pocket facing along the curved outer edges only. Make this pocket bag using ⅝-in. (15mm) seam allowances. Sew all of the layers together at the waist. Don't sew the pocket bag to the pant front's side seam yet.

8 Now for a trick to avoid pocket gaposis: Place the pant front and pocket bag right side up on a tailor's ham. A tailor's ham simulates the body's shape. When worn, the finished pocket fits the pants and body perfectly.

Starting at center front, run your hand over the pant front and pocket bag to

STEP 6

mold them to the rounded shape. Let any excess pocket bag fabric roll out past the side seam. The excess can be ⅛ in. to ¼ in. (3mm to 6mm), depending on the thickness of the fabric.

9 Pin the pocket to the pant front at the side seam with the excess outside the side seam. Still pinned, remove the pant front and pocket bag from the tailor's ham. Baste the pocket bag to the pant front at the side seam. Proceed with the garment construction.

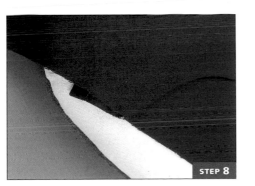

STEP 8

NO-TEAR LINING

Pant linings are well worth the small amount of extra effort it takes to make them. My favorite pant lining fabric is Bemberg rayon, also known as Ambiance. It's more comfortable than polyester lining because the fabric breathes. China silk is another good choice because it also breathes, although it's more prone to wrinkling. Often, the only available choice is polyester, which is suitable for cold-weather but not warm-weather pants, since this fiber traps heat. Peach-colored lining is less obvious in white or cream pants. If you have olive or darker skin, match the lining to your skin color.

Payback for the time you spend lining pants is fabulous—the pants wear better and are more wrinkle-resistant. What a bonus if you sit at a desk all day. With dark-colored fashion fabric I enjoy a color surprise, like this purple lining. These black crepe pants were made from Burda 3586.

TRICK
of the TRADE

ATTACK THE SNEAK PEEK

I like to attach the lining to the pant hem with a swing tack. This prevents the pant lining from peeking out when you sit down. A swing tack joins the lining to the pants at two points: the inner and outer leg seams. A traditional swing tack is made by finger-crocheting a length of doubled thread. Stitch one end to the lining and the other to the top of the pant hem. Instructions for making a swing tack are on p. 98.

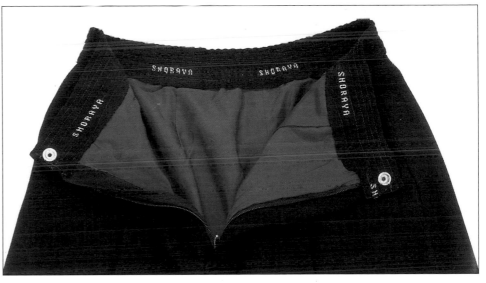

TRICK *of the* TRADE

LINING LIFESAVER

I used to sew pant-lining seam allowances ⅛ in. (3mm) deeper than the garment pieces. It made sense to me because something that fits inside something else must be smaller. Soon enough I knew that something was wrong with this logic. Once the pants were worn, the lining separated from the garment at the zipper and stress lines showed up at the darts and pleats.

Most pant fabric has sufficient resiliency for the stretch and recovery we need to move. Because lining fabric lacks give, the lining needs to be slightly larger than the pants. You don't have to cut the lining pieces larger—simply cut the lining the same size as the garment pieces, then sew the lining together using narrower seam allowances.

1 Fold up the hem allowance at the bottom of the pant pattern.

2 Cut the pant lining from the garment pattern pieces. The lining and fashion-fabric pieces start out the same size.

3 Join the inner, side, and crotch seams of the fashion-fabric pants. Insert the zipper and finish the pockets. Don't attach the waistband yet.

4 Sew the darts and pleats ⅛ in. (3mm) narrower than the marked width for the lining pieces. Join the lining front and back at the inseams and side seams using ½-in. (1.3cm) seam allowances.

5 The seam allowances are narrower than the garment so that the lining is slightly larger than the pants, which is necessary to prevent the lining from tearing at the seamlines or pulling away from the zipper. Press the seam allowances open.

6 Sew the lining crotch seam with a ½-in. (1.3cm) seam allowance. At the end of the seam, backstitch and remove it from the machine.

7 Place one hand at each end of the seam and pull it taut. Called "cracking," this forces weak stitches to break.

STEP 7

8 Sew the seam again. Make ¼-in. (6mm) deep clips into the lower crotch curve at 1-in. (2.5cm) intervals. Trim the seam allowances to ¼ in. (6mm) at the center 6 in. (15.2cm) of the crotch seam.

9 On the lining, press back the seam allowances at the zipper opening. To ease in the excess waist fabric, sew an ease line around the pant lining ½ in. (1.3cm) from the raw edge.

10 When it's time to join the lining and pants to the waistband, they'll fit together because the excess lining ease is drawn in with ease-stitching.

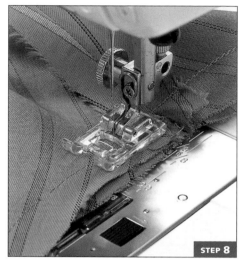
STEP 8

11 With wrong sides together, slip the lining inside the pants. Using a ½-in. (1.3cm) seam allowance, machine-baste the lining and pants together at the waistline with the pants against the presser foot. The lining goes on the bottom so that the feed dogs ease the extra lining fabric.

12 Attach the waistband. Using thread strengthened with beeswax, hand-sew the lining to the zipper seam allowances.

TIP To reinforce thread, pull it through the beeswax and press it with a warm iron. The heat forces the beeswax into the thread fibers. In addition to strengthening the thread, the melted beeswax won't flake off on the garment you're sewing.

13 Try on your pants and set the hem for the fashion fabric only. Hem the pants. See "Taming Pant Hems" on p. 84 for guidance on applying interfacing, avoiding puckers, and making invisible stitches.

14 The lining pieces were cut to the finished pant length. To ensure that the lining isn't visible at the pant hem, double-turn the lining hem (fold it up twice). Make each fold ½ in. (1.3cm) deep so that the lining is 1 in. (2.5cm) shorter than the finished pant length.

15 Remember, if you shortened the fashion-fabric pant, the lining must be shortened by the same amount.

TRICK of the TRADE

PUTTING ON THE RITZ

Apply preshrunk petersham ribbon over the side seams of pants for a decorative tuxedo effect. Start with a pant fabric that has some body, like three- or four-ply silk crepe de Chine, wool crepe, or wool gabardine. If the fabric is too lightweight, the petersham draws up the side seams.

Preshrinking the petersham in hot water is very important. You can iron it dry to save time, but don't stretch the petersham as you press. Attach a narrow strip of Stitch Witchery to one side of the petersham. Now fuse the petersham to the side seams. This makes it easier to topstitch the sides of the petersham to the legs. One raw end of the petersham extends into the waistline seam. The opposite raw end turns under with the garment hem allowance. These pants were made from Burda 5289.

TAMING PANT HEMS

How can a procedure as simple as hemming a pair of pants turn into such a nightmare? Instructions too often tell you simply to hem the pants, without offering any advice for achieving fabulous results. Often the hem seems too small for the pant. The following section has a variety of tips and techniques to help you avoid puckers, imprints, limp hemlines, and obvious stitching.

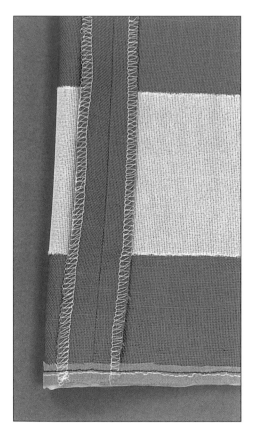

Hem Interfacing

I highly recommend that you interface the hem area of almost all pant legs. In my sewing room, only pants made from the most drapey fabrics escape this treatment. With interfacing, pant hems are crisper and hang better with the extra weight, the hem allowance won't show on the right side of the garment, and the hand stitching is invisible. These results are certainly worth the extra effort.

1 Cut out your pant pieces. Decide on the length of your pants. (See "Going to Great Lengths" on p. 49.) Allow a 1½-in. (3.8cm) wide hem allowance and trim the excess length off your front and back garment pieces.

2 Cut a length of crossgrain or bias-cut fusible tricot interfacing that's ½ in. (1.3cm) wider than the hem allowance. If fusible interfacing isn't suitable, use a bias-cut length of sew-in interfacing, hand-tacked at the top and bottom. The width difference allows you to anchor the hem allowance to the interfacing rather than the fashion fabric. This way the hem is truly invisible.

3 Trim the lengthwise edges of the interfacing with pinking shears.

TIP Don't interface the hem on white or cream pants because the layers make the hem more obvious.

4 If you already know your finished length, interface before sewing the inner leg seam. This is easier to do before the leg becomes a tube.

5 Place one long edge of the interfacing at the hemline on the wrong side of a pant leg. Position the width of the interfacing on the pant—not on the hem allowance. Fuse the strip to the leg.

STEP 5

TRICK
of the TRADE

PUCKER CONTROL

There's nothing more frustrating than finishing a beautiful pair of pants only to be disappointed by a hem that puckers. Whether your pant leg is straight or tapers from knee to hem, the hem-allowance circumference must measure the same size as the bottom of the pant leg.

With straight-leg pants, you often unwittingly reduce the hem-allowance circumference. Serging the raw edge of the hem allowance or using a Hong Kong finish slightly draws in the fabric. To compensate for the shrinkage, sew the inner leg with a standard ⅝-in. (15mm)

seam allowance to the hem crease. Gradually reduce the inner leg seam from ⅝ in. (15mm) at the hem crease to ⅜ in. (1cm) at the raw edge. Finishing the raw edge of the pant uses the additional width, so the circumference of the hem allowance and pant match.

If your pants are already hemmed but the edge of the hem allowance is drawing in the pant leg, you don't need to start all over again. Merely open the inner leg seam at the bottom of the pant. Let the seams spread slightly and conform to the larger pant leg circumference.

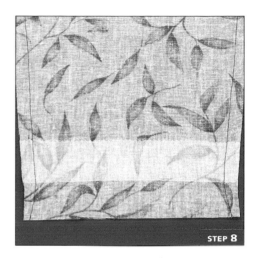

STEP **8**

6 Finishing the raw edge of the hem allowance slightly reduces the circumference, so it needs to start off larger than the pant. This ensures a smooth fit inside the bottom of the finished pant leg.

7 Serge or use a Hong Kong finish on the raw edge of the hem allowance. Sew the inner leg seams with a ⅝-in. (15mm) seam allowance from the waist to the hem crease.

8 Continue stitching, gradually reducing the seam allowance width to ⅜ in. (1cm) at the bottom of the pant. Turn up the hem allowance.

9 Check the circumference. Hand-stitch the hem in position. (See "Invisible Hand Hem" on p. 86.)

WEST COAST HONG KONG FINISH

A beautiful way to finish the interior of your hem is to apply a Hong Kong finish to the upper, raw edge of the hem allowance. It's a clean effect that doesn't add bulk. Unfortunately, the mere act of applying the bias fabric strip draws in the fabric edge. You can reduce the width of the seam in the hem allowance, as described in "Pucker Control" on p. 85.

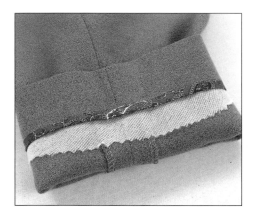

1 Select your material for the finishing strips. Use charmeuse, lining, or silk crepe de Chine for woven-fabric pants.

2 Cut a 1¼-in. (3.2cm) wide finishing strip on the crossgrain to the same length as the pant leg circumference.

TIP Don't use a Hong Kong finish on a knit fabric. The edge finish has less give than the pant leg. Instead, serge the hem using Woolly Nylon in the upper looper.

3 Place the right side of the strip against the right side of the bottom of the pant leg (the raw edge of the hem allowance).

4 Sew the strip to the pant with a ¼-in. (6mm) seam allowance.

5 Trim the seam allowance to ⅛ in. (3mm). Enclose the raw edge of the narrow seam allowance by wrapping the finishing strip to the wrong side of the pant. Don't turn under the raw edge.

6 From the right side, straight-stitch in the well of the seam.

STEP 6

Invisible Hand Hem

You're only a few steps away from making a wonderful hand-stitched hem that's practically invisible. Attaching and hiding the stitches between the top of the hem allowance and the wrong side of the garment (or the fused interfacing) is a simple process.

The true secret to an invisible hem is a fine needle and a light touch. Don't pull the thread too tight; a loose hand stitch is sufficient to hold the hem allowance in place. Beyond these important considerations, there are many things you can do to achieve the effect of a couture finish.

If you applied a lightweight interfacing to the bottom of the pants following

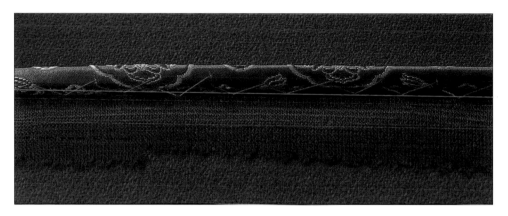

the instructions in "Hem Interfacing" on p. 84, your hem will look even better. You can anchor the hem to the fusible rather than to the pant fabric itself. This produces a truly invisible hem because the stitches don't prick the fashion fabric. The interfacing cushions the garment from the bulk of the hem and hides the hand stitches.

1 Set the hem allowance, placing the pins 1 in. (2.3cm) below the upper edge. Leave the top of the hem allowance free so that you can hide the hand stitches you make in a later step.

2 Prepare your hand-sewing needle with a single strand of thread. Don't double or wax the thread or it will become so bulky that the finished stitches will show. Anchor the start of the thread at the top of the hem allowance.

[TIP] Silk thread is the most invisible for hems because it marries well with the fabric.

3 At the start of the stitching, fold down the top ¼ in. (6mm) of the hem allowance with your thumb. Take one stitch on the inside of the hem allowance, move forward ¼ in. (6mm), and take one stitch on the pant.

STEP 3

If the hem is interfaced, take the stitch through the interfacing rather than the pant fashion fabric. By catching only the interfacing with the stitches, your work is nearly invisible. Don't pull the thread too tight as you stitch.

4 Move forward ¼ in. (6mm) and take one stitch on the back of the hem allowance. Continue in this manner until the hem is secured. Never pass the needle through the garment and the hem at the same time.

[TIP] Pant hems take such a beating. Every time you slip your pants on or off, there's a chance you'll catch a thread and take down the hem allowance. To control the damage, knot the thread every 4 in. (10.2cm) as you stitch around the hem.

Chapter 4

SKIRTS

A skirt can be simple or complex, and there's bound to be a flattering style for you—no matter what your figure type. You may need to experiment a little to find a perfect pattern, but the search is worth it because you can make it again and again. Then you can mix and match techniques, silhouettes, and hem lengths for exactly the look you want.

Sewing is all about enjoying the process, learning new techniques, and making one-of-a-kind garments. With this in mind, some of my all-time favorite techniques, plus wonderful new ones, are included in this chapter. There's a selection of waistbands, different kinds of hems, and ways to create shape. Most important, each technique gives you the information you need to decide when and how to use the method.

Combining interesting fabrics and innovative assembly techniques gives our sewn garments an edge over the clothes we see hanging in the stores. But before you get down to the nitty-gritty, why not explore the creative side of skirts? Women who sew have a great opportunity to create one-of-a-kind garments with striking details and shaping. On the next few pages, you can browse through some of my favorites.

WORTHWHILE WRAP

A wrap skirt is exotic, sexy, and stylish—but inappropriate if it's too revealing when you walk. Yet so many ready-to-wear garments and wrap skirt patterns set you up to show too much leg. To prevent this problem, make sure there's enough fabric to keep you covered while in motion (called walking ease) before you cut out your garment pieces. While you're at it, also check the fit through the waist and hips.

How I Made This Skirt

You can make a skirt like mine using the step-by-step instructions in the following features:

Solving the Flap about Wraps (see p. 104)
Designer Waistband That Grows (see p. 115)
Twin-Needle Hem (see p. 162)

Medium-weight wool jersey or challis fabric makes a fabulous wrap skirt. It doesn't cling and it isn't stiff.

Walking Ease

By far the most important concern with wrap skirts is walking ease. This is the amount of extra fabric that you need for coverage when you sit or move.

The amount of walking ease to add to a wrap style depends on its length. If it's hemmed at the knee, you only add ¾ in. (1.9cm). A midcalf wrap skirt needs 1 in. (2.5cm) of extra fabric. A long version should have even more walking ease—about 1½ in. (3.8cm). For fit and movement ease, make sure that the pattern has 1 in. to 2 in. (2.5cm to 5cm) of ease at the tummy and, depending on the style, 2 in. to 4 in. (5cm to 10.2cm) at the hips.

Hemming

A wrap skirt made in knit fabric looks fabulous with a stretch twin-needle hem. Depending on the style, you may need to hem the overlap part of the skirt before the underlap. Because the overlap is in the way, start and stop your twin-needle stitching at the side seam where the overlap piece is joined. Merely fold the overlap piece out of the way when you start and stop your hemstitching.

BEAUTIFUL BIAS SKIRT

Put a little glamour in your life with a gorgeous bias-cut skirt. While the grainline creates some challenges, over the years I've discovered numerous—and easy—ways to overcome the over-fitted look. Using wider seam allowances, stretching the garment pieces before you sew, and allowing more tummy and hip ease are just a few of my solutions for ensuring a flattering fit and preventing rippled seams and uneven hems.

The beautiful drape of bias fabric looks incredible on a fit figure, but it can be a little too revealing for the rest of us. This isn't to say that we can't wear a bias skirt—just follow my instructions for adding a bit more ease so that your skirt is figure-flattering.

Wouldn't it be wonderful to have a midcalf-length bias skirt in some sensational fabric, for instance, the satin side of silk charmeuse? You can get it in any color and it will fit fabulously if you make it yourself. Select a bias skirt pattern, preferably one with few seams, as in the skirt at right. A soft wool plaid cut on the bias shows off the fabric to its best advantage (see the skirt on p. 92).

Pattern Improvements

Measure the skirt pattern pieces between the seam allowances at the tummy and the full hips. For a flattering fit, you need 4 in. (10.2cm) of ease. If you have a fuller figure, you may prefer 6 in. (15.2cm) of ease. If your figure is well proportioned, you need only 2 in. (5cm) of ease. If the pattern circumferences aren't big enough, simply add the amount you need at the side seams.

[TIP] **The temptation may be strong, but never use a selvage for the seam allow-ance on any pattern piece. The selvage often draws up—even after preshrinking—and makes the seamline pucker.**

Garment Piece Preparation

Secure the pattern pieces to the fabric with fine, sharp pins placed only in the seam allowances. As you position the pieces, leave extra room for wider seam allowances on bias. I find that 1½-in. (3.8cm) seam allowances press better and prevent rippled seamlines. Besides, as the bias stretches in subsequent pressing, the seam allowances often shrink.

Before you start sewing, press each garment piece from top to bottom to lengthen it. By removing some of the bias stretch before seaming, you reduce the uneven, ever-lengthening hemline problem that's so common in bias-cut garments.

[TIP] **When interfacing on bias, always cut the interfacing on the bias as well. Otherwise, the bias will relax and the facing will not.**

Interfacing Decisions

A good rule of thumb for any garment sewing is to avoid fusible interfacings on any fabric with sheen. Fusibles make these fabrics stiff, which is very unattractive. However, all bias-cut skirts, even garments made from shiny or silky fabrics, need extra support at the zipper opening.

Interface the zipper seam allowances with strips of ½-in. (1.3cm) wide fusible interfacing that are 1 in. (2.5cm) longer than the zipper. This stops ripples and prevents the bottom of the zipper from pushing out. Because the interfacing is only on the seam allowance, fusibles are acceptable.

Seam Adjustments

Fabrics with sheen tend to make a body look larger, so stick to darker colors unless you're slim. If you don't plan to

stretching at the seamline. A small, narrow zigzag stitch (1mm wide and 2.5mm long) helps the seamlines relax with the bias fabric. Press open the seam allowances if the skirt is made from a heavy fabric. For a lighter-weight fabric, serge or zigzag the seam alowances together and press them to one side. This simple step allows the seams in the finished garment to relax without drag lines.

Weighted Hemming

I can't emphasize enough how important it is to let a bias skirt hang overnight before you hem it. Years ago, scrap fabric strips were pinned or basted to the bottom of the skirt, and it was left to hang for up to three days. Now that drapery weights are so easy to find, I prefer to baste a cord of these to the bottom edge. When it's time to set the hem, remove the drapery weights and mark the new hemline. Don't be surprised if the skirt bottom, which started out nice and even—weaves up and down by 3 in. or even 4 in. (7.6cm to 10.2cm). That's bias! Shiny fabrics look best with a bulk-free look, so I use a fine rolled hem.

TIP **If you're in a hurry, turn up a ½-in. (1.3cm) hem allowance and fuse it with Steam-A-Seam II.**

How I Made This Skirt

You can make a skirt like mine using the step-by-step instructions in the following features:

Petersham Waist Facing (see p. 71)
Bias Grainline Adjustment (see p. 97)
Fine Rolled Hem (see p. 120)

hand-wash your finished garment, forget about preshrinking it. By the way, silk charmeuse washes beautifully in warm water and a mild hair shampoo. All shiny, satinlike fabrics have a nap, which means all pieces need to be cut in the same direction. This affects the amount of fabric that you need, so use a "with nap" layout.

TIP **Cutting slippery fabrics is a pleasure with Gingher serrated shears.**

For sewing satin bias on your machine, use a new 70/10 H-J or Microtex needle with good quality cotton thread. Attach an even-feed foot (or engage the machine's differential feed) to control

TERRIFIC TUBE SKIRT

I love long, skinny tube skirts because they're so flattering and a snap to make. A few years ago (it seems like 50!), I would pull one on with a cropped or boxy blouse, but these days I pair mine with a tunic top or long sweater. This way I get a lean look without worrying about my tummy showing.

Since knit stretches, you can make a tube skirt with an elastic waist in less than two hours. Always position the fabric with the greatest stretch going around the body. It isn't necessary to use a pattern, just start by cutting a knit fabric 5 in. (12.7cm) wider than your hip measurement. Seam the center back, leaving the bottom open 9 in. (22.9cm) for a slit.

Set your machine for a narrow zigzag stitch (0.5mm long and 2.5mm wide, 10 spi). With right sides together, join the two long fabric edges with a 1½-in. (3.8cm) wide seam allowance (see the photo below). This gives you 2 in. (5cm) of ease. Then turn down the top to make a casing and insert the elastic. The garment on the facing page was made without a pattern. (See "Thoughtful Assembly" on the facing page.) For an interesting hem treatment, consider ruching the bottom of the seam instead

of making a center-back slit. Zigzag over ¼-in. (6mm) wide clear elastic stretched to a 2:1 ratio.

Fabric Selection

Look for more than stretch when you shop for tube skirt fabric. Good recovery is just as important; otherwise, your garment won't maintain its sleek silhouette for long. Wool or cotton double knit are good choices. Lycra woven blends are also suitable. Wool jersey is a single knit, which is too weak to hold its shape.

Yardage Decisions

Depending on your height and the desired hemline location, you need one or two lengths of fabric. It's nice to use a single length of fabric that's seamed only at center back. Buy a single length if your hip measurement plus 5 in. (12.7cm) is less than the fabric width. Some Lycra blend fabrics are only 42 in. (106.7cm) wide. In this case, you may need two lengths. If you want a snug fit, reduce the ease; the slimmer version will stretch to fit after seaming.

If you find fabric that wraps around you with 5 in. (12.7cm) of ease, order yardage for your finished skirt length from waist to hem, plus a 2½-in. (6.4 cm) wide waistband casing and a 1-in. (2.5cm) hem allowance. For example, if you want a 36-in. (91.4cm) finished skirt length, buy 1¼ yd. (1.1m) of wide fabric or 2½ yd. (2.3m) of narrow fabric.

Thoughtful Assembly

If you need two fabric lengths, you make two side seams. You can ruch one (see "Ruched Hem" on p. 121) or leave the bottom 10 in. (25.4cm) open for a side slit on a midcalf-length skirt. If you're using a single length of fabric, all you need is a center-back seam.

While still at the serger, overlock the bottom and top of the skirt. Sew a 1½-in. (3.8cm) wide center-back seam. Turn up a 1-in. (2.5cm) hem allowance and fold back the slit facings. For built-in walking ease at the slit, taper the depth of the facing ½ in. (1.3cm) at the hemline. This means that while the center-back seam is 1½ in. (3.8cm) wide, the fold-back facings at the slit are only 1 in. (2.5cm) wide. Miter the corners of the slit and hem allowance. (See "Mitered Hem with Walking Ease" on p. 105.)

Hand-sew the skirt hem, pausing every 4 in. (10.2cm) to slightly stretch the fabric and knot the thread. This cautious hemming prevents your allowance from falling down too easily. You can also hem by machine with a stretch twin needle, using hand-wrapped Woolly Nylon on the bobbin.

How I Made This Skirt

You can make a skirt like mine using the step-by-step instructions in the following features:

Mitered Hem with Walking Ease (see p. 105)
Back Slit or Vent (see p. 107)
Cut-On Elasticized Waistband (see p. 114)
Ruched Hem (see p. 121)
Twin-Needle Hem (see p. 162)

ANATOMY *of a Skirt*

There are many assembly methods you can use to sew quickly and still achieve professional results. Many of these techniques are featured in this book, so it's worthwhile to browse through the pages before starting your next project. There is, however, an assembly method that really stands out as a time-saver: a procedure that's adapted from some skirt manufacturers. As the saying goes, time is money, and the following construction order gives you great results fast.

Using satin brocade immediately places this skirt in the upscale category. To enhance the effect, use the time you saved during assembly to make a hand-picked zipper. (See "Hand-Picked Zipper" on p. 112.)

1 Sew all the darts and pleats.

2 Easestitch ⅜ in. (1cm) from the waist's raw edge of the garment pieces. This draws in the skirt to fit your waist while giving you a little extra fabric over the tummy and high hip. Stabilize the easing with twill tape and press over a tailor's ham to eliminate puckers.

3 Sew the seam below the zipper opening. Baste the opening closed if you plan to insert a centered zipper. If you're using an invisible zipper, sew it in before making the seam.

4 Insert the zipper, positioning the top of the teeth 1¾ in. (4.5cm) below the top edge of the skirt if you're planning to face the waistband with petersham ribbon rather than attaching a waistband. (The petersham waist treatment is explained on p. 71.) Use a zipper that's 2 in. (5cm) longer than the opening you would use for other insertion methods.

5 Baste the side seams together using a contrasting thread color. Try on the skirt and refine the fit. Sew the side seams with a regular stitch length and press open the seam allowances. Twill tape at the waist gives you an accurate reading of how the skirt will fit when the waistband is on.

6 Cut the skirt lining from the pattern pieces. Fold up the hem on the pattern pieces before cutting out the lining. The lining is cut to the finished length of the skirt so that it's shorter than the garment.

7 Lining fabric is stable, lacking the "give" characteristic of fashion fabric. Lining often pulls away from the zipper and shows stress at the seams. Give it some extra ease by cutting with ⅝-in. (15mm) seam allowances but sewing with ½-in. (1.3cm) seam allowances and reducing dart and pleat widths by ⅛ in. (3mm) on the sides.

8 Easestitch around the waistline to help the lining fit the skirt's waist. Don't push too hard on the back of the presser foot or the lining will gather rather than ease.

9 Join the lining pieces at the sides and back. With wrong sides together, sew the lining to the skirt at the waist. To ease the slightly larger lining waist into the garment, stitch with the lining against the feed dogs.

10 Hand-stitch the lining to the zipper tape using doubled thread reinforced with beeswax. (Press the thread before sewing.)

11 At the waistband, attach a facing or petersham finish. Trim out the seam allowance bulk, especially near the ends, so that the closure "seats" properly.

12 Add buttonholes or snaps at the waist. Avoid hook-and-eye closures because they fall off after repeated wearing.

13 Hem the skirt as desired. You can miter the corners of a slit and add weights, as explained in "Mitered Hem with Walking Ease" on p. 105.

Master Construction Methods

A skirt is never just a skirt. It's a combination of interesting techniques and wonderful details. How you choose to assemble your garment will dictate the options that you choose.

A full-cut bias skirt can have a petersham waist treatment and a hand-sewn or twin-needle hem. A flowing georgette skirt looks superb with a shirred waist and a rolled hem, while a straight slit skirt looks best with a tailored waistband and a weighted hem.

Whatever your preferences, the instructions in this chapter give you the information to make your vision a reality. The chapter sections are arranged in the order you would follow to assemble your garment.

FLATTERING GRAINLINE CHOICES

Who wants to spend hours making a skirt that hangs in the closet because it's unflattering? Regardless of the construction and fabric quality, if a skirt's fullness isn't distributed evenly, it's never going to make it out of the closet.

The skirt needs to drape so that it minimizes your lumps and bumps while accentuating your best features. Changing the grainline on your pattern pieces can do wonders for the garment's final shape. The best skirt for all figures positions the grainline in the middle of each skirt panel. The fullness is evenly distributed around the perimeter of the skirt. If you want to try this, see the step-by-step instructions in "Centered Grainline" on p. 96. But just in case you want to consider the merits of other grainline options, descriptions and advice follow.

In the skirt at left below, the grainline is parallel to center front. Most of the skirt's fullness hangs at the sides with a flat center front and center back. This is disastrous for full-hipped women because extra folds at the sides draw attention to the figure problem.

In the skirt at right below, the grainline is parallel to the side seam. The fullness hangs at center front and center back, which leaves the sides of the skirt flat. This makes your figure look deep, which is unflattering if you have a tummy or a protruding derriere.

If the grainline is at a 45-degree angle, the bias skirt's fullness is well distributed, but flattering only on the perfect body unless you add extra ease.

(See "Pattern Improvements" on p. 91.) A bias-cut skirt takes considerably more fabric and the hemline becomes uneven after the first wearing.

The grainline on the skirt below is centered in each skirt panel. Fabric fullness is evenly distributed, which is flattering to all figures. You need a bit more fabric, but it's worth the investment: You'll look 10 pounds slimmer in a skirt with a centered grainline. See the following step-by-step instructions.

Centered Grainline

Examine your skirt pattern carefully before you cut. For a flared style to hang well, it may be necessary to change the grainline. A grainline centered on each skirt panel is the most flattering style for all figure types. The same rule applies to gored skirts. On a straight skirt, position center front and center back on the straight grain to prevent the skirt's seat from stretching. A centered grainline evenly drapes the fabric's fullness around your body.

After the grainline revision, you may not be able to cut a full-skirt pattern on the fold. Just add a center-front seamline, as in the photo at right. This consumes a bit more fabric, but the effect is so pleasing that most ready-to-wear skirt manufacturers prefer this grainline. It's almost magic: Drawing one simple line on each of your skirt panels turns your garment from frumpy to fabulous.

1 Fold a pattern piece in half lengthwise, matching the cutting lines on the lengthwise edges or the center-front fold line to the side seam. Align the fold at the bottom hemline. The waistline curve won't match.

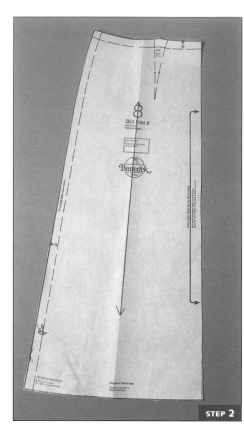

STEP 2

2 Crease the fold, then open the pattern. Draw a new grainline along the newly created lengthwise fold. Use this for laying out your pattern pieces, and disregard the grainline printed on the pattern.

3 If your pattern piece is cut on the fold, disregard the "Cut on Fold" instructions on the pattern piece. After your adjustment, the grainline won't be parallel to the fold, so you need to cut two of each pattern piece.

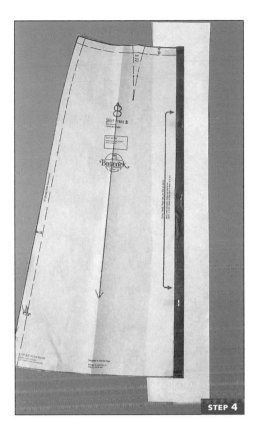

STEP 4

BIAS GRAINLINE ADJUSTMENT

If your pattern grainline isn't on the bias but you want this type of skirt, merely shift the grainline. Draw the crosswise grainline on the pattern piece so that it's perpendicular to the lengthwise grainline. The bias is midway between the crosswise and lengthwise grainlines. Draw the bias grainline in both directions on the pattern piece. Position the new bias grainline on the fabric so that the bias is parallel to the selvage.

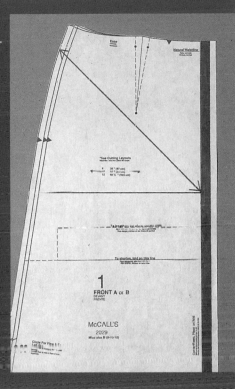

4 Now add a ⅝-in. (15mm) seam allowance at the former "Cut on Fold" line. Draw a new grainline on all skirt panels in the same manner.

5 A skirt cut with the new grainline needs more yardage because the pattern pieces can't be squeezed together on the yardage without going off grain. It's important to find out if you need more yardage before you purchase the garment fabric.

6 Measure across the widest part of the skirt pattern piece. Divide the fabric width in half. If the pattern piece is wider, you need to buy extra yardage. Measure the panel length and multiply by 4 for the yardage. The waistband or other pattern pieces can usually be cut on the fabric between the main pattern pieces.

SWING TACKS

A free-floating lining gives the best drape to a lined garment because both the lining and the fashion fabric can hang free without inhibiting each other. It's one of the easiest ways to finish the inside of a skirt. You can keep the lining from twisting by linking the garment to the lining at the side seams near the hem.

Assemble and hem the garment and lining separately, as though you were making two garments. Hand-tack the lining to the zipper tape. Now machine-baste the lining to the garment at the waist and apply the waistband in the customary manner. Make a 1-in. (2.5cm) long crocheted chain from doubled sewing thread.

At one of the side seams, sew one end of the chain to the top of the garment's hem allowance. Attach the other end of the chain to the lining. Link the remaining side seam with another crocheted chain. A free-floating lining in a coat or dress can be attached at the bottom in the same manner.

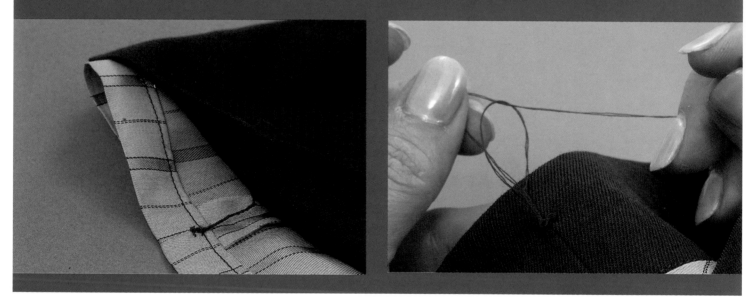

LINING VS. UNDERLINING

Deciding when to use a lining or an underlining for a skirt can be confusing. However, the purpose of lining and underlining, as well as the types of fabrics used with each, are substantially different. Usually a skirt is lined or underlined—not both.

A lining is attached at the waistband and sometimes at the hem if the skirt is straight; it hangs free from the garment at the side seams. It's like a built-in slip, added to conceal figure faults and control seam allowances that are prone to ravel (if the lining is attached to the bottom of the hem). An underlining supports weak fabric and reduces wrinkles in the finished garment.

Linings and underlinings are both a second "skirt"—cut from the same pattern pieces as the garment, but without the hem allowance. Both are easy to make.

COUTURE UNDERLINING

If you get joy out of making the interior of your garments truly beautiful, this is the technique for you. The interior of this finished garment looks as if you went to the trouble of stitching in an underlining and applying a Hong Kong finish to the seam allowances. In reality, you attached the underlining and created a mock Hong Kong effect at the same time. Apply this finishing technique only to a straight skirt or a fitted pair of pants. Margaret Islander was the first to show me this fabulous technique.

1 Pretest your pattern in scrap fabric. This is important because you can't make fitting adjustments later in the process. Alter your pattern pieces to fit. Choose your underlining fabric: silk organza for a crisper look or cotton batiste for a softer effect.

2 Using 1-in. (2.5cm) seam allowances everywhere except at the waist, cut the garment pieces from your fashion fabric.

3 Cut out the skirt underlining with 1-in. (2.5cm) seam allowances, except at the waist. Use the same pattern pieces, but with the hem allowances folded up. The extra-wide seams are used up in the following steps, so don't count on them to give you a better fit.

[TIP] You retain the standard seam allowance width because you cut the lining and fabric pieces with 1-in. (2.5cm) seam allowances, and because subsequent steps nibble away at the extra width. You still have an extra ⅛ in. (3mm), but this will be used up by turn of cloth.

4 Sew and press the darts and pleats in the skirt garment pieces. Do the same with the underlining pieces. Each skirt panel will be lined before you join them together to form the skirt.

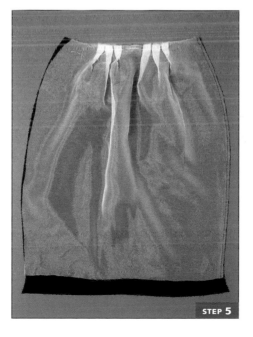

STEP 5

5 Place one skirt panel and the corresponding lining piece right sides together with the raw edges matching at one side seam. Join the pieces with a ¼-in. (6mm) seam allowance. Press them open, and then closed, to slightly favor the fashion fabric.

6 Fold the skirt and the lining wrong sides together to enclose the seam allowances. Pin vertically down the center of the skirt, through both the fashion-fabric and underlining layers.

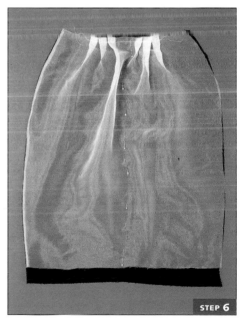

STEP 6

7 Fold the skirt and lining along the pin line, rolling the unsewn part of the skirt and underlining piece right side out along the seamline. Let the underlining creep slightly past the raw skirt edge at the side seam that isn't joined.

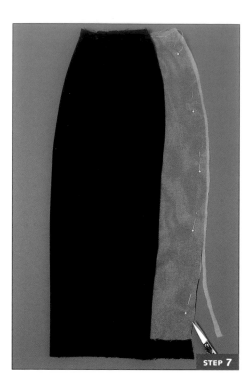

STEP 7

8 At the unattached side, pin along the seamline. Place the joined pieces on a flat surface and trim off any underlining that extends beyond the raw, unattached edge of the skirt's side seam.

9 Remove the pins that are holding the fashion fabric and underlining together. Refold the skirt and underlin-

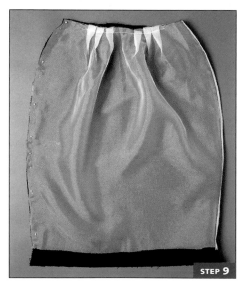

STEP 9

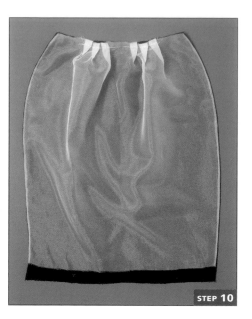

STEP 10

ing with right sides together and the raw side-seam edges even. Join the underlining and skirt pieces at the remaining side seam with a ¼-in. (6mm) seam allowance. Press the seam allowances open. Don't do anything at the waist or hem yet.

10 Turn the joined pieces right side out with the underlining rolling slightly to the underside. Press the skirt piece flat. The waist and hem still aren't seamed. Join the remaining underlining and skirt pieces in the same manner.

11 Now assemble your skirt according to the pattern instructions, using ⅝-in. (15mm) seam allowances. Apply a true Hong Kong finish to the skirt hem and inner edge of the waistband. (See "West Coast Hong Kong Finish" on p. 86.)

12 Sew the top of the hem allowance inside the garment, handstitching only through the lining and the hem allowance, not the skirt.

BASIC UNDERLINING

Underlining supports a weak or wrinkle-prone fabric. The underlining is basted to the garment pieces, then handled as one shape for construction. Cotton batiste and lawn are good choices for underlining, since neither is slippery. Silk organza adds a crisp effect to a straight skirt and is most effective for preventing wrinkles. The number one rule to remember when underlining a garment is to treat the underlined garment shapes as a single unit.

1 Cut the underlining exactly the same size as the outer garment, without the hem allowance. Transfer all pattern marks, such as darts, to the right side of the underlining fabric. There's no need to mark the fashion-fabric garment pieces.

2 Use long hand-basting stitches to join the underlining and the fashion-fabric pieces, wrong sides together, around all of the outside edges. This holds the two pieces together until the seams are sewn.

TIP If you don't like to baste, temporarily affix the underlining to each skirt piece with dots of fabric glue within the seam allowances of the garment fabric. This saves time, and it has never damaged any of the many fabrics I've worked with. Nevertheless, I still prefer hand-sewing with a glazed cotton basting thread; the seam allowances are more pliable this way.

LINING WITH A TAKE-UP TUCK

This technique is most suitable for a straight skirt in a fabric that's extremely prone to raveling. The inside of the garment doesn't look much different from other lined garments, except that the lining no longer hangs loose. Instead, it's attached to the skirt's hem allowance. A hang-loose treatment is still the best option for flared skirts. A take-up tuck, just like the type featured on lined jackets, allows the lining to move somewhat freely so that it doesn't tear.

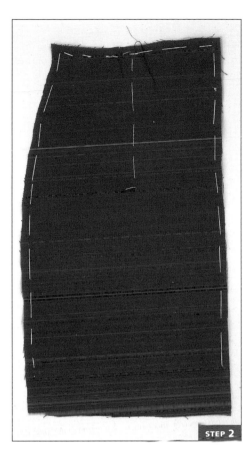

STEP 2

3 Once the underlining and fashion fabric are joined, handle and seam them as if they were a single unit as you sew your skirt. After the skirt is completed, you can zigzag or overlock the raw edges together for a more finished appearance.

For this method, the skirt is hemmed and the lining is attached before you add the waistband. If your fashion fabric ravels, this lining method prevents your seam allowances from raveling. The seam allowances are completely encased by the lining, which is attached at both hem and waist.

1 Cut the lining pieces as long as the garment's finished length (the length of the garment piece minus the hem-allowance width.) Simply fold up the pattern hem allowance when you cut out the lining pieces.

TIP If you decide to shorten the skirt, don't forget to shorten the lining by the same amount.

2 The lining and the skirt are assembled separately, as if you were making two skirts. However, the lining is shorter so that it doesn't show at the bottom of the finished skirt.

3 Although the top of the hem allowance will be attached to the bottom of the lining, it's important to anchor the hem. Hem the skirt by pressing up the hem allowance to the desired length. Hand-stitch ½ in. (1.3cm) from the raw edge, leaving the top edge free for seaming.

TIP Fuller skirts take narrow hems, while straighter styles need a more substantial hem to hang properly. Run an ease line close to the edge of a flared skirt to draw in the extra fullness and keep the hem flat.

4 Pull the top, raw edge of the hem allowance away from the rest of the garment. Match this edge with the right side of the lining's hem. With right sides together, sew the raw edge of the skirt hem to the raw edge of the lining using a ¼-in. (6mm) seam allowance.

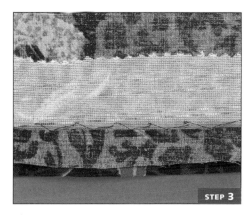

STEP 3

STEP 4

5 Pull up the lining to the waist so that the wrong side of the lining and the wrong side of the skirt are facing each other. The lining is intentionally loose—not taut—from hem to waist. The excess fabric forms a take-up tuck at the hem. This gives you extra movement ease, thus preventing the lining fabric from tearing when you sit.

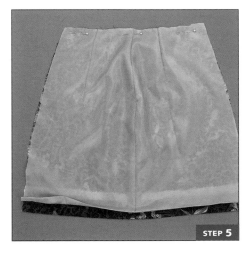

STEP 5

6 Hand-tack the lining to the zipper tape. Machine-baste the lining to the skirt at the waist and apply the waistband in the customary manner.

KNIT SKIRT LINING

If your knit skirt fabric is lightweight and a bit too transparent for your liking, consider adding a lining to your skirt. You'll end up with better coverage and get to eliminate the sew-on waistband. Instead, the lining and skirt are seamed at the waist and the elastic is butted against the seamline so that it's sandwiched between the two fabric layers. Keep in mind that the skirt's waist has to be big enough to pull over your hips without a zipper opening.

You won't believe how easy it is to make a lined skirt with lightweight knit. You can make the lining for the skirt from another layer of the fashion fabric or from bathing suit lining if the lining and the skirt are the same length. This skirt was made from Vogue 7025, Today's Fit by Sandra Betzina.

1 Cut two identical skirts, one in the knit fashion fabric and one in the lining fabric.

2 Sew together two separate skirts, one in lining and the other in fashion fabric. Seams can then be serged together with a three- or four-thread overlock stitch. Or you can opt to simply press open the seam allowances, since knit fabric doesn't ravel.

STEP 2

3 Set your machine for a 0.5mm-wide and 2.5mm-long zigzag stitch. With right sides together and raw edges even, join the two skirts at the waistline. Woolly Nylon on the bobbin will prevent popped stitches on a pull-on knit garment. Trim the seam allowances to ¼ in. (6mm).

4 Turn the skirt right side out so that the waistline seam allowances are encased. Press and edgestitch ⅛ in. (3mm) from the folded seamline.

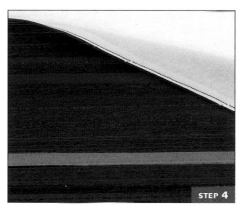

STEP 4

5 Cut a length of nonroll elastic to your honest waist measurement minus 3 in. (7.5cm). (For an explanation of how to take your "honest" waist measurement, see "Designer Waistband That Grows" on p. 115.)

6 Butt the ends of the elastic together over a piece of ribbon. Zigzag the elastic ends to the ribbon. Slide the circle of elastic up from the bottom of the skirt between the two layers. Butt the top edge of the elastic against the waistline seam.

7 With the elastic sandwiched between the two layers, pin the fashion fabric and lining together around the circumference of the skirt waistline, underneath the elastic. Join the skirt layers, forming a casing by sewing with a small

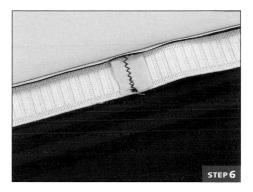

STEP 6

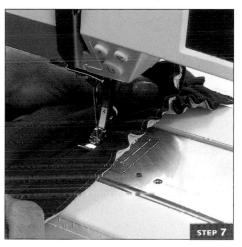

STEP 7

zigzag stitch directly under the elastic, once again with Woolly Nylon on the bobbin. Don't catch the elastic in the stitching.

8 Prevent the elastic from rolling when you wear it by sewing in the well of the side seams, stitching through the elastic and the newly sewn casing. Hem the two skirt layers separately with a stretch twin needle with Woolly Nylon on the bobbin.

[TIP] **For an alternate hem, press up ½ in. (1.3cm) with Steam-A-Seam II between the layers. You can also serge a rolled hem with the differential feed engaged (or place your finger behind the presser foot, as when easing).**

SOLVING THE FLAP ABOUT WRAPS

As explained in "Worthwhile Wrap" on p. 90, a poorly designed wrap skirt can be a nightmare to wear when it reveals too much when you walk and sit. The solution is simple: Add walking ease and make sure that the underwrap isn't too skimpy.

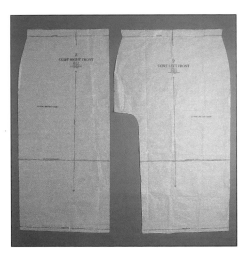

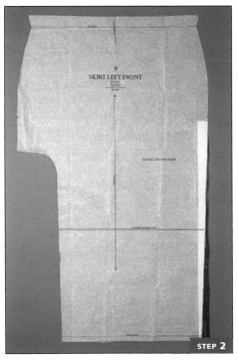

STEP 2

Faux Wrap

The best wrap skirt is a faux wrap; designed to include the top third of the underwrap (the skirt panel closest to you) in the side seam. The hemline is very high on the underside, sloping steeply to a longer length at the opposite side seam. The top wrap covers this. Study the line drawings on the backs of patterns to find one shaped like this (see the photo at top left).

You don't need two full skirt fronts with the faux wrap—a great benefit if you're using costly fabric. Less fabric does not translate into less coverage, because both sides of the underwrap are secured in the side seams. Nevertheless, you still need to add walking ease.

1 Measure around your body at the tummy (2½ in. to 3 in. [6.4cm to 7.6cm] below the waist) and at the full hips. Add 3 in. (7.6cm) to the larger of the two numbers. Compare this to the flat-pattern measurement at the corresponding location. Alter the pattern to fit.

2 Walking ease is added only to the side seams of the front (overlap and underlap) pattern pieces, tapering to nothing at the waist. It's important to position walking ease at the hemline, where it's needed most. Don't make any addition to the skirt back, or the garment shape will change.

3 Now add your walking ease. See "Walking Ease" on p. 90 to determine the amount you'll need for the skirt length you're using.

Traditional Wrap

As the name suggests, this type of skirt wraps around the body, secured with a button, snaps, or a tie. The underlayer doesn't get attached at the side seam.

Walking ease is just as important for the wrap skirt that looks more like a length of fabric than a garment until you put it on. When the two fronts—the underlap and overlap pattern pieces—are placed on top of each other and measured, you may discover that there isn't enough fabric to wrap around your body. This is fine for a beach cover-up, when it doesn't matter if you show too much leg—but you need more fabric on other types of wraps.

Even if there's enough coverage when you're standing still, there may not be when you walk or sit, not flattering if you have ample thighs or a bit of a tummy. If you think the fronts will spread apart when you move, measure your pattern pieces and add walking ease.

1 Measure across your body, from side to side, at the tummy (2½ in. to 3 in. or 6.4cm to 7.6cm below the waist) and at the full hips. Add 3 in. (7.6cm) to the larger of the two numbers.

2 Place the front underlap on a table with the front overlap on top of it, matching them at center front. Measure across the locations that correspond to the body measurements, excluding the seam allowances.

3 Compare the pattern measurements to the body measurements plus ease. If the pattern pieces aren't big enough, alter them to fit by adding at the side seams. Make the same adjustments to the back pattern piece.

4 Add 2 in. (5cm) to the loose (usually straight) edge of the underwrap. Lengthen the waistband to match. This extension to the loose edge of the underwrap offers additional coverage, but a side seam addition is still necessary.

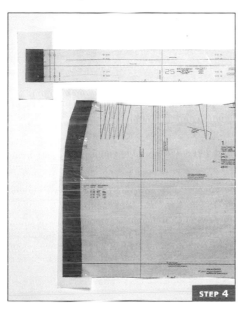

STEP 4

5 Now it's time to add walking ease to your skirt. See Steps 2 and 3 under "Faux Wrap" on the facing page for detailed instructions.

MITERED HEM WITH WALKING EASE

Mitered corners have a flat, professional touch that quality garments demand. A miter reduces bulk and creates a clean diagonal seamline where the fabrics are joined on the wrong side of the garment. It's a polished, professional look for garment locations like the hem of a vent in a skirt, even if it's visible only to you.

Whether you're sewing a skirt with a slit or vent—or a faced blouse or jacket—you have the opportunity to miter a corner where the hem allowance meets the facing. This mitering technique works when the hem-allowance depth is ½ in. (1.3cm) narrower than the width of the facing on the pattern piece. Plan a 1½-in. (3.8cm) hem depth before cutting out your garment pieces, and make the facing 2 in. (5cm) wide.

Is there a trick to keeping a vent closed in the back of a skirt? You bet there is—walking ease. In the case of a vent, the garment pieces are cut out without changes, then ½ in. (1.3cm) is "stolen" from the lower portion of the inner edge on both sides of the vent. Complete instructions for a mitered, no-gap vent are included in the following instructions.

1 Assemble your garment. Press the hem allowance to the wrong side. On your garment piece, the vent facing is the same width from top to bottom, usually 2 in. (5cm) wide.

2 Press the facing to the wrong side, starting with a 2-in. (5cm) width at the top of the vent opening and tapering to 1½ in. (3.8cm) at the bottom of the hem allowance.

Folding back a smaller facing near the hem, however, helps the vent hang closed. This ½-in. (1.3cm) "addition" on each side fills in the vent opening when the skirt is on the body.

3 Fold open the facing and interface it.

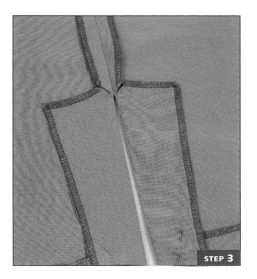

STEP 3

STEP 4

4 Unfold the hem and facing. Fold the corner of the garment diagonally to the wrong side, matching the crease lines. Press the fold to make a diagonal line for sewing the miter. The crease lines create guides for your straight stitching.

5 If this is the first time you've mitered a corner, try Steps 6 and 7 with basting stitches and don't trim away any excess fabric. When you're happy with the results, repeat the steps using permanent stitching.

6 Unfold the corner. Fold the right side of the hem allowance to the right side of the facing with the raw edges even. Set your machine for small, straight reinforcing stitches, and sew diagonally along the crease you made in Step 4. Trim the triangular hem allowance to ⅛ in. (3mm).

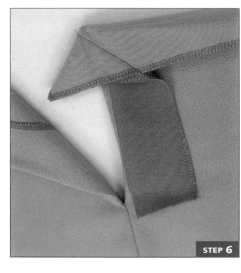

STEP 6

7 Turn the hem allowance and facing to the wrong side of the garment. The hemline and facing foldlines are now the garment edges. To prevent an imprint on the outside of the garment, slip an envelope or a Dritz EZY-Hem guide into the corner before pressing or pounding the corner flat.

8 Hem the garment and secure the facing with small, invisible stitches.

BACK SLIT OR VENT

An Eastern-style, embroidered satin skirt begs for a slit at the hem. This fabric makes a wonderful pegged skirt, which needs a slit so that you can walk and sit. However, without reinforcement at the release point, the slit would soon tear.

Often, center-back and side-seam slits are secured at the top with decorative reinforcement stitching. Depending on the fabric, this stitch could be a basic bar tack, a satin-stitched triangle, or merely a straight-stitched silhouette of a triangle. You can have a lot of fun making an interesting bit of stitching at the top of the slit (called the release point).

Whatever your fancy, the release point for your slit deserves elegant and subtle reinforcement and support that extends

> [TIP] **A slit hangs smoothly when you stitch circular weights into the folds.**

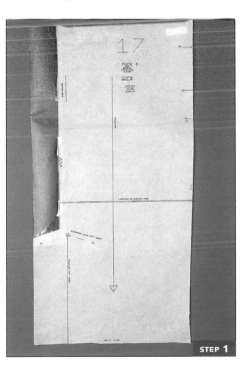

STEP 1

all the way to the waist. Here's a great way to prevent the slit from tearing higher when you walk or sit. The technique involves extending the facing all the way to the waist, which also prevents sagging at center back.

1 Alter your pattern pieces to fit. If you plan to miter the hem and slit facing according to the instructions in this chapter, make the hem allowance ½ in. (1.3cm) narrower than the facing for the slit, or 1½ in. (3.8cm) wide. Alter the pattern piece so that the 2-in. (5cm) vent fold back extends all the way up to the waistline.

2 Cut out the garment pieces and serge the raw edges of the slit extension (the facing) with a three-thread overlock stitch. When cutting out the garment pieces, don't use the fabric selvage as the edge of the center-back seam allowance. The selvage may shrink in subsequent washings, which makes the seamline pucker.

3 Sew the center-back seam with 2-in. (5cm) seam allowances/vent facings. Use small stitches (15mm) for the last ½ in. (1.3cm) before the release point. To reinforce your fabric at this high-stress area, sew over ¼-in. (6m) wide twill tape.

4 Press the seam allowances/vent facings to the wrong side of the fabric all the way to the hem. Miter and hem

the skirt. (See "Mitered Hem with Walking Ease" on p. 105.) The facing is ½ in. (1.3cm) narrower in the slit opening for walking ease.

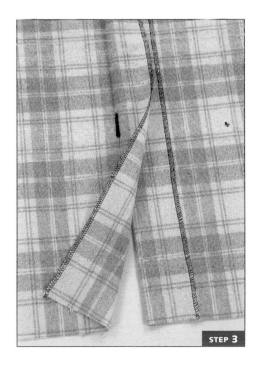

STEP 3

GREAT GODETS AND YOKES

Whether you want to insert a pointed yoke or a godet, the technique is the same. A yoke on a skirt, a Western-style top, or a pair of pants is sewn exactly like a godet. It's amazing that a simple triangle of fabric can have such an impact on the styling of a garment.

Insert several godets at the bottom of vertical skirt seamlines, and the hemline will flare as you walk. Alternatively, add them to the bottom of a sleeve for fullness. Whether the godet is in a skirt, a dress, or a jacket, the effect is stunning. For even more drama, consider using contrasting fabric for the godet.

[TIP] **An insert can go in any seam. Just decide on the length and width and cut the fabric triangle with the grainline running lengthwise through the point and the center of the base. The stitching starts about 2 in. (5cm) below the point, which affects the height that you cut your godets. On a skirt, try cutting the godet piece with an 8-in. (20.3cm) base and a 16-in. (40.6cm) height from the center of the base up to the point.**

1 Cut out the garment pieces. Apply a lightweight interfacing to the wrong side of the yoke for a skirt or pants. The interfacing strengthens the point and prevents it from stretching. Don't interface a godet or yoke on a blouse because this will interfere with the garment's drape. The following instruc-tions explain how to insert a pointed godet or yoke (called an "insert" in sub-sequent steps).

2 At the point on the wrong side of the insert, draw a line ⅝ in. (15mm) from one edge. Make a second line in the same manner on the other edge. The two lines intersect at the exact center of the insert.

[TIP] **Lines drawn in pencil or a temporary fabric-marking pen are better than chalk lines because they're thinner, more accurate, invisible from the right side of the fabric, and don't wear off as quickly.**

3 Transfer the pattern marks to the skirt pieces, including a dot to mark the insert's point. Keep in mind that the dot goes at the point's seamline, not at the raw edge of the point. For example, if the side of the insert is 16 in. (40.6cm) long, place the dots 14 in. (35.6cm) above the bottom of the skirt at the seamlines.

4 Finish the raw edges of all the pat-tern pieces—including the inserts—with a three-thread overlock or zigzag stitch. (Don't worry about making a perfect serged point; it's cut off in a subsequent step.)

5 With right sides together, sew the seam. Stop 1 in. (2.5cm) before the insert placement dot. Switch to small reinforcing stitch-es (1mm) and sew up to the dot. End the seam by breaking the threads without backstitching.

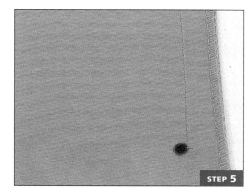

STEP 5

[TIP] **Avoid backstitching as much as possi-ble. The extra lines of stitching add bulk and prevent the seam from pressing uniformly.**

6 Place one side of the insert against the garment, with right sides together and matching the marked point with the garment's seamlines. Pin the

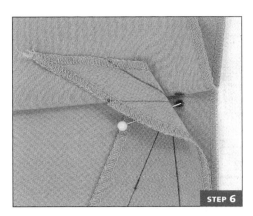
STEP 6

pieces together with the insert on the bottom. Don't try to pin the second side of the insert into the triangular opening yet. This causes a tuck at the point.

7 Still using a very small stitch length (1mm) and ⅝-in. (15mm) seam allowances, place the pieces on the machine bed with the insert against the feed dogs. Insert the needle at the point where the seamlines intersect.

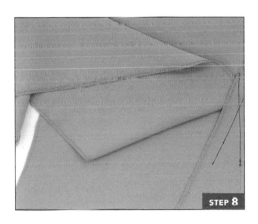
STEP 8

8 Sew for ½ in. (1.3cm) without backstitching. Backstitching at the point can ruin an attractive insert. The extra stitching adds bulk and prevents a flat application. Very small stitches are sufficient to secure the point of the insert. Switch to a regular stitch length.

StyleMaker

ROUND ABOUT

Who says that the top of a godet has to be pointed? A rounded godet adds a wonderful design element to a garment. The shape is just as easy to insert as a triangular pattern piece, although the insertion technique is slightly different.

Staystitch the skirt ½ in. (1.3cm) from the raw edge, then clip the seam allowances to the stitching. Make ⅜-in. (1cm) deep snips into the seam allowance every inch (2.5cm) at the uppermost rounded portion of the insertion location. Pin the godet into the skirt with right sides together and with the clipped side on top. The clip allows the skirt to conform to the shape of the godet. This technique also works for princess seams, which join two reverse curves.

With the godet against the feed dogs, sew it into the skirt. Use small stitches as you work around the top of the godet. Press the seam allowances together and away from the godet. If desired, topstitch next to the godet seamline on the right side of the skirt.

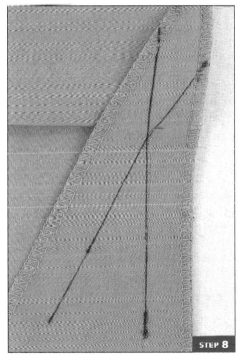
STEP 8

STEP 9

Be sure to always place the insert on the bottom, against the feed dogs, and sew from the point down.

9 Match and pin the remaining side of the insert into the opening. Sew the second side of the insert, again using a 1mm stitch length near the point and sewing from the point to the wide end.

10 If you're happy with the results, serge across the point (only the point—through a single layer of fabric) to trim off the excess. Press the seam allowances away from the insert. Topstitch if desired.

PEGGED
SIDE SEAMS

A straight skirt doesn't have to be straight. Nipping it in at the hem gives you almost the same silhouette, but is far more flattering. Pegging, as it's called, reduces the hem's circumference until it's smaller than that of the hips. The amount you take in the bottom (at the side seams) depends on your hip measurement and your personal taste.

1 Sew the back and front seam on your skirt. Baste the side seams. You can peg a skirt that has side-seam pockets. If you've attached the pockets, the tapered side seams must revert to the original seamline where the bottom of the pocket bags are stitched into the seam.

2 If you haven't added the pockets yet, simply follow the steps below and insert the pockets before stitching the side seams in Step 5.

STEP 3

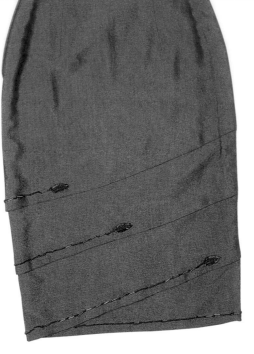

3 Pin in the amount by which you want to narrow the hem. If your hips are 39 in. (99.1cm) or less, pin out ½ in. (1.3cm) at each side seam, tapering to the original seamline at the hips. This reduces the hem circumference by 2 in. (5cm).

4 If your hips are larger, deepen both side seam allowances by 1 in. (2.5cm) at the hem, tapering to the original seamline at the hips. This reduces the hem circumference by 4 in. (10.2cm).

5 Try on the skirt. Pin in less or more at the hem until the silhouette flatters you. Sew the side seams and finish making the skirt.

[TIP] **Side seams in drapey fabric are more successful when they're joined with a narrow zigzag stitch, with machine settings at 0.5mm wide and 2.5mm long (10 spi). This stitch relaxes with the fabric, rather than drawing up the seam, which happens with a straight stitch.**

CENTERED ZIPPER

During my first few years of sewing, I relied entirely on the centered zipper application for my dresses, pants, and skirts. As my skills and confidence increased I moved on to lapped and fly-front applications, but I didn't entirely reject the centered version. It's still a great closure for center-back locations.

All the time I've spent on the centered zipper has reaped rewards. Through experimentation, I've come up with a way to "baste" the zipper with clear tape and invented a simple, easy-to-remove stitching guide.

1 Cut two ½-in. (1.3cm) wide strips of fusible interfacing, in the nonstretch direction, 1 in. (2.5cm) longer than the zipper. Fuse one strip to the wrong side of each seam allowance at the zipper opening.

2 Place one edge of the interfacing close to the basted seam. The interfacing stabilizes the seam and keeps it from rippling as you sew in Steps 3 and 4. When you press the basted seam open, you won't see the interfacing.

TIP **If the fabric is stable, you can insert the zipper without the strips.**

STEP 2

3 With right sides together and raw edges even, join the garment pieces that have the zipper opening. Start at the bottom of the seam using a regular stitch length.

4 At the bottom of the zipper opening, switch to machine-basting stitches. Continue the basting to the top of the zipper opening. Backstitch a little at the end of the basting to prevent the seam from opening during the application. Press the seam allowances open.

5 Close the zipper. Place it, face down, on the wrong side of the seamline. Temporarily pin the zipper to the garment. Apply several pieces of clear tape horizontally across the seam allowances and zipper. Remove the pins.

STEP 5

6 Turn the garment right side up. Center a piece of ½-in. (1.3cm) wide clear tape over the length of the basted seamline. Insert a zipper foot in the sewing machine and set the zipper tape to the right of the needle.

7 With the garment right side up, start topstitching at the upper left of the zipper. Use the edge of the tape as your guide, being careful not to stitch through it.

TIP **Clear tape is a fabulous stitching guide, as well as a great pin substitute.**

STEP 7

8 Sew down the left side of the zipper, through all thicknesses. At the bottom of the opening, stop with the needle down, pivot, sew across the bottom, and stop with the needle down at the oppo-

TRICK of the TRADE

INSTA-PIN SOLUTION

Try using a strip of ¼-in. (6mm) wide double-sided tape on each side of the zipper tape for positioning. This way, you don't need to pin the zipper to the garment.

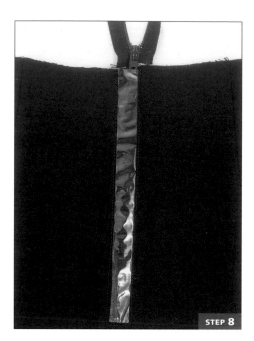

STEP 8

site edge of the tape. Pivot the garment and sew up the remaining side of the zipper.

9 Peel off the tape on both sides of the garment. Remove the machine basting. Press the zipper area with an up-and-down motion to avoid fabric ripples.

TRICK of the TRADE

STOP JOGGING

Here's a great way to avoid a jog at the top of a zipper. Use a zipper that's 2 in. (5cm) longer than the garment opening. Let the upper end extend beyond the top of the opening, and cut off the extra length after the waistband or facing is attached. Hand-walk the waistband seam through the zipper teeth.

HAND-PICKED ZIPPER

This type of zipper is an excellent choice for a fine, tailored skirt or dress. Tiny hand stitches, visible from the right side of the garment, add an elegant touch to your closure—regardless of the treatment you choose.

For a special touch on an evening skirt, try this tip from Susan Khalje, author of *Bridal Couture* (Krause Publications, 1997). Thread one small pearl or seed bead every time your hand-sewing needle comes to the right side of the fabric. This embellishment looks best when the pearls or seed beads are paired on each side of the zipper. Mark the stitch locations before sewing. Because each pearl takes up a scant ¼ in. (6mm), space the stitches ½ in. (1.3cm) apart, rather than the standard ¼ in. (6mm) (see the photo below).

One of the important features of a hand-picked zipper is the subtle line of hand stitching that's visible on the right side of the garment. On the burgundy dress shown on p. 147, you sew in a manner that makes the hand stitching practically invisible. You still retain the striking hand-picked effect because the beads accent the work.

Hand picking is typically applied to a centered zipper. At the side seam, however, experts prefer to hand-pick a lapped zipper treatment.

1 Cut out your garment pieces. Stabilize each seam allowance at the zipper opening with a ½-in. (1.3cm) wide strip of interfacing that's cut with the grainline parallel to the length. You can also use a narrow strip of straight-grain, fusible seam stabilizer (fusible interfacing on a roll).

2 Seam the garment below the zipper opening. Press back the seam allowances in the opening.

[TIP] **Don't press back seam allowances on velvet. Hand-baste them in position.**

3 From the right side of the garment, position the closed zipper with the folded edge of one side of the opening centered on the zipper teeth. As you approach the upper tab stop, undo the zipper and position the remaining teeth ¼ in. (6mm) away from the pressed fold. This creates room to hide the zipper pull when the garment is closed.

[TIP] **If the garment is snug-fitting, like a bustier or a strapless dress, let the pressed fold overlap the entire length of the zipper by ⅛ in. (3mm). This overlap hides the zipper teeth when the closure is under stress.**

4 Pin well both sides of the zipper in position.

STEP 3

5 Pull a double length of thread through beeswax. Press the thread to set the wax. This strengthens the thread and allows it to glide through the fabric without wax buildup.

6 Hand stitch the zipper by sewing through all of the fabric layers. Use a simple backstitch ¼ in. (6mm) away from the folded edge. When the thread is on the right side of the fabric, reinsert the needle into the fabric two garment threads behind where it came out.

7 Inside the garment (on the zipper tape), move the needle forward ¼ in. (6mm). Pull the needle and thread to the right side of the garment again. Don't pull the thread too tight or the fabric will pucker between the stitches.

8 For a decorative effect, add a bead at every stitch on the outside of the garment, moving forward ½ in. (1.3cm) rather than ¼ in. (6mm) for large beads or pearls.

[TIP] **It's easier to stitch the beaded decorations in pairs, one on each side of the zipper, if you close the zipper after working the first side.**

9 Continue to the end of the zipper, then stitch the remaining side of the zipper in the same manner.

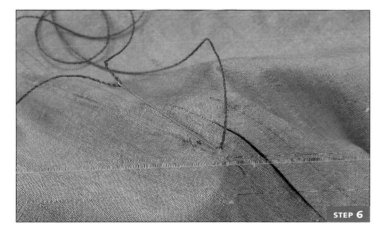

STEP 6

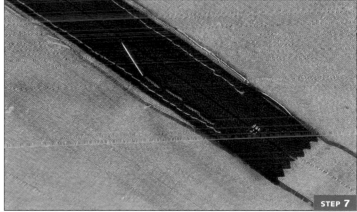

STEP 7

CUT-ON ELASTICIZED WAISTBAND

When time is limited—or when you're working with a difficult fabric—this is a good way to finish the top of a tube skirt made in stretchy fabric. After serging the raw fabric edge, the top of the skirt is folded to the wrong side and stitched down to make a casing. Then 1-in. (2.5cm) wide elastic is inserted through the casing. This is simple, elegant, and easy. There's no need to attach a waistband. It's ideal for those times when you want to make a garment in a few hours.

Almost any stretchy skirt is a good candidate for this simple waist treatment. Just ignore the separate waistband pattern piece. Make an elastic casing by extending the top of the skirt front and back.

TRICK
of the TRADE

TUG-AND-MARK EASY FITTING

Whether you have a bit of a tummy, full hips, or uneven hips, there's an easy way to get an even hemline. Try on the skirt. Tie an elastic around your waist (or put on a narrow belt). Tug on the top of the skirt until there's 3 in. (7.5cm) above the elastic around your entire waist.

Now look at the bottom of the skirt in the mirror. If the hemline isn't straight, pull sections of the skirt up or down to even it out at the bottom. Draw a chalk line at the bottom of the elastic. Take off the skirt and cut off the fabric 2⅜ in. (6cm) above the chalk line for a casing.

STEP 3

all layers, to make the casing for the elastic. Leave a 2-in. (5cm) opening at center back for inserting the elastic.

4 Cut a length of 1-in. (2.5cm) wide nonroll or Banroll stretch elastic to match your waist measurement minus 3 in. (7.5cm). Insert the elastic through the casing.

5 Butt the ends of the elastic together on top of a piece of ribbon or a small square of garment fabric. Anchor the edges with two rows of zigzag stitching through all layers of the fabric and elastic. Butting elastic ends reduces bulk and partially reduces the flat spot when the waist fabric gathers.

6 Straight-stitch through the casing along the center-back seam to prevent the elastic from twisting. Pull the waistband several times to distribute the fabric fullness evenly around the elastic. If you want a shirred effect, use Banroll stretch elastic and sew two horizontal rows through the elastic with a 75/11 HS needle.

1 Extend the top of the skirt at least 3 in. (7.5cm) above the natural waistline. Cut out the garment pieces and join the side seams.

2 Finish the raw edge at the top of the skirt with a three-thread overlock or zigzag stitch. Turn the skirt wrong side out.

3 Fold the top 2⅜ in. (6cm) of the waist to the wrong side. Using a stretch stitch or narrow zigzag stitch (0.5mm wide and 2.5mm long) and Woolly Nylon on the bobbin, sew ¼ in. (6mm) from the finished edge, through

STEP 5

DESIGNER WAISTBAND THAT GROWS

Achieve the ease and sophistication of a tailored waistband without compromising comfort. The front looks like a traditional waistband while hidden elastic provides stretch. It's the best of both worlds.

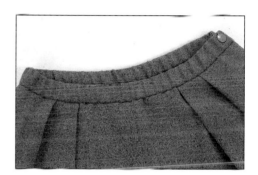

Although the waistband is slightly gathered on the hanger, it's smooth and comfortable on your body. This is an ideal treatment for someone who wants the look of a tailored waistband but loves the comfort and ease of an elasticized treatment. You can use this waistband on any skirt or pant.

I started using the Designer Waistband that Grows on leather pants and skirts. It was so easy that I started using it for all of my garments.

1 Fold out the darts and pleats on the pattern pieces. Measure the pattern at the waistline seam.

2 Alter the skirt pattern so that the garment's finished waistline equals your waist measurement plus 3 in. (7.6cm). Make the darts and pleats narrower or add a bit at the side seams so that the waistline of the garment equals your waist measurement plus 3 in. (7.6cm).

TIP It's certainly tempting to cheat when you take your waist measurement, but the results can be disastrous. To avoid fudging the numbers, take a measurement with the metric side of the tape measure facing out, then flip it over to discover the truth in inches. If you're making your waistbands too tight, take the measurement sitting down.

3 Cut the garment pieces from your fashion fabric. Don't cut out the waistband yet. Transfer the pattern markings. Stabilize the seam allowance at the zipper opening with a ½-in. (1.3cm) wide strip of interfacing that's cut with the grainline parallel to the length. Assemble the garment up to the point where you attach the waistband.

4 Cut a waistband length to your waist measurement plus 6 in. (15.2cm). If you can cut one long side using a selvage, all the better. If you're using 1-in. (2.5cm) wide elastic, cut the waistband 3¾ in. (8.6cm) wide. With 1½-in. (3.8cm) wide elastic, cut a 4⅜-in. (11.1cm) wide waistband. And for 2-in. (5cm) wide elastic, cut the waistband 5¼ in. (13.7cm) wide.

5 If you didn't cut one long side of the waistband on a selvage, serge or use a Hong Kong finish on one long raw edge. (See "West Coast Hong Kong Finish" on p. 86.)

6 Open the zipper. Pin the unfinished long edge of the waistband to the skirt's waist with the right sides together and the raw edges even. Use as much waistband as it takes to go around the skirt, letting ⅝ in. (15mm) extend past the overlap side of the zipper and the rest at least 1 in. to 1¼ in. (2.5cm to 3.2cm) past the underlap side.

7 Sew the waistband to the skirt. Close the zipper to ensure that the waist seamline meets on both sides of the zipper. If one side of the seamline is higher than the other at the zipper opening, reposition the waistband now. Otherwise, one side will be higher when the finished waistband is closed.

8 Cut the elastic to the same length as your waist measurement plus 1¼ in. (3.2cm). Chalk-mark the elastic ⅝ in. (15mm) from one end and 1⅝ in. (4.1cm) from the other end. Leave the right side of the waistband against the right side of the skirt with the seam allowances exposed.

STEP 7

9 Place the elastic on top of the seam allowance so that one long edge is almost on top of the waistband seamline and the opposite edge isn't on any fabric. Match the chalk marks with the zipper teeth.

10 The side of the elastic that's marked 1⅝ in. (4.1cm) from the end goes at the underlap side of the waistband. The elastic is shorter than the waistband, so just pin the ends and midpoint to the seam allowances.

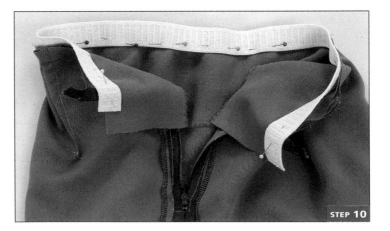

STEP 10

11 Set your machine to a 4mm-long and 4mm-wide (6 spi) zigzag stitch. With the elastic on top and stretching it gently as you proceed, sew one edge of the elastic to the waistband seam allowances. Remove the skirt from the machine and turn the garment right side out.

12 There's an easy way and a hard way to finish the ends of the waistband. For the easy way, see p. 77. This photo shows the start of the hard—but very professional—method.

STEP 12

13 To machine-stitch the ends of the waistband starting inside the waist seamline, you need to get the body of the skirt out of the way. The easiest way to do this is to roll up the portion nearest the zipper until it's on the waistband, and the waistline seam allowances are exposed.

14 Working on the overlap side of the zipper, roll up the skirt in the zipper area below the waistband seamline to the right side of the garment. Continue rolling the fabric and zipper until they're on the waistband and above the seamline.

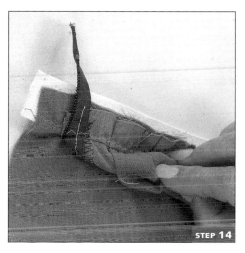
STEP 14

15 Still holding the roll on the waistband, work on just the first few inches of the waistband for this step. Flip the waistband back on itself so that the finished edge is even with the waistband seam allowances. Enclose the rolled portion of the garment inside the waistband.

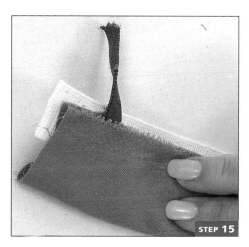
STEP 15

16 Set your machine to a 2mm straight stitch (12 spi). On the overlap side of the garment and with the elastic facing you, begin sewing over the waistband seamline, starting 2 in. (5cm) away from the end of the waistband.

17 Sew through the seam allowances, without catching the lengthwise edge of the elastic or the fabric roll in the stitching. Sew to the closest short end of the elastic.

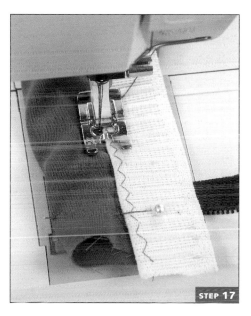
STEP 17

18 Stop sewing ⅛ in. (3 mm) past the end of the zipper placket. Pivot and sew across the end of the waistband, through all of the layers (including the elastic). This end of the band is flush with the edge of the skirt opening.

19 Trim all of the seam allowances to ¼ in. (6mm) along the two seams you just made. Trim the end of the elastic in the seam allowance to ⅛ in. (3mm).

20 Turn the end of the waistband right side out and unroll the skirt fabric that was trapped inside. Use a screwdriver to make sharp points and push the elastic flat inside.

21 Roll the opposite side of the skirt onto the waistband, adjust the seam allowances, and fold the waistband as explained in Steps 13 through 15.

22 Starting at the fold, sew across the end of the waistband and the elastic 1¼ in. (3.2cm) from the zipper teeth, or else lined up with the fly-front placket. This allows for an extension closure. Stop ⅝ in. (15mm) from the raw edge and pivot. Don't backstitch or break the threads.

23 Make sure the skirt roll is tucked inside the waistband, away from the waistband seamline. With the elastic facing you, sew the extension together, starting at the pivot point and using a ⅝-in. (15mm) seam allowance. Be careful that the rolled skirt isn't caught in the stitching.

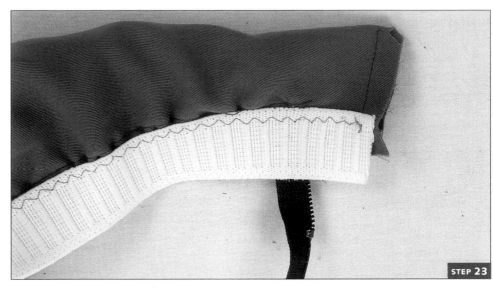

STEP 23

24 At the edge of the skirt opening, continue stitching on top of the waistband seamline for about 2 in. (5cm) past the zipper teeth. Trim the seam allowances and elastic. Turn the end right side out as explained in Step 20.

25 Clip through the seam allowances on the long edge of the band for about 1 in. (2.5cm) right where the stitching finishing the ends stops. This allows the band to lie flat. Wrap the remainder of the waistband snugly around the elastic and waistband seam.

26 Let the finished edge of the waistband extend past the waistband seamline inside the garment. From the right side of the garment, sew the waistband in place by stitching in the well of the waistband seamline.

STEP 26

FACED HEM

When hemming a skirt in bulky fabric, you'll get a less cumbersome hem if you trim the hem allowance to ½ in. (1.3cm) and make a hem facing from a light-weight fabric.

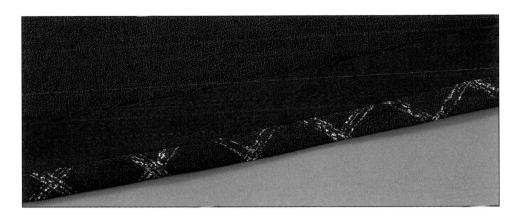

1 Assemble your skirt and mark the hemline. Measure ½ in. (1.3cm) down from the hemline, and trim off any hem-allowance fabric beyond this point.

2 Choose a lightweight fabric such as silk charmeuse or lightweight cotton for the facing. A striped cotton cut on the bias makes a nice surprise. Look up the finished skirt hem circumference on the back of your pattern, or measure around the hemline of your skirt. Add 1¼ in. (3.2cm). Cut a 4-in. (10.2cm) wide facing strip on the true bias.

3 Press the bias strip in half length-wise, taking care not to stretch the strip. Sew the doubled raw edges to the right side of the bottom of the skirt. Use a ½-in. (1.3mm) seam allowance and an even-feed foot to avoid stretching the seamline. Join the ends of the bias strip so that the skirt is faced with a continuous strip. Trim the seam to ¼ in. (6mm).

4 Press up the seam allowances, then press up the facing to the wrong side of the skirt along the hemline. The seam joining the skirt and facing stabilizes the hem crease.

5 Hand-hem the facing to the skirt with a single thread. Don't pull the thread too tight, and knot it every 4 in. (10.2cm).

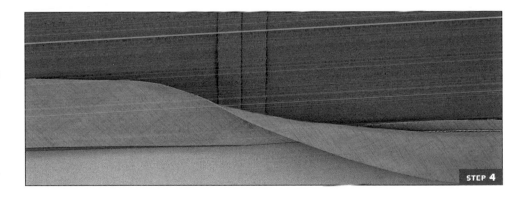

STEP 4

FINE ROLLED HEM

This is a wonderful treatment for a bias skirt; full, drapey pants; or any garment made from fabric that needs a tiny, narrow hem—even a scarf. Lightweight fabrics, such as chiffon and georgette, and bias-cut edges look fabulous with a crisp edge finish.

This is a very easy technique—you don't even need a serger. And you don't have to fiddle around trying to feed a raw fabric edge evenly into a rolled-edge presser foot. Thanks to fusible thread, this is the easiest and best-looking rolled hem you'll ever make.

1 Load fusible thread on the machine's bobbin. Staystitch along the garment ½ in. (1.3cm) from the raw edge, with the fabric right side up.

2 Press up the hem allowance along the line of staystitching. As the fusible thread melts, it forms a sharp crease at the fold.

3 Trim the hem allowance to ⅛ in. (3mm). Satin-stitch over the fold, or roll the edge and hand-stitch or machine-sew it. When machine-stitching, press your finger behind the presser foot to prevent the edge from stretching.

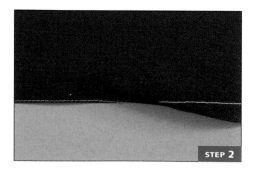

STEP 2

RUCHED HEM

A small investment of time yields top results for this sportswear detail. Often positioned at center back at the bottom of a skirt, you can also apply the treatment to side seams. Basically, all you're doing is drawing up a short length of a seam—usually from the hem up a few inches—so that the fabric gently gathers along the vertical seam and the hemline is no longer even.

The old way of ruching is to draw up two lines of basting, then straight-stitch the gathers to Stay Tape. Try this easier method, which gathers and stabilizes at the same time. This technique is most suitable on lightweight fabrics such as knit or challis because they have enough body to gather nicely, yet they aren't heavy enough to stretch out the elastic. Avoid using a ruched hem treatment on heavier fabrics such as gabardine and linen.

[TIP] To flatten out the ridge between lines of stitching when using a twin needle, loosen the top tension.

1 Hem your skirt to the desired length. A narrow hem works better for this treatment, so consider turning up only ½ in. (1.3cm) and topstitching the edge with a twin needle.

2 Cut a 6-in. (15.2cm) long piece of ¼-in. (6mm) wide elastic. You can use regular or clear elastic. Fold the elastic in half lengthwise and mark the midpoint. Inside the skirt, mark the seamline 6 in. and 12 in. (15.2cm and 30.5cm) above the bottom of the hem at center back.

3 Pin one end of the elastic to the hem about ½ in. (1.3cm) above the hemline. Leave the very bottom of the hem flat to give the skirt a nice, clean finish. Pin the remaining edge to the 12-in. (30.5cm) seamline mark. Pin the elastic's midpoint to the seamline at the 6-in. (15.2cm) mark.

4 Set your sewing machine to a medium width and -length zigzag stitch. Insert the elastic under the presser foot and take several stitches in place to anchor one end of the elastic to the center-back seamline just above the hemline.

5 Sew the elastic to the seamline, stretching it so that the fabric and elastic are flat as they're stitched. If you feed the elastic through the front of the presser foot, it's easier to center it on the seamline.

STEP 3

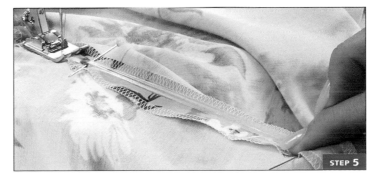

STEP 5

121

Chapter 5

DRESSES

Separates diversify and expand your wardrobe, but no closet is complete without a few dresses. They're the ultimate in no-fuss dressing: You just slip one on, toss a vest or jacket over it, and head out the door.

My absolute favorite dress is a T-shirt style made in stretchy fabric. Since I've made so many, I have a great variety of knit fabric techniques to share with you. But there's more to this chapter than knits. You'll also find advice on bound edges, facings, necklines, sleeves, and a foolproof invisible zipper.

Since you can lengthen any top pattern into a dress or shorten any dress pattern to make a top, I've combined the two garments in this chapter. I'll show you how to convert a top to a dress and share numerous techniques that apply to both types of garments.

Sandra's Closet

It's my hope that you'll use the ideas in this chapter to develop an exciting new wardrobe. To get you started, I'd like to explain some techniques I've incorporated into several of my favorite garments.

How I Made These Wraps

You can make a dress or top like mine using the step-by-step instructions in the following features.

No-Gap Wrap (see p. 140)
Twin-Needle Hem (see p. 162)
Cornering with a Twin Needle (see p. 163)

WONDERFUL WRAP

The wrap dress is back! For those of you who yearn to feel sexy again, a wrap dress or top just might do the trick, regardless of your size. If it fits properly, this style flatters all figures, so give it a try even if you're full busted. You'll look fabulous as long as you use my "No-Gap Wrap" technique on p. 140 so that the dress covers your body sufficiently.

I used Vogue top pattern 7024 and lengthened it by 22 in. (56cm) to make this dress. It's so easy to assemble, you can make this basic in no time at all.

A wrap top is equally flattering. The one below, made from Vogue 7024, has a peplum below the waist to cover the tummy.

Fantastic Fabric

A wrap dress is especially beautiful when made in wool jersey or wool double knit. You can make a fabulous wrap top in a stretchy, lightweight knit using Vogue 7024, but a wrap dress needs fabric with a more substantial hand. The extra weight helps the wrapped front layers hang properly without sticking together.

Style Maker

SHOP FOR INSPIRATION

Clothes off the rack seldom fit, but they can give you some wonderful ideas for your next garment. I always carry a small notebook with me so that I can write down or sketch interesting design ideas I see. Before I start my next project, I look for inspiration in the notebook's pages.

Stable Construction

Patterns vary, but you should be able to do most of the assembly on a serger. Use a narrow, four-thread stitch with Woolly Nylon in the lower looper to give the seams some stretch. You'll work on your conventional sewing machine for stabilizing and hemming.

I highly recommend stabilizing the shoulder and neckline seams. First staystitch the seamline of each pattern piece, then sew a length of twill tape or ¼ in. (6mm) wide, tightly woven fabric selvage on top of the staystitching on the wrong side of the fabric. The shape and stability of the diagonal front is very important. Review "No-Gap Wrap" on p. 140 before making your dress.

Wrap dresses and tops usually have cut-on sleeves. To stabilize them, sew ¼-in. (6mm) wide elastic over the shoulder. Use a strip of elastic cut to the same length as the shoulder and be careful not to stretch it during stitching.

The Hem

Hem the garment with a twin needle especially designed for knits. The correct needle prevents skipped stitches, so look for one with a blue band. To flatten the bump between the two rows of top-stitching, loosen the top tension. I strongly advise against adding weights to the hem of a wrap skirt. The weights fly around too much.

TERRIFIC T-SHIRT DRESS

Every season I peruse the pattern books for the perfect basic dress. While I find many great tops, terrific dress patterns tend to be more elusive. The hunt isn't as frustrating as you might imagine, though, because I stop as soon as I find an appealing top. Then, back in my sewing room, I extend the top pattern to make a dress. You can turn any top into a dress merely by adding an extension to the bottom. It's a simple process, although you'll have to do a bit of shaping so that the extension doesn't turn your garment into something that looks like a paper bag.

You need to make a few decisions about length, desired fit through the hips and tummy, and a zipper insertion. The garment at right is made from the T-shirt pattern included in my book *No Time to Sew* (available from the author; see Resources on p. 226).

You may not need a zipper. Measure the neck seamline on the pattern. If it's 22 in. (56cm) or larger and you're working with a knit, just sew straight up the center-back seamline. If the pattern measurement is too small to eliminate the zipper, consider lowering the neckline at center front. Taper back to the original cutting line at the shoulders.

Lengthy Decision

Once you find an attractive top pattern, compare the back-length measurement to a favorite dress. I always check the finished length on the back of the pattern envelope because fashion illustrations and pictures can be misleading. The difference between the pattern and the dress is the length of the extension. I'm 5 ft. 6 in. tall, so I usually tape 20-in. to 24-in. (50.8cm to 61cm) extensions to the bottom of my pattern.

How I Made This Dress

You can make a dress like mine using the step-by-step instructions in the following features.

Movement Ease and Design Ease (see p. 12)
Back Slit or Vent (see p. 107)
Pegged Side Seams (see p. 110)
Neckline Stabilizing (see p. 130)

Hem Contouring

For a top with a straight hem, I simply draw a straight line across the bottom of the dress pattern. A curved hem is a bit more work. In this case, slash the pattern and add the length between the top and the hemline.

Quick Fitting

A flattering fit depends on having enough fabric to wrap comfortably around your lower torso. After you trace your size on a multisized pattern, take a flat-pattern measurement in the areas that correspond to your body's trouble spots. (Don't include seam allowances in your measurements.) The pattern measurements should equal your body dimensions plus fit and movement ease. For a straight dress in a knit, I like 2 in. (5cm) of ease at the bust and 3 in. (7.6cm) at the tummy and the hips. If your pattern doesn't measure at least that much, add to the side seams.

If the top has shaped side seams and you have a large waist, you can fill in the waist curve a bit. Too much hassle for you? Then simply add 1 in. (2.5cm) to every side seam. This gives you 4 in. (10.2cm) of extra fabric to play with. Machine-baste the side seams in a contrasting color thread, then refine the fit as desired.

Terrific Tapering

For a tapered look, peg the side seams from the fullest part of your hips to the hem, taking in ½ in. to ¾ in. (1.3cm to 1.9cm) on each side. Keep in mind that a very narrow pegged skirt needs a slit so that you can walk easily.

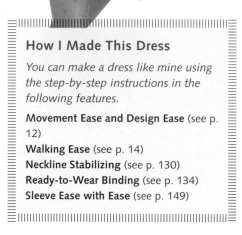

How I Made This Dress

You can make a dress like mine using the step-by-step instructions in the following features.

Movement Ease and Design Ease (see p. 12)
Walking Ease (see p. 14)
Neckline Stabilizing (see p. 130)
Ready-to-Wear Binding (see p. 134)
Sleeve Ease with Ease (see p. 149)

BASIC BACKDROP DRESS

Jackets and vests are wonderful garments for trying out interesting style details. But this poses a problem because you need to wear a simple dress underneath them—something that doesn't draw attention from the jacket or vest. A dress with clean lines and a bit of shaping is the ideal solution. In my case, a brown knit fabric was the best choice because there's a lot of copper and olive in my wardrobe.

A simple dress is ideal for a hot summer day or a tropical vacation. Easy and fast to make, you can dress it up with an elegant vest or add a fun belt for a casual look. This garment was made from Vogue 7055.

Fabric Selection

What fabrics make a great T-shirt dress? Look for cotton knit in a substantial weight, slinky knit, or stretch velour. Wool jersey is a bit too thin unless the dress is quite full. You can also use a linen Tencel blend, matte rayon jersey, or wool double knit. The fabric needs a bit of weight so that the finished dress hangs properly. Lightweight, filmy knits work well for tops but not for dresses because the material clings at the tummy and hips. If you have any doubt about the fabric, it's probably too lightweight. Look around for a high-quality cotton knit that's at least 10 percent Lycra.

Constructive Ideas

You have the option of eliminating the neckline facing pattern pieces. Binding the raw fabric edge is a classy alternative for the neckline. Staystitch these locations ½ in. (1.3cm) from the raw edges. Sew a ¼-in. (6mm) wide length of twill tape or fabric selvage to the neckline directly on top of the staystitching. Before attaching the binding, serge the raw edges at the neck and armholes, trimming off ¼ in. of the seam allowance.

Stylish Back Slit

Walking ease is an important but often overlooked feature in dresses and skirts. I don't know how many times I've discovered that a pattern doesn't include a slit (or call for enough fabric) so that I can walk and sit without straining the bottom of the seamlines.

ANATOMY *of a T-Shirt Dress or Top*

This type of garment can be one of the most versatile pieces in your wardrobe. The simple neckline and trim silhouette make this style a wonderful backdrop for jewelry, or a companion piece for a great jacket or vest.

My favorite pattern for a T-shirt dress is Vogue 7055, shown here. The pattern includes waistline shaping with pintucks at the waist. There are two sleeve choices, or you can eliminate them altogether.

The following step-by-step is a summary, intended to give you an at-a-glance reference while constructing your garment. All of the procedures outlined below are explained in detail throughout the chapter.

1 **Take flat-pattern measurements** of the pattern piece at locations that correspond to the problem areas of your body. Make any necessary alterations—including ease adjustments. If your pattern doesn't have a dart, lengthen the pattern and widen it at the bust.

2 **Cut the garment pieces** from the fashion fabric.

3 **If your pattern has a V neck,** cut and interface the neck facing pieces. If your pattern has a circular neck, stabilize the neckline. Staystitch ½ in. (1.3cm) from the raw edge, then apply ¼-in. (6mm) wide twill tape or fabric selvage over the staystitching.

4 **Set your serger for a four-thread overlock stitch** with Woolly Nylon in the upper looper and regular thread in all other positions. This gives your seamlines a bit of stretch, a must when sewing knits.

5 **Join the shoulder seams** with a four-thread overlock stitch. Let the serger knives trim the seam allowances to ¼ in. (6mm). Press the seam allowances toward the front.

6 **On sleeveless styles,** crowd (ease) the fullness into the lower half of the front armhole to eliminate gaposis. Serge the armholes and the neck with a three-thread overlock, trimming off ¼ in. (6mm) as you stitch. If you have a rounded back, also crowd the back armhole.

7 **Press under a ⅜-in. (1cm) seam allowance** on a circular neckline (and on the armholes of a sleeveless dress) if you plan to finish with twin-needle stitching. Topstitch the neckline.

8 **Bind or face the neckline.** If you decide to use facings, machine-sew the facings to the garment. Press and pound the neckline flat.

9 **If the dress has sleeves,** ease each sleeve cap and sew the sleeve to the armhole before joining the garment's side seams. Sew with a small zigzag stitch (5mm wide and 2.5mm long). Overlock the armhole seam allowances together.

10 **Ease the shaped portion** of the front side seams if the garment doesn't have darts.

11 **Machine-baste the side seams** with a contrasting color thread on the bobbin. Try on the dress to check the fit, then permanently join the side seams. Overlock and trim the side seam allowances to ¼ in. (6mm). Press the side seams to the front of the dress.

12 **If your dress is sleeveless,** topstitch or bind the armholes. Press and pound the stitching flat.

13 **Decide on the dress length.** Cut off any excess fabric beyond the 1½-in. (3.8cm) hem allowance. Serge the raw hem edges with a three-thread overlock stitch, using differential feed or pushing your finger against the back of the presser foot to prevent the serger from stretching the knit fabric edge. Press under the hem allowance.

14 **To build elasticity into the hem,** hand-wrap Woolly Nylon on the bobbin and topstitch with two rows of twin-needle stitching. Sew close to the edge of the hemline, using the side of your presser foot as a guide. Again, if your fabric stretches, crowd it by pressing your finger against the back of the presser foot, on top of the fabric.

15 **Sew a second row of twin-needle stitching** close to the top of the hemline. Trim off the excess hem allowance above the twin-needle topstitching. Press and pound the hem flat.

Master Construction Methods

Pull-on tops, blouses, and dresses can be as unique and as stylish as you want. Yet beyond the various embellishments and color choices, there's often a solid foundation of similar assembly methods. For example, you can use the same technique to apply a bias binding to a casual top or an evening dress. Likewise, you follow the same instructions to prevent a gaping neckline on a jumper or a V-neck blouse.

Over the years I've discovered some wonderful ways to attach collars, make perfect necklines, add pockets, create dynamic sleeves, and hem dresses. The best are presented here. To make it easy to find a suitable technique, the topics are arranged in the order you would follow to assemble a garment.

TRICK of the TRADE

STOPGAP EASING

An ease line is all you need to prevent a front armhole from gaping on a sleeveless dress, whether it's made in knit or woven fabric. Run the straight-stitch easing ½ in. (1.3cm) from the raw edge on the lower half of the front armhole. Also ease the facing if you aren't applying a binding. Steam-press any puckers flat. A rounded back needs a longer ease line. Run the ease line along the entire back armhole so that it conforms to the body.

CONTOURED T-SHIRT DRESS

Many patterns for T-shirt dresses or knit-only tops are created with equal-length side seams and no darts. On a full-busted woman, a finished garment made with this pattern design pulls up at center front and stands away from the body. But even if you wear a C cup or larger, you can still make a great garment from this pattern with a few adjustments. Simply add length to the front to go over the bust, and shape the straight side seams of your stretchy top or dress.

1 To build curves into the straight form, cut through the front pattern piece horizontally across the bust. Insert a ½-in. (1.3cm) wide piece of pattern paper. Connect the side seam with a curved line built out ¼ in. (6mm) at the widest part.

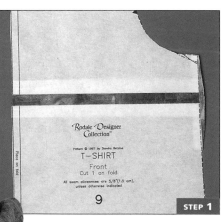

Rodale Designer Collection

T-SHIRT
Front
Cut 1 on fold
All seam allowances are 5/8"(1.5 cm), unless otherwise indicated

9

STEP 1

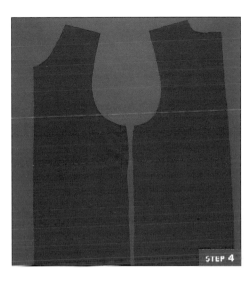

STEP 4

2 Cut your garment pieces from the fashion fabric and prepare them for assembly. Don't sew the side seams yet. At both front side seams, run an ease line over the curved portion for about 5 in. (12.7cm) below the armhole.

[TIP] You may want to add a wider extension, but resist the temptation. No more than ½ in. (1.3cm) can be eased into the back at the side seam.

3 Press each ease line to flatten the fabric and eliminate gathers. Don't stretch the eased portion to its original length.

4 Now you're ready to join the front and back at the sides. Because the addition on the front was eased, the pieces match at the side seams.

[TIP] Always cut pattern pieces from knit fabric with the greatest stretch going around the body whether you're cutting lengthwise or crosswise.

HIGH OR LOW BUST DARTS

Fed up with horizontal wrinkles above or below your bust on a finished garment? Horizontal wrinkles above your bust usually mean you have a low bust or the garment is too tight in the bust area. If the wrinkles appear below your bust, you have a high bust—very rare indeed. The ideal position for the point of a bust dart is 1 in. (2.5cm) from your bust point.

This flat-pattern alteration is easy. Simply make the existing dart into a movable cutout, then shift it up or down until you're happy. I got the idea for this technique from a sewing book I used in high school, which featured a similar alteration called a "bust box."

1 Starting at the side-seam cutting line on your front pattern piece, draw a straight line going through the middle of the dart and stopping 1 in. (2.5cm) beyond the dart point.

2 Now draw a second line, parallel to and the same length as the first, where you want the center of the dart to be, whether this is higher or lower than the first line.

It's best to assess the location of the bust point on your pattern piece before altering the bust area. Using a well-fitting bra, measure from the middle of one shoulder to the nipple. On your front pattern piece, mark 1 in. (2.5cm) past the dart point toward center front. This is where your nipple should be positioned underneath a garment. Still working on the pattern piece, measure from the midshoulder seamline to the bust point. The difference between this measurement and the corresponding body measurement is the amount you need to raise or lower the dart on the pattern piece.

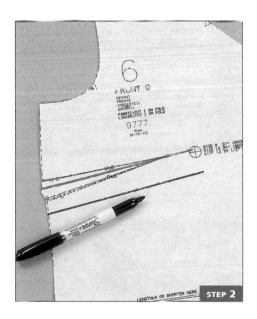

LENGTHEN OR SHORTEN HERE   STEP 2

TRICK
of the TRADE
GOOD SHOULDER FIT

If you alter your pattern to fit a wider back, the lengths of the front and back shoulders no longer match. One of the simplest ways to solve this problem is to ease the longer seam into the shorter one. On light-weight fabrics, sew the shoulder seam with the back against the feed dogs and the front against the presser foot. The feed dogs draw in the excess length. Heavier fabrics usually need a small dart in the middle of the back shoulder. Make the dart 3½ in. (8.9cm) long and ⅜ in. (1cm) wide at the shoulder seam.

STEP 4

3 Draw a three-sided box, just slightly larger than the dart legs and dart length, around the existing dart. Don't include the extension you drew beyond the dart point in the box.

4 Cut out the box and slide it up or down until the center line of the existing dart matches the line that marks the new dart position.

5 Tape the box in position and fill the empty spot on the pattern piece with spare pattern paper. Tape a bit of pattern paper on the side so that you can correctly position the dart extension.

6 Fold out the dart and fold it down as it will be pressed. Redraw the side-seam cutting line.

NECKLINE STABILIZING

Necklines on collarless dresses and tops can be a disappointment if they're stretched during the construction stage. No amount of pressing or steaming can restore a neckline to its original size or make it conform to the shape of your body. The Power Sewing solution to this problem is simple: Stabilize the neckline with a stabilizer cut to the size of the pattern before you attach a binding or facing. This eliminates neckline distortion.

Staystitching near the raw edge is insufficient unless the fabric is very crisp.

1 Cut a length of lightweight, narrow twill tape or ¼-in. (6mm) wide fabric selvage the exact size of the front and back necklines on the pattern pieces. Determine the size by measuring the neck seamlines, not the cutting lines. The measurement needs to include the seam allowances for the shoulders and the center-back seam, if there is one.

2 Cut the garment pieces from the fabric. Before sewing the shoulder or center-back seams, pin the stabilizer to the wrong side of the neckline. Position it ¼ in. (1.3cm) from the raw edge.

3 If the stabilizer is smaller than the neckline when you pin it in place, don't be concerned; as you sew, the feed dogs will draw in the excess fabric to fit the length of the stabilizer.

4 Place the work on the machine bed with the garment against the feed dogs. Sew the center of the stabilizer to the neckline using a regular straight stitch (2.5mm or 10 spi). Press the neckline flat. It's now stable enough to continue with construction.

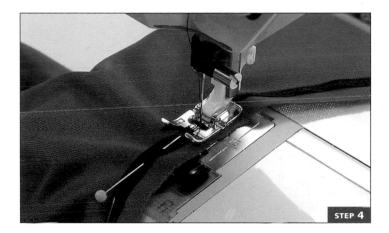

STEP 4

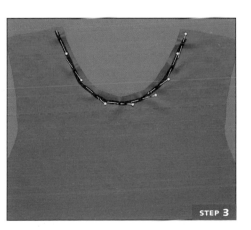

STEP 3

TRICK
of the TRADE

STRONG YET SOFT

To bind the neckline of a chiffon dress, couture seamstress Lynda Maynard suggests the following method to prevent the neckline from stretching. Before sewing the shoulder seams, pin tissue paper to the wrong side of the neckline. Lynda prefers tissue paper because it's lighter than tear-away stabilizers.

Sew the neckline of each garment piece separately with a small (2mm or 12 spi) stitch through both layers ⅝ in. (15mm) from the raw edge. Staystitch another row through the tissue paper and fabric 1⁄16 in. (1.6mm) to the right and then to the left of the initial stitching line. Leaving the tissue paper between the rows, tear away the excess outside the stitching lines. Cut away the neckline seam allowance close to the staystitching.

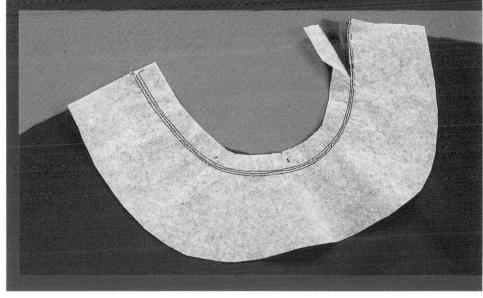

FOOLPROOF INVISIBLE ZIPPER

Always popular in close-fitting skirts and pants, an invisible zipper is equally attractive at the center back of a dress. It's elegant and subtle. Invisible zippers are perfect for garments made in knit or Lycra blends, such as stretch denim, and stretch wool gabardine. Some of my students avoid this type of zipper because they think the insertion is complicated. Actually, it's one of the easiest zipper techniques.

Normally, you can't use this zipper on lightweight garments because the fashion fabric is too limp to support the closure.

You can get around this problem by using interfacing in the seam allowances of the garment's zipper opening. A complete explanation follows. Keep in mind that an invisible zipper is inserted before you sew the seam below the zipper.

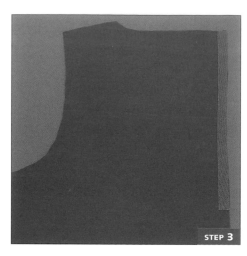

STEP 3

1 Open the zipper and press the coils flat. To stabilize the opening in light-weight or stretchy fabric, cut two ½-in. (1.3cm) wide strips of light-weight interfacing along the grain-line that has the least stretch. The strips need to be 1 in. (2.5cm) longer than the zipper.

2 Press the strips to the wrong sides of the seam allowances at the zipper opening.

TIP If the fabric is very stretchy, such as slinky knit, cut the interfacing strips 1½ in. (3.8cm) wide so that the seams are also supported. Pink the lengthwise edges of strips wider than ½ in. (1.3cm).

3 Fold under (don't press) the seam allowances at the zipper location on the garment. Open the zipper. With the garment pieces right side up, slide the zipper under the folded seam allowances so that the zipper pull is facing you

4 Temporarily pin each seam allowance to the corresponding side of the zipper tape. Leave the pieces pinned until you're ready to position and attach the zipper tape, or mark the seam allowances and zipper tape so that you know which sides are joined.

5 Now it's time to attach the zipper. Unpin and unfold the seam allowance on one garment piece. Position one side of the zipper tape on the fabric with right sides together and the coil on the seamline, the zipper tape next to the garment opening, and the upper stop ¾ in. (1.9cm) below the top edge of the fabric.

6 To prevent the presser foot from pushing the top of the zipper out of position, hand-tack the top of the tape to the seam allowance.

7 Sew the first side of the zipper tape as pinned. Position and sew the right side of the remaining zipper tape against the right side of the other garment section in the same manner.

TIP If you have a buttonhole foot with two grooves, you can use it instead of an invisible zipper foot. Fit the zipper coil into one of the grooves so that you can sew close to the coil.

8 This is the only zipper method that joins the garment pieces after insertion. Switch to a regular zipper foot (so that you can sew close to the zipper), and sew the garment seam below the zipper opening. Use small reinforcing stitches for the final ½ in. (1.3cm) of the seamline, at the bottom of the zipper opening.

STEP 4

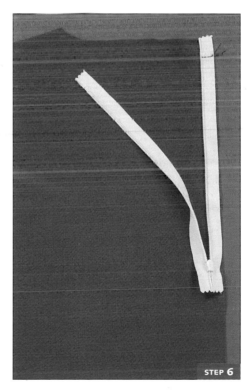
STEP 6

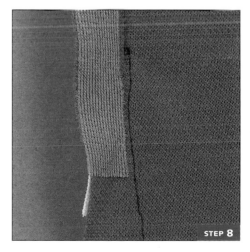
STEP 8

READY-TO-WEAR BINDING

Boutiques are full of stretchy T-shirts and sheer dresses with narrow satin binding along the neck, and around the armholes of sleeveless versions. This fabulous look isn't difficult to achieve. Simply styled garments, such as pull-on, collarless shirts or dresses, are far less bulky and more professional-looking when you substitute a narrow binding for the facings.

StyleMaker

BOUND TO PLEASE

Fabric for finishing a raw edge can be made from silk charmeuse, handkerchief linen, or almost any material that isn't too heavy. When using a woven fabric, true bias is preferable, but you can get away with using significantly off-grain scraps if the material is soft. Use at least ½ yd. (0.5m) of fabric so that seamlines in the binding aren't too frequent.

In the knit category, wool jersey and cotton knit are excellent choices for binding. Little fabric is required since you cut the strips along the greatest stretch, which is the crossgrain; ⅛ yd. (0.1m) is usually enough.

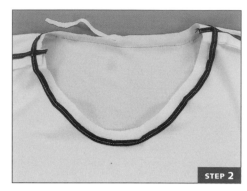

STEP 2

Consider using silk charmeuse or handkerchief linen—self-fabric binding is too predictable. Even if your dress fabric isn't sheer, you may find this binding procedure preferable to attaching a facing.

Although the binding process is simple, you need to stabilize the raw edge prior to the application. My method, which involves hand-stitching the binding's inner fold to the neck seamline, leaves the stitching practically invisible. See "Bound to Please" at left for suggestions on fabric for binding.

1 Join both shoulder seams and press the seam allowances to the front. If your garment fabric is unstable, sew narrow twill tape, Stay Tape, or a strip of ¼-in. (6mm) wide lining or woven fabric selvage cut to the exact size of the pattern at the seamline.

2 No matter what type of fabric you're using, prepare the neckline by staystitching over a stabilizer ½ in. (1.3cm) from the raw edge. Trim the seam allowance to ¼ in. (6mm). (See "Neckline Stabilizing" on p. 130 for comprehensive instructions.)

3 Cut your binding strips 1¾ in. (4.5cm) wide, on the bias in woven fabrics and on the crossgrain in knits. Measure the raw edge of the neckline (or armholes) on the garment and add 4 in. (10.2cm) to determine the length of binding you need. If necessary, seam your strips to this length. Don't bother piecing the ends on an angle—a straight seam is sufficient. Press the seams flat and trim them to ¼ in. (6mm).

TIP Lightweight fabrics are a must for flat, bulk-free bound edges.

4 Fold the strip in half lengthwise. Press, shaping the bias strip with your iron and slightly stretching the outside, cut edges. Let the inner, folded edge curve in—or even shrink a bit.

5 Stiffen the binding fabric with spray starch. This gives the strip additional body, making it easier to handle and mold to the neckline's shape.

STEP 4

6 With right sides together, place both raw edges of the folded binding against the trimmed neckline. Start 1 in. (2.5cm) away from the shoulder seam, leaving a 2-in. (5cm) tail free past the seamline. Since you already trimmed the neckline, sew a ¼-in. (6mm) seam allowance. The new seamline ends up just inside the line of stitching for the stabilizer.

STEP 6

7 Continue stitching around the neckline, stretching the bias slightly. The stretching helps the finished binding conform to the shape of your body. When you get about 4 in. (10.2cm) from the start of the stitching line, take the garment out of the machine.

8 Hand-walk or pin the last of the binding around the neckline. Clip into both ends of the binding where the ends join.

9 Open both ends of the binding. With right sides together, match the clips on the binding. Seam the ends together ⅛ in. (3mm) inside the clips. This makes the binding circumference ¼ in. (6mm) smaller, which helps flatten the seam against the neckline.

10 Press the seam allowances open. Trim the binding seam allowance to ¼ in. (6mm). Stitch the remaining bias to the neck edge.

11 Let the binding wrap around the neck seam allowances. The binding wraps to the wrong side of the garment and encloses the seam allowances.

12 Pin the fold at the neck seamline.

13 Hand-stitch the fold to the neckline. Hand-stitching the inner edge of the binding to the neckline seam is quick and well worth the minimal effort. The stitching, which is hidden inside the binding, gives a near-perfect finish. Start by hiding a thread knot in the seam. Take one stitch on the neckline seam, slide the needle ¼ in. (6mm) forward inside the binding fold, bring the needle out, and take the next stitch in the neck seamline.

[TIP] **Not a fan of hand stitching? Then let the binding's inner fold extend slightly past the neck seamline inside the garment and pin it in position from the right side. Now topstitch in the well of the seam, through all layers, from the right side. This works better if you trim the neck seam allowances to ⅛ in. (3mm).**

14 Place the neckline over a tailor's ham. Press and pound it flat.

[TIP] **If a neckline is smaller than 22 in. (56cm), it must be able to stretch to go over the head. Stabilize the neckline seam with ¼-in. (6mm) clear elastic cut 1 in. (2.5cm) smaller than the seamline on the pattern. Ribbing can then be applied or the neck can be turned under and top-stitched with a twin needle.**

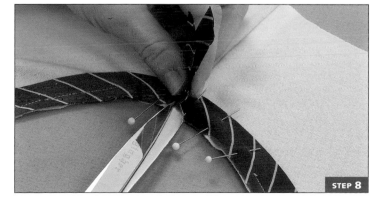

STEP 8

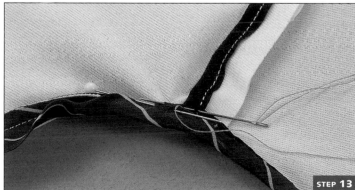

STEP 13

MITERED SQUARE-NECK BINDING

Yes, you can apply a bias strip to a square neck on a dress or blouse. This technique gives the garment a ready-to-wear look. You don't see this treatment too often in patterns because applying bias fabric strips to a square neckline can be tricky. With other methods, the inner corners are a problem because the bias strip has too much bulk. My technique eliminates the excess bulk by making tiny miters (see the photo below).

To make a round neckline square, simply leave the neckline the same at the shoulders and square off the front and back as desired. Start the binding process by sewing the shoulder seams and then preparing bias-cut fabric strips. With this procedure, careful preparation ensures success.

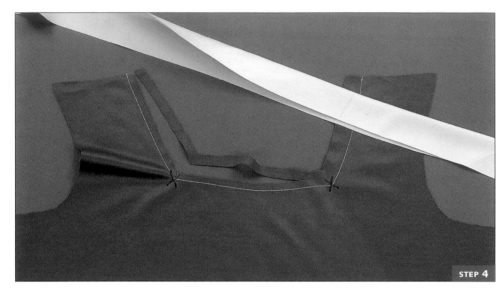

STEP 4

1 Mark the corners of the neck seamline on the front and back garment pieces with tailor's tacks. Sew the front and back together at the shoulders.

2 Unless fabric is very stable, stabilize the entire neck seamline with a

length of ¼-in. (6mm) wide cotton twill tape, selvage from lining fabric, or straight-grain fusible tape, cut to the exact size of the pattern neckline on the seam.

3 Straight-stitch the center of the stabilizing strip to the neckline ⅝ in. (15mm) from, and parallel to, the raw fabric edge. Use a regular stitch length. To reduce bulk, cut away the stabilizer in the corners.

4 Trim the neckline seam allowance to ¼ in. (3mm). Clip into the seam allowances at the corners to within ¹⁄₁₆ in. (1.6mm) of the staystitching.

5 Measure the length of the front and back neck seamline, excluding the seam allowances. Cut a bias strip 2 in. (5cm) longer than the seamline and 2 in. (5cm) wide. Press the strip in half lengthwise. With all three raw edges even, place the folded bias strip on the right side of the garment neckline.

6 Sew the bias strip to the neckline with the garment on top, starting at the back neckline so that the seams joining the ends of the bias are less obvious on the finished garment. Use 1.5mm (15 spi) stitches and a ¼-in. (6mm) seam allowance.

7 Leave the first 1 in. (2.5cm) of the bias strip unstitched. Sew directly on top of the neck staystitching. Stop sewing at the corner with the needle in the fabric. Spread the neckline at the corner.

If you clipped far enough into the seamline in Step 4, you can open the fabric until the edge is straight. The clips in each corner make it easy for you to spread the fabric until the raw edges are straight. Now it's easier to sew the neck corner to the straight edge of the bias strip.

8 Continue sewing around the neckline, spreading each corner as explained in Step 7. Stop sewing about

4 in. (10.2cm) from the start of the attached binding. Hand-walk the binding together so that you can predict where the two ends will join.

9 Make ⅛-in. (3mm) deep snips into the bias strip where the ends join. Sew the ends of the bias strip together ⅛ in. (3mm) inside the snips. The finished binding will lie flat because the neckline circumference is ¼ in. (6mm) smaller than the bias-cut strip.

10 Trim the seam allowances to ¼ in. (6mm) and press them open. Pull the bias strip away from the neckline and seam allowances. Fold the garment and the attached bias strip right sides together at one of the neckline corners. Make sure the fold is exactly at the corner.

11 Sew across the folded bias strip from the seamline to the pressed edge. Don't make a straight line. Instead, straight-stitch two ¼-in. (6mm) deep V shapes. Clip into the center of both V shapes. Miter the bias strip at the remaining corner in the same manner.

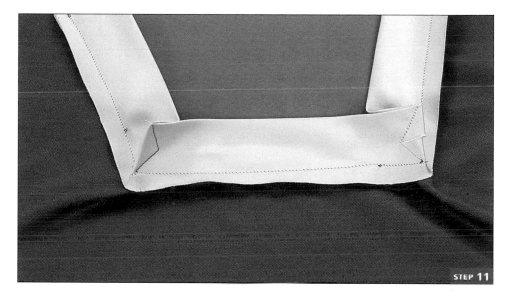

STEP 11

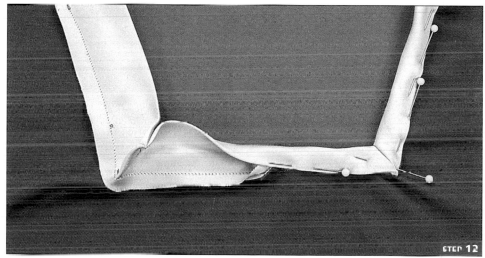

STEP 12

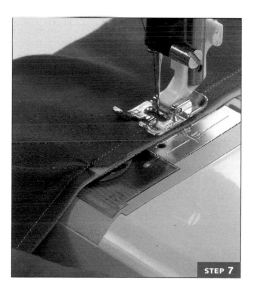

STEP 7

12 Press the neckline seam allowances toward the bias strip. Wrap the bias strip to the wrong side of the garment, enclosing the seam allowances by folding the bias strip to the wrong side of the garment so that the pressed edge extends just past the seamline. Hand-sew the folded edge of the bias strip to the neck seamline.

SHAPELY V NECKLINE

Unless a V neckline has some shape, it won't lie flat against the upper chest. The front of our body isn't flat, so we shouldn't expect a neckline with straight sides to fit us perfectly. However, there's an easy, subtle way to shape the neckline so that it conforms to the body.

This neckline looks perfectly straight, but it isn't. Just below the shoulders, it starts to curve out, to a maximum of ¼ in. (6mm) midway between the shoulder and the point of the V.

Build a curve into the neckline, making it slightly convex or concave to suit your body and the size of your bust. If you're full busted, this gives you more coverage and a flattering neckline.

1 Before cutting out the garment pieces, shape the neckline on the front and front facing pattern pieces. Mark the midpoint between the shoulder and the point of the V on the neck cutting line.

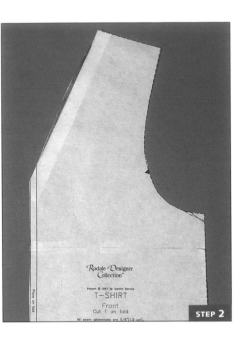

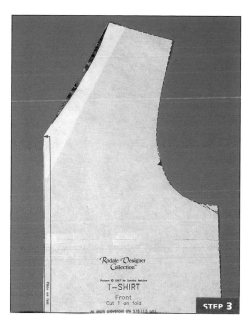

STEP 3

2 For a large bust, draw a gentle arc from the shoulder. Curve the new cutting line out ¼ in. (6mm) at the midpoint and tapering back to the original cutting line 1 in. (2.5cm) before the point of the V.

3 If you have a small bust, draw the arc so that it curves inward ¼ in. (6mm) at the midpoint.

4 Sew the dress and facing shoulder seams separately. Don't join the side seams—it's easier to work on the neck while the garment is flat. Cut a ¼-in. (6mm) wide length of twill tape or fabric selvage to prevent the neck from stretching.

[TIP] **Twill tape is too heavy for a silk dress. Instead, use ¼-in. (6mm) wide selvage cut from your silk yardage.**

5 Mark the exact point of the V on the wrong side of the facing. Pin the facing and garment right sides together.

6 Pin the twill tape to the facing seamline, stopping 1 in. (2.5cm) from the point of both sides of the V so that there's less bulk in the V of the finished garment.

7 Sew the garment neckline to the facing starting at a shoulder seam, stitching through the twill tape or selvage. Stitch the neckline with the facing on top. This makes the neckline more stable, plus it's easier to sew a curved seam. Switch to small stitches 1 in. (2.5cm) from the point and sew to the point.

8 Hand-walk two stitches across the point. Slightly squaring off the point gives you enough room to turn the point right side out. Stop with the needle down and pivot the work.

9 Still using small stitches, sew up the neckline for 1 in. (2.5cm). Continue sewing the remaining side of the neckline and around the back of the neckline with a regular stitch length.

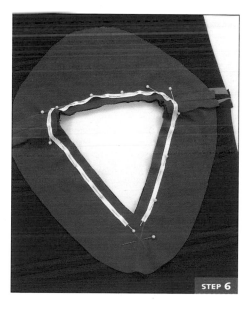

STEP 6

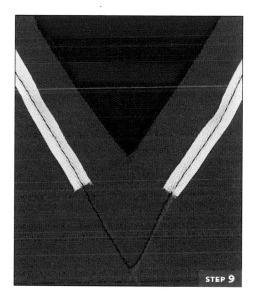

STEP 9

10 Slash through the seam allowances at the point to within a few threads of the stitching. Trim the neckline seam allowances to ¼ in. (6mm) and clip at the curves.

11 Press the seam allowances away from the garment and toward the facing, and understitch them to the facing. To reduce bulk at the point, don't understitch the facing for 1 in. (2.5cm) on both sides of the point.

12 Press and pound the neckline with a tailor's clapper.

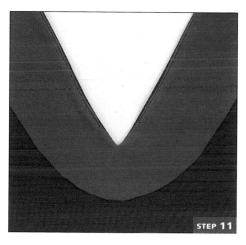

STEP 11

NO-GAP WRAP

Few garments are as flattering and sexy as a wrap dress or top. But you can easily sabotage the entire effect if the wrap front (called a surplice neckline) doesn't lie flat against the body. My sewing experience has proven that adding a strip of stabilizer cut the size of the pattern seamline along the diagonal neckline eliminates all gaping. Another important construction detail, which is often omitted in pattern instructions, is building ease into the neckline. The effect is subtle, and varies according to your bust size.

I'm such a fan of wrap-style dresses and tops that I designed one for my collection of Vogue patterns, Today's Fit. The dress I made from this wrap top (Vogue pattern 7024) is particularly flattering because the waist is defined with a tie while the peplum hides the tummy. It's designed to fit bust sizes 32½ in. to 55 in. (81.6cm to 139.7cm).

1 Measure the length of the back neckline and front diagonal neckline on the pattern pieces. Cut strips of ¼-in. (6mm) wide twill tape or fusible straight-grain Stay Tape to match the measurements. Pin each stabilizer strip to the area where it will be applied so that the pieces don't get mixed up.

TIP **You can stabilize the shoulders or long dolman shoulder seams with a ¼-in. (6mm) wide strip of clear elastic.**

2 Cut the garment pieces from your fashion fabric. Don't move them off the cutting surface yet. Take the pattern pieces off the fabric shapes. Separate the layers of the front garment pieces and flip one over so that they're both wrong side up.

StyleMaker

CUPPING THE CUPS

Before sewing a stabilizer strip to the front neckline, slightly shorten the strip. When applied to the garment, the shorter strip will draw in the neckline for a better fit. The amount you need to cut off the strip depends on your cup size: A cup, none; B cup, ¼ in. (6mm); C cup, ½ in. (1.3cm); D cup, ½ in. (1.3cm). Never cut off more than ½ in. (1.3cm) no matter what your cup size. The neckline will pucker.

3 Pin a stabilizer strip to the back neck and diagonal front neckline ½ in. (1.3cm) from the raw edge. Don't worry if the garment piece is slightly longer than the stabilizer. You want to draw in the neckline, particularly in the middle third of the front. This helps the front conform to the shape of your body.

4 Place the start of the stabilizer under the presser foot with the garment against the feed dogs. Straight-stitch the stabilizer to the neckline as pinned. Don't stretch the stabilizer. Instead, let the feed dogs ease any extra fabric into the seamline.

5 At the end of the stitching, the garment fits the stabilizer. Gently press the puckers out of the neckline stitching. Finish assembling the garment.

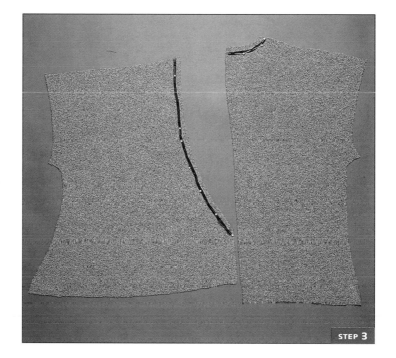

STEP 3

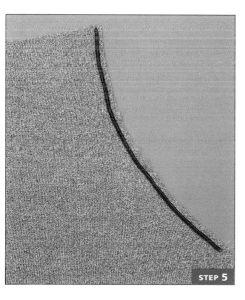

STEP 5

TRICK
of the TRADE

IT'S A WRAP

While a lightweight single knit works well for a wrap top, a wrap dress needs to be made in a knit with more body for two reasons: so that the fabric does not seat out and so that it has enough weight to hang properly. St. Johns or slinky knits work well in tops and dresses because they have stretch and weight. Wrap garments are more flattering in knits or stretch wovens because these conform better at and under the bustline. A woven such as silk charmeuse lacks this stretch, giving a puffy, weight-gaining appearance when made in wrap styles.

CLEAN EDGE FACING

My favorite method for completing a facing is a clean finish that doesn't have a single visible stitch. The effect is professional and the construction is simple. The best part of this technique is that you interface the facing and clean-finish the outer edges at the same time. I think you'll agree that this technique produces a high-quality finish with very little effort.

Basically, a clean edge treatment "faces" the facing with interfacing. Using a sew-in interfacing, enclose the

Style Maker

LET'S FACE IT

You never see the wrong side of the fabric when a high-quality, unlined garment is on a hanger. A deeper facing hides the seams and is less likely to roll to the outside of the garment when you're wearing it. Get into the habit of adding 1 in. (2.5 cm) to the outer edges of the facing.

Deepen a center-back facing to 5 in. (12.7cm), but blend the outer edge back to the original width plus 1 in. (2.5cm) at the back shoulder seams. This gives you enough room at center back to stitch in your label. If your garment has a deep front opening, you may need to lengthen the back facing even more.

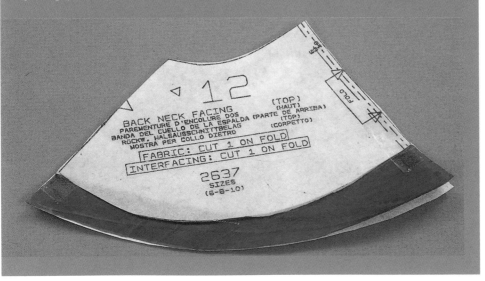

seam allowances between the layers. Add a label for the finishing touch. (My favorite labels come from Bach Label Company; see Resources on p. 226.)

I prefer silk organza interfacing when using this method on a blouse or dress because it isn't bulky. On the facing of an unlined jacket, use a sew-in like Veri-Shape on the bias for a crisp effect or medium-weight organza for a softer hand.

1 Cut the garment fabric and the interfacing shapes from the same facing pattern pieces. (Ordinarily, the interfacing for a facing is cut slightly smaller than the fabric pieces. Don't do this for the clean edge treatment. The fabric and interfacing pieces are cut—and remain—the same size throughout the process.)

2 Join the fabric front and back facings at the shoulders and press the seam allowances open. Join the interfacing front and back facings in the same manner. Trim the interfacing seam allowances to ¼ in. (6mm).

3 Place the facing and interfacing right sides together with the raw edges even. Using a ¼-in. (6mm) seam allowance, sew around the outside edges, which are opposite the neckline. Trim the seam allowance to ⅛ in. (3mm).

4 Turn the facing right side out and press. You're now ready to sew the facing to the garment, treating the fabric and interfacing as a single layer.

MACHINE-ANCHORED FACING

How many times have you hand-tacked a facing at the back zipper or underarm, only to find that your hand stitches pull out shortly after? In areas of stress, hand tacks don't hold up as well as these two machine-tacking techniques. Both treatments are invisible and will last the life of the garment.

Attach an armhole facing with right sides together, then trim the facing seam allowances to ¼ in. (6mm). Cut a triangle shape out of the seam allowances at the seam joints to eliminate even more bulk. Fold and press the facing to the inside of the garment. Sew in the well of the garment side seam through all layers for 1 in. (2.5cm), starting at the top of the underarm. Position the garment right side up on the machine to reduce the appearance of a seamline that strays from the well (see the top photo at right).

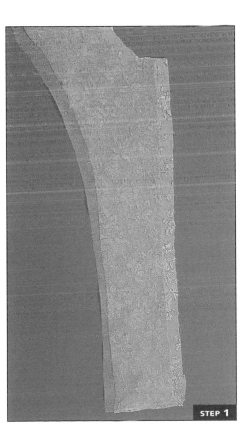

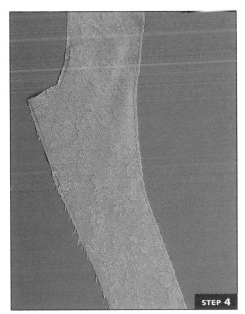

STEP 1

STEP 4

A neckline facing or a back zipper needs an invisible technique. Sew the facing to the garment, placing it in the finished position. Fold away the garment and the facing while holding the facing and dress seam allowances together. Sew the two seam allowances together about ¼ in. (6mm) from the raw edges. Start at the bottom and stitch as far as you can to the neckline, as shown in the bottom photo above.

BANDED COLLAR SANDWICH

Here's a neat way to attach a collar to a neckband, another technique I learned from Margaret Islander. I like it because it eliminates the bump you usually find at the end of the neckband.

Sew together the collar pieces, then baste them to the inner neckband. Attaching the neckband creates a fabric "sandwich," which traps the collar and part of the garment between the neckbands and enables you to seam the start and end of the neckband to the garment by machine. This technique clean-finishes the neckband and neckline at the front opening with machine stitching.

1 Interface all of the collar and neckband pieces. This prevents the pieces from stretching, thus keeping them the same size. With right sides together, join the collar pieces by sewing around all of the edges except the (notched) neck edge, which joins the neckband.

2 Trim the seam allowances on the neckline, neckband, and collar to ¼ in. (6mm). (The garment industry uses this narrow width at the neckline because it's easier to sew.)

3 Clip ⅛ in. (3mm) into the seam allowances at the collar's unseamed edge. The released seam allowances help the collar mold easily to the shape of the neckband. Turn the collar right side out.

4 Staystitch the shirt neckline ⅝ in. (15mm) from the raw edge. Trim the garment neckline to ¼ in. (6mm). Clip ⅛ in. (3mm) into the seam allowances at 1-in. (2.5cm) intervals through the curved portion of the neckline.

5 To eliminate a wrinkled neckband, trim an additional ¹⁄₁₆ in. (1.6mm) off the outer edges and ends of the inner neckband so that it's slightly smaller than the outer neckband.

6 On the inner neckband, don't trim the seam allowance at the neckline edge. Since the inner neckband is closer to the neck and therefore has less distance to travel, it needs to be smaller to prevent wrinkles. Later, when you seam the inner and outer neckbands, place the outer neckband against the feed dogs to draw in the excess fabric.

7 Place the right side of the upper collar against the right side of the trimmed inner neckband. Baste the pieces together at a scant ¼ in. (6mm). Now sew the right side of the inner neckband to the wrong side of the neckline using ¼-in. (6mm) seam allowances (see the top left photo on p. 146).

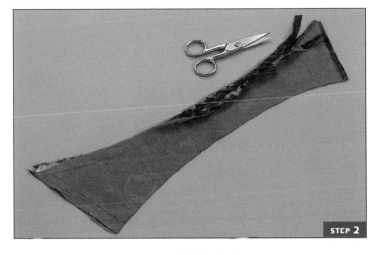

STEP 2

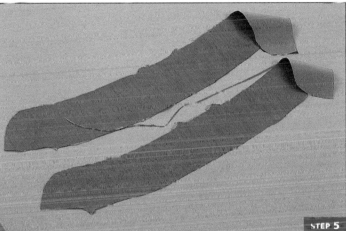

STEP 5

8 Tightly roll up the ends of the collar and pin them to the inner neckband so that they're clear of all neckband seamlines. This allows you to seam the outer and inner neckbands without catching the collar in the stitching.

9 With right sides together and raw edges even, place the outer neckband against the inner neckband and pin them together with the inner neckband on top.

STEP 7

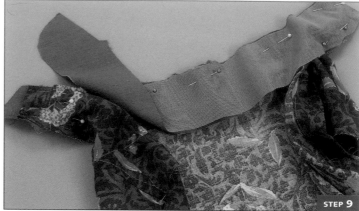

STEP 9

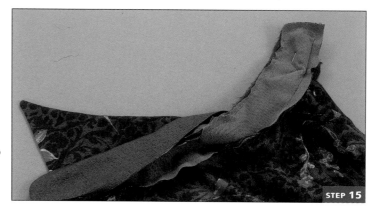

STEP 15

10 Roll and tuck the front edges of the shirt and collar inside the neckband pieces for 2 in. (5cm) at the end of the neckband on the right-hand side of the garment.

11 With the collar and neckband out of the way, sew together the last 1 in. (2.5cm) of the bottom of the neckband. Start 1 in. (2.5cm) inside the garment neckline and sew toward the front edge using a ¼-in. (6mm) seam allowance.

12 Stop with the needle down when you can feel the end of the shirt front, approximately ¼ in. (6mm) from the edge of the neckband. Be careful not to catch the collar and garment in the stitching.

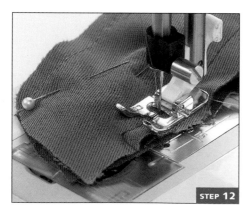

STEP 12

13 At the front edge, pivot the work and continue sewing all around the collar—including over the basting line that attaches the collar to the inner neckband. Remember, you're using ¼-in. (6mm) seam allowances since the seams were already trimmed. The feed dogs draw in the slightly larger outer neckband to fit the trimmed inner neckband.

14 At the opposite end of the neckband, sandwich about 2 in. (5cm) of the shirt and the collar inside the neckband pieces. Pivot the work and sew across the bottom of the neckband into the neck for 1 in. (2.5cm).

15 Trim away bulk at the ends of the neckband and turn the neckband right side out. Turn under a ¼-in. (6mm) seam allowance on the outer neckband and pin it to the garment's neckline.

16 Topstitch around the entire neckband ⅛ in. (3mm) from the edges. Press and pound the collar and neckbands flat with a tailor's clapper.

TIP It's easiest to pin the outer collar in position by placing the work over a tailor's ham.

TRICK of the TRADE

BIAS BONUS

Certain parts of a garment should always be cut on the bias unless this interferes with the fabric's design. In particular, cuffs and mandarin collars mold into a smooth circle when cut on the bias.

MANDARIN COLLAR

From the Nehru style of the 1960s to the mandarin version that's again gaining favor among the fashion-forward, the stand-up collar is back. It's a dramatic treatment, especially when cut for extra height. I'm a fan of Asian satins, so I love the sexy look of a slim, side-slit dress with a mandarin collar. Four children and a couple of decades of traveling and teaching have left me with a tummy that shows in a slim dress, but I still use mandarin collars on tops and dresses. This tunic was made from McCall's 7412.

There are several Power Sewing tips and insertion methods that give a stand-up collar a professional look. Similar to the banded collar instructions on p. 141, the mandarin collar is attached to the garment neckline with a sandwich technique.

1 Collars are far easier to sew if you first trim the seam allowances and garment neckline to ¼ in. (6mm), the width used by the garment industry to join the collar and neck. Interface both collar pieces.

TIP **I prefer a fairly stiff interfacing, like Veri-Shape, for stand-up collars.**

2 Trim ¹⁄₁₆ in. (1.6mm) off the ends and the inner curved (upper) edge of one of the collars. Don't trim the neck edge. Label this piece the inner collar.

3 Staystitch the garment neckline ¼ in. (6mm) from the raw edge and make ⅛-in. (3mm) deep clips through the seam allowance at 1-in. (2.5cm) intervals.

TIP **As you staystitch, stabilize loosely woven fabric with ¼-in. (6mm) wide twill tape or fabric selvage cut to the size of the pattern neckline.**

4 Sew the right side of the inner collar's neckline edge (the long, outer curve with notches) to the wrong side of the garment neckline using ¼-in. (6mm) seam allowances. The clips in the seam allowances help the garment neck conform to the curve of the collar.

TRICK
of the TRADE

SHAPELY CHOICES

Depending on the patternmaker's preference, the pattern pieces for your stand-up collar can be straight or curved. The curved pattern pieces are the only ones to use to ensure that the finished collar conforms to the neck. If the pattern you're using has straight pieces, search your other patterns for a shaped piece you can use as a substitute.

7 Start on the neckline, 1 in. (2.5cm) away from the end of the collar and using ¼-in. (6mm) seam allowances. Stop with the needle down at the end of the garment neckline, about ¼ in. (6mm) from the end of the collar. Pivot the work and sew the end of the neckline to the outer and inner collars.

8 Sew the end of the collar. Continue stitching along the top edge of the collar, using a ¼-in. (6mm) seam allowance and sewing the opposite side with the same method.

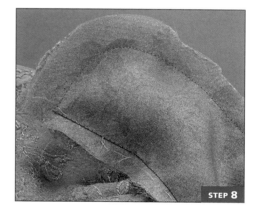

STEP 8

5 Place the inner and outer collars right sides together. Pin them from the inner collar side so that the feed dogs ease in the slightly larger, untrimmed outer collar.

6 Roll up one side of the front of the dress neckline and tuck it between the collar pieces for about 2 in. (5cm). With the garment out of the way, you can sew the inner and outer collars together.

9 Trim away any bulk at the ends of the collar and turn it right side out. Fold under a ¼-in. (6mm) wide seam allowance on the long edge of the outer collar and pin it to the outside of the garment neckline, just covering the previous seamline.

[TIP] **If you have trouble pinning, shape the neckline over a tailor's ham as you work.**

10 Topstitch the neck edge—or all the way around the collar—⅛ in. (3mm) from the edge. Press and pound the collar with a tailor's clapper over a tailor's ham.

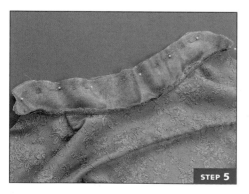

STEP 5

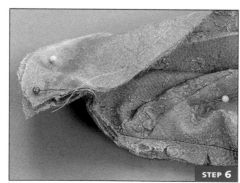

STEP 6

SLEEVE EASE WITH EASE

Industry sewers who insert sleeves day in and day out have some fabulous tricks for building ease into the caps without creating seamline puckers. But it doesn't take years of practice to set in a pucker-free sleeve cap. You can apply industry methods—crowding, staystitch plus, and shaping—to your projects. All three of these methods achieve the same results in slightly different ways. You may find that one or another is most suitable for certain fabrics, or you may feel more comfortable with a certain technique.

Flat Assembly

Borrowing from the ready-to-wear industry, insert the sleeve flat before sewing the side seams. This is easier on sleeves with shallow (flatter) caps, but it can work on any sleeve other than those on coats or jackets. These are more comfortable set "in the round," after the underarm seam is sewn.

1 Ease the slightly larger sleeve into the armhole as you make the seam. Crowding and staystitch plus, described on pp. 150 and 151, are both effective. If you staystitch, prepare the sleeve before pinning it to the garment.

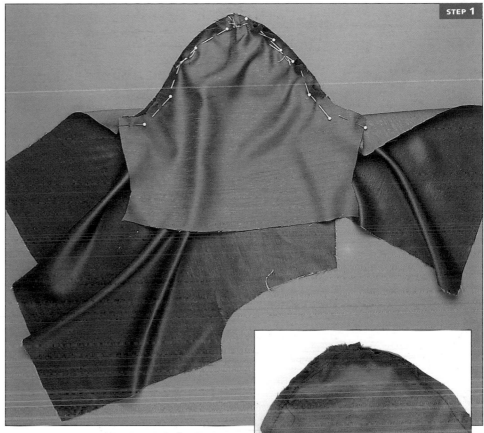

2 Sew the garment shoulder seams. Don't sew the side seams or the sleeve's underarm seam.

3 Open the garment armhole flat and right side up. Match the right side of the sleeve to the garment armhole with raw edges even.

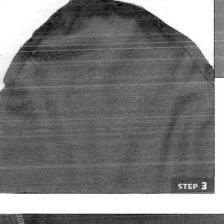

4 Sew the garment's side seam and the sleeve's underarm seam in one continuous line of stitching. Repeat on the remaining side and underarm seams.

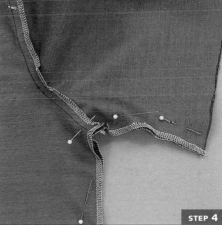

TIP Knits don't need as much ease as other fabrics, so don't overdo the sleeve cap easing.

Crowding

This technique employs the flat assembly method. Join the garment shoulder seams but don't stitch the side or sleeve underarm seams. Match the raw edges of the sleeve to the garment armhole and place them on the machine with the sleeve against the feed dogs (see the photo below).

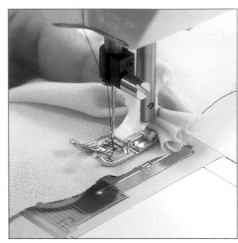

As you stitch, let the feed dogs draw in the extra fabric in the sleeve cap. The machine's feed dogs move a bit faster than the presser foot, so the bottom fabric layer is shortened. You can help the process by slightly lifting the top layer (the garment) with your left hand and using your right hand to gently push the sleeve cap toward the feed dogs. This may take a bit of practice, but it's certainly a time-saver (see the photo above center).

Staystitch Plus

This is my favorite method for inserting a sleeve in the round or flat. Sew ⅜ in. or ½ in. (1cm or 1.3cm) from the sleeve's raw edge, placing your finger on top of the fabric behind the presser foot and pushing with medium pressure. Your finger, acting like a fence, keeps the fabric from coming out the back of the presser foot. If you can't feel the pressure of the presser foot against your finger, you're not doing the process correctly (see the photo above right).

Fabric weight determines the stitch length and finger pressure for staystitch

plus. A lightweight fabric calls for a regular stitch length (2.5mm or 10 spi) and light pressure. A heavy fabric calls for more pressure and a long stitch length, about 4mm or 6 spi. If the fabric is very heavy, you may need two rows of staystitch plus next to each other (see the photo below).

After easing, check the sleeve fit in the armhole. If the cap is too small, tug gently on the seamline to remove some of the excess ease. If the cap is too large, it needs more ease. Try pulling on the bobbin thread or make another row of staystitch plus (see the photo at top left on the facing page).

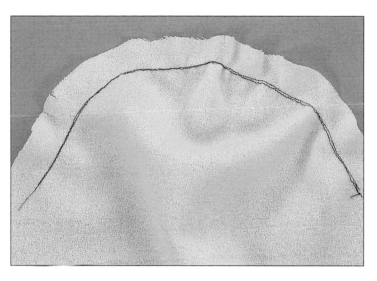

Shaped Cap

Before sewing a sleeve into an armhole, steam-press the sleeve cap over a tailor's ham. This sets the ease and shrinks the cap a bit, as shown in the photo at top right. This is the best way to eliminate seamline puckers.

Insert the sleeve with the sleeve on top, flattening the sleeve cap as you sew. Place your fingers on each side of the stitching line and pull it apart, as shown in the photo at bottom right. Don't worry if the sleeve seems to have too much "ease" for the armhole.

Style Maker

GO BACK

More ease is needed at the back of the sleeve, so don't crowd the same amount between the front and back notches. European ready-to-wear manufacturers start the ease line 2 in. (5cm) in front of the shoulder placement dot. Continue easing down the back of the sleeve cap until you reach the back notch—about 4 in. (10.2cm) down from the shoulder dot, or beyond if the sleeve has a lot of ease.

If a fabric is very difficult to ease, such as wool gabardine, ease all the way around the sleeve, from underarm to underarm. The option I prefer is altering the pattern to reduce the cap ease.

DOUBLE DELIGHT

Short sleeves are a super option for a summer dress or blouse. They're cool, yet they offer a bit of coverage for the upper arms. Unfortunately, lightweight wovens and knits give you limp sleeves and curled hems. The best way to fix this is by doubling the sleeves. You'll love this high-quality finish. Doubled short sleeves are professional-looking and easy to make. The finished sleeves don't ripple at the hem edges and they conform better to the shape of your arm.

For doubled short sleeves, cut four sleeves from the garment fabric and make one of each pair into a "lining." After seaming, set the sleeves into the garment armholes.

1 Trim off the hem allowance on the sleeve pattern so that only 1 in. (2.5cm) extends beyond the hem crease line.

2 Cut four sleeve pieces from your fashion fabric. If you're short on fabric, you can use lining fabric for the second set (except in the case of knits, where self-fabric is recommended).

3 Cut an additional 1 in. (2.5cm) off the bottom of the lining (inner sleeve) set. The inner sleeves must be shorter to pull up the hem on the outer sleeve.

TIP To reduce bulk in a crisp fabric like linen, cut the second set of sleeves from a lining fabric.

4 Treating each of the four sleeve pieces as a separate unit, sew the underarm seams. Press the seam allowances open.

5 Pair the sleeves and turn the lining pieces right side out. With each set, place one lining "cylinder" inside the garment sleeve with right sides facing and raw edges even.

6 Sew together the bottom edges of each set using a ⅝-in. (15mm) seam allowance. Trim the seam allowances to ¼ in. (6mm).

7 Turn the joined sleeve right side out so that the wrong sides are together in each set. Pull up the sleeve lining so that both layers match at the cap. The shorter lining pulls the garment sleeve hem allowance into the sleeve.

8 Slip a sleeve over a seam roll and press the bottom edge. There's no need to hem the bottom of your sleeves, since you've already seamed the bottom edge of the layers.

9 Working on one sleeve at a time, ease the sleeve cap through both layers and shape it over a tailor's ham. (See "Sleeve Ease with Ease" on p. 149.) Set the sleeve into the dress armhole.

Style Maker

ARMED AND BEAUTIFUL

Sometimes, a beautifully draped sleeve doesn't require special shaping or pattern alterations. Cutting the garment piece with the grainline running on the bias (a 45-degree angle) is all that's necessary to make your sleeve hang perfectly. However, unless you're seeking an unusual effect, don't try this cutting idea on plaids, stripes, or one-way designs. It works best for plain wovens, and is especially beautiful in a full sleeve.

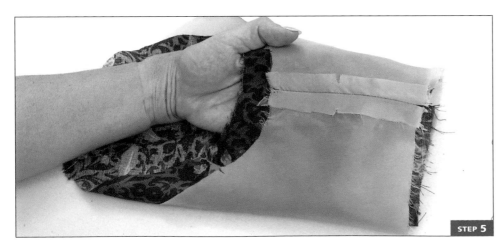

STEP 5

FULL-SLEEVE SUPPORT

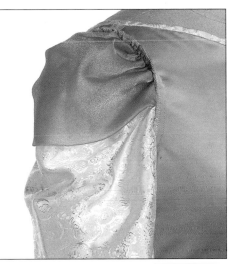

Bridal or evening dresses often feature dramatic poufed sleeves. To create this effect, each of the sleeves needs a firm sleeve head. This gives you volume at the shoulder but allows the remainder of the sleeve to drape gracefully on your arm. The effect need not be excessive. Made from two layers of organza, the head sits only in the cap area of the sleeve. It's added before you insert the sleeve into the garment (as shown above).

Whether you underline the entire sleeve or merely add a head for subtle volume at the shoulders, organza is a wonderful support fabric. In this situation, nylon organza is better than silk organza. Silk organza loses its stiffness with wear. Nylon organza, on the other hand, never loses its original body.

[TIP] If you want the whole sleeve to be poufy, it's best to underline the entire sleeve piece with organza.

Style Maker

RUCHED SLEEVE

You can easily draw up the bottom portion of a sleeve underarm seam to create ruching in a lightweight fabric. The technique is usually done on the outer, most visible, seam of a two-piece sleeve.

Sew the outer seam and turn up the hem allowance at the bottom of the sleeve. Leave the underarm seam open. Cut two strips of ¼-in. (6mm) wide and 4½-in. (11.4cm) long clear elastic. Stretch one elastic strip to fit the lowest 9 in. (22.9cm) of the sleeve piece below the elbow.

Straight-stitch the center of the elastic to the wrong side of the sleeve. The elastic draws up the fabric as it moves out the back of the presser foot. Sew the remaining sleeve seam and the hem allowance.

1 First make a pattern for the sleeve head by tracing the top of the sleeve pattern from the front to the back notches. On the tracing, draw a straight line from front to back near the notches.

2 Fold a piece of organza on the bias. For extra fullness, don't press the folded edge. The folded fabric edge gives the sleeve head a bit of volume.

3 Place the straight, lower edge of the sleeve head pattern on the fabric fold. Cut out the doubled organza without cutting through the fold.

4 To attach the sleeve head, fold it and place it on the wrong side of the sleeve. Match the raw edges at the cap, then hand-baste the layers together.

5 Insert your sleeve according to the pattern instructions. Run the gathering stitch through all thicknesses of the sleeve and sleeve head. Set the sleeve into the garment.

[TIP] To get the maximum benefit from the sleeve head, gently tug the head and sleeve apart at the stitching line after the sleeve is inserted. This gives the sleeve and sleeve head independent shaping.

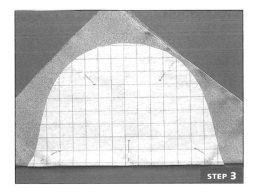

STEP 3

MAN-TAILORED SLEEVE PLACKET

Men's shirts feature beautiful sleeve plackets. Unlike the continuous bias strip you see on most women's wear (except the very best), a menswear sleeve placket is wide and attractively topstitched. In fact, it's so attractive that an elongated version looks great in the neck opening of a shirt or a dress. This treatment immediately says a garment is upscale.

Like better-quality ready-to-wear, this shirt has a wide sleeve placket above the cuff. It's easier to insert this placket before sewing the sleeve's underarm seam.

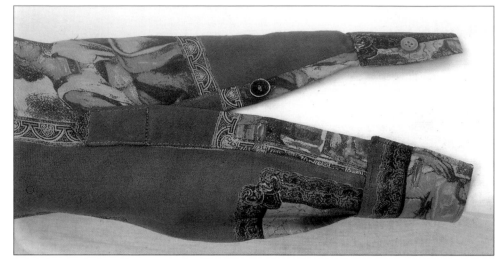

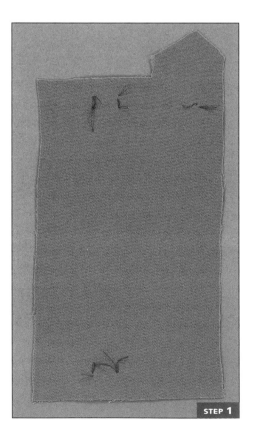

1 Cut the sleeve placket from your fashion fabric. You can either use one from a man's shirt pattern or make your own. Interface the wrong side of the placket.

[TIP] Interface a silk placket with silk organza, hand-basting it to the wrong side of the placket. It's perfectly acceptable to interface the entire placket of a light-weight cotton or slightly heavier fabric with a lightweight fusible interfacing.

2 Fold under ¼-in. (6mm) seam allowances along both lengthwise edges of the placket. Hand-baste or press them in place.

3 Place the right side of the placket against the wrong side of the garment, exactly matching the placement lines. Sew the placket to the garment along the stitching lines indicated on the pattern, using 1mm (18 spi) straight stitches.

4 As you reach the top of each line of stitching, pivot the work and hand-walk two diagonal stitches across each corner.

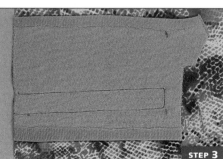

STEP 3

5 Slash through the placket and the garment between the stitching lines. Cut diagonally into the corners to within a few fabric threads of the stitching. Press the newly cut edges away from the opening so that they face the placket.

[TIP] Don't worry about cutting too close. The small stitches don't come undone easily. Cutting close to the stitching line is very important for a perfectly smooth placket.

6 Turn the placket to the outside of the garment through the new opening. First place the side that doesn't have the point by bringing the folded edge just over the stitching. Topstitch it in position.

STEP 5

STEP 8

7 To complete the placket, fold the remaining side in the same manner. Position the triangle placket so that it's suitable for the bulk of your fabric. Trust your judgment. Your goal is a smooth, bulk-free placket.

8 Fold the placket, and hand-baste it in position. Trim away any unnecessary bulk. Topstitch the triangle.

TIP When completing the triangle at the end of the placket, you don't have to use the placement position indicated on the pattern. Let your fabric relax for a pucker-free placket.

EASIEST SLEEVE VENT

This sleeve placket treatment is found on women's dresses and blouses with cuffed sleeves. I also find it an especially handy treatment for difficult fabric.

A simple welt is the easiest way to make a professional-looking sleeve placket. In most instances, sewing instructions tell you to make a 3-in. (7.6cm) long slash at the bottom of the sleeve, open it so that the cut edge is straight, then bind it with a strip of fabric. Finally, you attach the cuff. This procedure can be frustrating, but I've developed several improvements that dramatically improve the results.

1 Cut out the sleeves and mark the placket location if there isn't one on the pattern. You can approximate its placement by dividing the sleeve into thirds. The placket opening goes about one-third the distance from the back of the sleeve.

2 Make a 3-in. (7.6cm) long vertical cut into the sleeve fabric at the marked location. To help with the subsequent binding, make a ⅛-in. (3mm) deep snip on either side of the top of the slash.

STEP 2

3 Cut a separate strip of fabric on the bias, 1½ in. wide and 8 in. long (3.8cm by 20.3cm). Interface the strip with bias-cut, fusible interfacing. Press under ¼ in. (6mm) on one long edge.

4 Spread the sleeve open at the slash so that it's completely straight. Place the right side of the unpressed long edge of the strip against the wrong side of the opened slash. Sew, using a ¼-in. (6mm) seam allowance and one continuous line of stitching.

5 Let the strip curve around the top of the slash. Wrap the strip around the seam allowances to enclose the raw edges. Pin, then topstitch, the strip in place from the right side. Press.

6 Fold the bound edge in half, placing the front of the sleeve on top. You'll see a small pleat at the top of the sleeve placket. Secure this by straight-stitching a triangle—through all thicknesses—on top of the pleat.

7 Press and pound your new placket with a tailor's clapper.

SMOOTH CUFFS

Smooth sleeve cuffs don't happen by accident. The key to a fabulous, hassle-free cuff is making the inner cuff smaller than the outer cuff, interfacing both cuff pieces, and cutting all cuff pieces on the bias.

For the cuff to circle the wrist without puckers, you need to cut both of the cuff pieces—and the interfacing—on the bias. Sometimes this isn't possible because the fabric has a distinct design, like a stripe, that looks odd when placed diagonally on a cuff.

In this situation, cut the outer cuff on the straight grain, and the inner cuff and both of the interfacing pieces on the bias. I like to apply Fusi-Knit to the wrong side of the inner and outer cuff pieces. The following instructions also include a great way to apply a cuff to a jacket.

1 Before applying the cuff to the sleeve, sew the underarm seam and insert the sleeve into the garment. Complete the placket for the sleeve vent.

TIP Fusibles make fabrics such as silk too stiff. Interface these fabrics with silk organza for a soft cuff or Veri-Shape for a crisp effect.

2 Cut out two cuff pieces on the bias, one for the inner cuff and another for the outer cuff. Interface the wrong side of both pieces. Label one of them the inner cuff.

3 Trim ⅛ in. (3mm) from all edges of the inner cuff. Making it smaller eliminates wrinkles when the finished cuff circles the wrist.

4 Place the right side of the inner (trimmed) cuff against the wrong side of the sleeve. Both ends of the cuff extend ⅝ in. (15mm) beyond the edges of the finished sleeve placket, unless you want a longer underlap.

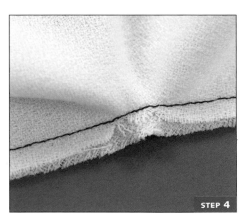

STEP 4

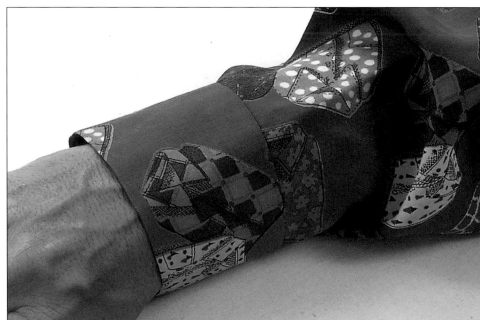

StyleMaker

STEP 5

5 Sew the inner cuff to the sleeve with a ⅝-in. (15mm) seam allowance. Press the seam allowances toward the cuff.

6 With the cuff opened away from the sleeve, place the right side of the outer cuff against the right side of the inner cuff with the raw edges even.

7 Pin the sides and top of the cuff pieces together, placing the pins on the inner cuff side. Sew the sides and top, letting the feed dogs ease the larger cuff to fit the trimmed one.

8 Tuck the bottom of the sleeve inside the cuff pieces so that 2 in. (5cm) of the seam allowances from the cuff/sleeve seamline (made in Steps 4 and 5) are visible. This makes it possible to join the bottom of the cuffs when the pieces are sewn together.

9 Pin the bottom of the outer cuff to the exposed inner cuff and sleeve seam allowances. Be careful not to catch the portion of the sleeve tucked between the cuff pieces.

10 At the pinned portion of the cuff/sleeve seamline, start sewing 1 in. (2.5cm) from the corner—on the seamline. Sew to the side of the cuff, stopping with the needle down ⅝ in. (15mm) from the corner.

11 Once again, sandwich about 2 in. (5cm) of the sleeve inside the cuff pieces. Pivot the work and sew along the cuff/sleeve seamline for 1 in. (2.5cm).

Trim off bulk in the seam allowances and upper corners.

12 Turn the cuff right side out. Use a point turner to push out the corners. Turn under the seam allowance on the loose edge of the outer cuff.

13 Pin the fold to the sleeve so that it just covers the cuff/sleeve seamline. Topstitch the fold to the garment, then continue topstitching around the entire cuff ⅛ in. (3mm) away from the seamed edges.

[TIP] To shape the cuff while pressing it, insert a sleeve roll or a rolled-up magazine inside the cuff. Pound the seams with a tailor's clapper.

STEP 7

STEP 10

STEP 8

CONTOURED SHOULDER PADS

Covered shoulder pads look great, but lack the shaping needed to make them invisible when worn. A covered pad is usually too bulky and never lies flat. Margaret Islander showed me a nifty way to cover a pair of shoulder pads when she was a guest on my television show, *Sew Perfect*.

This technique lets you cover and contour a shoulder pad in about 10 minutes using an industry-proven method. The entire process is done by machine, and the results are fabulous. No matter what size or type of shoulder pad you want to use, the following method shapes the pad to your shoulder, even if the pad starts out as flat as a pancake.

1 Cut a large square of lining or light-weight fashion fabric with the edges parallel to the grainlines. Place the shoulder pad diagonally across the

STEP 1

square with the fat (shoulder) side in the middle and diagonal to the corners. Fold the other half of the lining square over the top of the pad. Pin.

TIP **If you're using a lightweight material such as silk, you can cover your shoulder pads with fashion fabric. Otherwise, lightweight cotton is suitable.**

2 Set your machine for the longest possible straight stitch. On the fat, wide side of the pad, start sewing 1 in. (2.5cm) from the folded fabric edge, halfway across the width.

3 Curl the front of the shoulder pad up toward the front of the presser foot. You build in shaping by rolling the pad as you stitch.

4 Sew a straight line along the pad toward the narrow end and the matched points on the fabric square. Release the rolled pad as it approaches the presser foot.

5 Continue sewing parallel rows of stitching ½ in. (1.3cm) apart, contouring half of the pad. Work from the center of the pad to the edges to build in as much shape as possible in the shoulder pad. Work on half of the pad at a time.

STEP 4

6 Once you finish the first half of the pad, turn it around and contour the second half, always sewing from the center of the pad out to the ends for maximum shaping.

7 After the straight stitching is complete, serge together the pad and lining around the cut edges. Let the knives cut off the excess lining as you serge around the pad's perimeter. Curl the pad as you serge so that it doesn't lose its contouring.

8 Position the shoulder pad no closer than 1¼ in. (3.2cm) from the neck seamline and extend it ½ in. (1.3cm) into the sleeve. Hand-sew the center of the shoulder pad to the shoulder seam allowances.

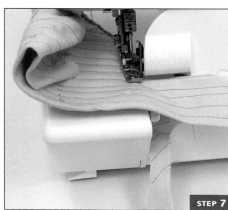

STEP 6

STEP 7

ELASTICIZED WAIST

Many loose dress and top styles need a belt to control the fullness. This is great, as long as you don't mind rearranging the gathers and the above-waist fullness every time you move. If you add a casing and insert elastic, however, you can evenly distribute the fabric fullness and the hem will always hang evenly. This dress was made from Burda 3743.

My method is sewing elastic to the waistline—without a casing. This is perfect for light- and medium-weight fabric. You can apply this simple procedure to a garment you're constructing or a finished piece of clothing. If possible, hold off on hemming until the waist is completed. The following steps explain how you can apply the elastic even if the garment wasn't in

tended to be belted, or if you want to change the garment to a blouson style.

1 Try on the dress or top. Tie a string or a piece of elastic around your waist. Let the garment hang straight, rather than pulling it up for a blouson effect. Pin-mark your waist at one side seam.

2 Take off the garment and turn it wrong side out. Transfer the pin at the waist to the wrong side of the garment. Insert another pin at the waist on the other side seam, placing it the same distance below the armhole as the pin on the opposite side.

3 To elasticize a waist, you need to lower the waistline so that the upper portion of the dress is fuller. This blouson effect can be as full or as subtle as you desire.

4 At the side seams, measure 1½ in. (3.8cm) down from the pin-marked waist. This is the location of the new waistline. Mark it with pins. Connect the new waist marks by drawing a line across the garment front.

5 Drawing a new back waistline isn't as simple as connecting the side-seam pins. To ensure that the garment hangs correctly, and to eliminate a droopy hem, lower the waistline at center back. Draw a temporary line across the back, connecting the lowest side-seam waistline marks.

Measure ½ in. (1.3cm) down at center back. Draw the new waistline by connecting the side seams to the lower center back with a gently sloping arc. The curve enables the hemline to hang evenly because the waistline slopes gently at center back.

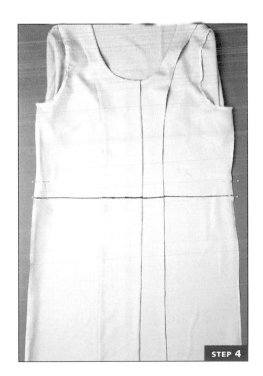

STEP 4

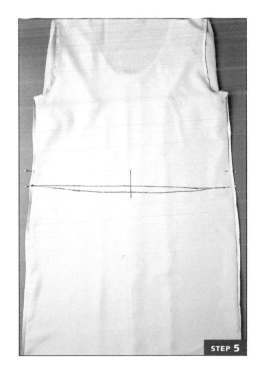

STEP 5

6 Cut a piece of ¼-in. (6mm) wide elastic to your waist measurement less 2 in. (5cm). Cut it smaller if the fabric isn't lightweight. Butt the ends of the elastic together over a piece of ribbon. Zigzag through all layers to make the elastic into a circle. Mark each quarter of the elastic circle.

7 Working from the wrong side of the dress, pin a marked location on the elastic to one of the side seams. Match the remaining quarter marks to the skirt's center front, center back, and remaining side seam.

8 Using a serpentine or zigzag stitch, sew the center of the elastic to the new waistline marked on the wrong side of the dress

Style Maker

CASE BY CASE

You can elasticize the waist of a garment made from heavy fabric. Simply use a more substantial elastic, cut 3 in. (7.6cm) smaller than your waist, and add a casing for it. Position the bottom of the casing 2 in. (5cm) below the waistline.

CONTINUOUS BUTTON LOOPS

Tiny, continuous loops are an eye-catching detail that need not require a lot of work to make. Here's an incredibly easy ready-to-wear method that gives you perfectly sized and spaced loops every time. The loops are first sewn to a strip of paper, which in turn is straight-stitched to the garment. When you pull off the paper, the loops remain intact on the garment. Very painless and professional, just the way we like it.

1 Cut a strip of paper 1½ in. (3.8cm) wide and the same length as the facing. Draw a line on the paper ¼ in. (6mm) from one of the paper's lengthwise edges.

2 Draw lines across the strip to indicate the location of every button loop. The spaces between small buttons are usually ¾ in. to 1 in. (1.9cm to 2.5cm).

3 Draw a second line on the paper ½ in. (1.3cm) away from—and parallel to—the first. Large buttons need longer loops, so place your second line a bit farther away from the first. The horizontal lines mark the location of each button loop, while the vertical lines show you the finished loop size.

4 Make a strip of bias-cut fabric cord for the loops. (A Fasturn Miniturn makes the cleanest, narrowest bias cord possible.) Narrow purchased cord is a great substitute for loops in dry-clean-only garments.

5 Place one end of the cord on the lowest horizontal placement line (the one that's ¼ in. [6mm] from the paper's lengthwise edges). The cord goes next to, not on, the placement line for the opening.

6 Loop the cord to the other vertical placement line and back to the starting point at the first line, leaving an opening for the button.

7 Straight-stitch the cording to the paper along the line ¼ in. (6mm) from the long side of the paper. Cut the cord at the edge of the paper, continuing the same line of stitching and placing and sewing the remaining cord to the paper as you go.

8 Once all of the loops are sewn to the paper, place the paper—loops down—on the right side of the garment. Match the vertical line that's ¼ in. (6mm) from the paper's edge with the first stitching line on the garment.

9 Align the stitching on the cording with the garment seamline so that your subsequent stitching catches the ends of each loop in the seamline.

10 Pin the paper strip to the garment from the paper side. Straight-stitch the paper strip and cording to the garment along the seamline, sewing right on top of the stitching line that attaches the cording to the paper.

11 Tear off the paper and attach the facing to the garment.

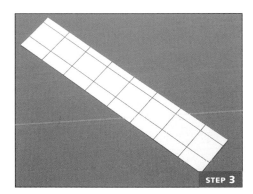
STEP 3

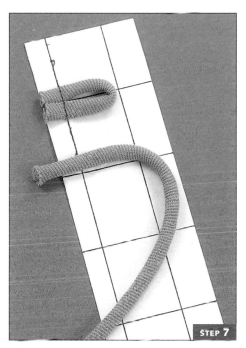
STEP 7

STEP 10

SHAPED CURVED HEM

Shirtdress styles often call for a thinly rolled hem that curves gently around corners to join slits at the side seams. The challenge with this hem is making the curves smooth and flat. For a roll that doesn't ripple, I recommend making the outside edge smaller. This is easily done with an ease line at the hem allowance.

You can apply this same technique to an overblouse, but a rounded shirttail hem is more suitable for a blouse or tailored shirt that's going to be worn tucked in. A shirt-dress or blouse with curved side slits is sexy yet functional. Your legs appear longer and the side slits give you the ease needed for walking and sitting. The curved corner—where the hem meets the bottom of the side slits—is less intimidating with this technique.

1 At each curve on the front and back hems, use a regular stitch length (2.5mm or 10 spi) to case-stitch ¼ in. (6mm) from the raw edge. Press your finger against the back of the presser foot as you stitch in order to draw in the fabric. Lengthen the stitch for heavier fabric.

STEP 2

2 Sew each garment piece separately, stopping at the top of the slit opening. This simple line of stitching makes the hem curl slightly to the wrong side, making it easier to press the hem to the wrong side of the garment.

3 Press up ½ in. (1.3cm) on the hem edge. If you need to pull in a little more fabric on the curve, pull slightly on the bobbin thread.

4 Now you're ready to finish the hem. On the wrong side of the garment, tuck under and pin the hem from the raw edge to just past the easing.

5 Press lightly, then sew the rolled hem to the garment with hand or machine stitching. Press and pound the hem with a tailor's clapper.

STEP 5

6 At the top of the slits on both side seams, make a ¼-in. (6mm) long bar tack over the seamline. Use a narrow, short zigzag stitch (1mm wide and 0.8mm long).

TWIN-NEEDLE HEM

Many tops and dresses, especially T-shirt styles made with a knit or a Lycra blend, look fabulous with a twin-needle hem. I use this hemming technique on knit or Lycra stretch pants and skirts as well. It's well worth considering for your next garment because it looks professional, provides stretch, and eliminates the need to hand-stitch the hem.

[TIP] Control very stretchy knit hems like slinky knit by reducing the hem width to ½ in. (1.3cm) and pressing a strip of Steam-A-Seam II between the hem allowance and the garment. Cover the hem area with a press cloth and steam-press for 10 seconds. Topstitching is optional.

Twin-needle hems may appear intimidating, but they aren't. Once the machine is set up, your stitching will look great: two evenly spaced rows of topstitching on the right side and a line of zigzagging on the wrong side. The fabric between the stitching lines will be flat (see the photo below).

Be sure to test the effect first on a fabric scrap so that the stitch length is cor-

rect and the fabric is flat between the rows of stitching. Using the correct twin needle for your fabric ensures that you won't end up with skipped stitches. Any machine that can make a zigzag stitch is capable of sewing with a twin needle.

1 A twin needle may have frustrated you in the past because it skipped stitches every 3 in. to 4 in. (7.6cm to 10.2cm), especially on knits. This isn't a problem anymore. Simply switch to a ZWI 130/705 HS twin needle with a blue band, which is designed for stretch fabrics. (The twin needle with the red band is for wovens.)

2 Needle spacing, which determines the distance between the two rows of topstitching, can range from 2.5mm to 4mm. The most attractive twin-needle hem has 3mm or 4mm spacing.

3 Stitches will pop on a knit dress if it was sewn together with regular thread on the bobbin. Woolly Nylon, a kinky-textured thread that's frequently used on a serger, builds stretch into the seamline. Hand-wrap Woolly Nylon on the bobbin and use regular thread in the needles.

[TIP] Don't machine-wind Woolly Nylon onto your bobbin; this will pull all of the stretch out of the thread.

4 Load the thread into the needles. For the best stitch quality, make sure that one thread goes on either side

of the tension disk. (Don't worry about this setup if you can't see the tension disk in your machine.) It helps if each spool unwinds in a different direction.

5 Now you're ready to test the stitching. Loosen the needle tension until the ridge between the stitching lines flattens. Also experiment with the stitch length.

6 Press up a 2-in. (5cm) hem allowance. With the garment right side up, sew with a twin needle around the hem ¼ in. (6mm) from the hem fold, using the side of your presser foot as a guide.

7 Sew another row of twin-needle stitching 1½ in. (3.8cm) above the first. Stacked rows of twin-needle stitching make a wonderful hem, particularly for knits. With two simple rows of sewing, you get four perfectly spaced stitching lines.

8 Turn the garment inside out so that you're working from the wrong side. Trim the excess hem allowance close to the uppermost line of stitching.

[TIP] It's easier to trim off the excess fabric using appliqué (pelican) scissors.

TRICK of the TRADE

CORNERING WITH A TWIN NEEDLE

When there are two lines of stitching at a corner, the one closer to the edge needs to be longer to get around the corner. Impossible with a twin needle? Not according to Patsy Shields, an educator for Sulky. The trick is to pivot the outer needle while keeping the inner needle in the same spot.

Switch to an open-toe presser foot so that you can see your stitches. Using the twin needle, sew to the corner. Stop with the needle on the inside of the corner, in the exact spot where you want to turn the corner. Pull the needle slightly out of the fabric and lift the presser foot.

Pivot the fabric just a little, so that the inside corner needle goes into the same hole while the outside corner needle swings out slightly. Make the stitch and pivot the fabric for another stitch. Again, let the inside corner needle enter the same hole. It takes four or five pivoted stitches to fully turn the corner.

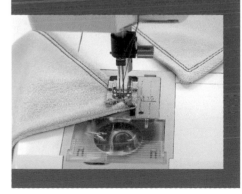

Chapter 6

JACKETS

Jackets are great for completing an ensemble. Choose a style that maximizes your assets and minimizes your liabilities. Spend a little time on the pattern so that it fits you to a T.

Decide what color jacket you need to pull some of your existing wardrobe pieces into the "wear-it-now" orbit. Take these pieces with you when you shop for fabric. Look for something that feels great and doesn't wrinkle a lot.

So what kind of time commitment are we talking about when you're ready to sew? One or two days of total pleasure. Take time to enjoy the process. This jacket will be in your wardrobe for years, so take the extra steps to make it special. A jacket can be the most rewarding and creative piece you make—especially if you add details like cuffs, interesting pockets, and piping. You'll remember the journey, not just the finished product.

Sandra's Closet

I don't work in an office (thank goodness!), so my jackets and coats can be unconventional. Nevertheless, I do need great-looking garments I can wear while teaching or hosting my television show. Luckily, this gives me opportunities to make a variety of styles. The jackets on the next few pages feature some of the techniques and ideas I like to explore when making a jacket. If you'd like to try any of the details, follow the accompanying step-by-step instructions.

EXTRAVAGANT EASTERN BROCADE

Rules are made to be broken, and fashion designers are adept at doing just that. Fabric use is a good example. At one time, fabrics were divided into distinct categories: day and eveningwear. Luxurious fabrics such as brocade, chiffon, satin, and velvet were reserved for clothes you'd wear for a night on the town. Today you can wear these wonderful fabrics during the day by making them into casual clothes, such as a chiffon anorak or a tailored velvet shirt.

The latest fabric to make the crossover from night to day is satin brocade. If you've always loved this fabric but felt that your lifestyle didn't warrant making a jacket just for the evening, you now have an excuse to work it up in a casual jacket or coat.

The Japanese-inspired Haiku Jacket pattern from the Sewing Workshop was perfect for my red-and-black satin brocade fabric. Since I wanted a fashionable but warm coat, I interlined the garment with a thermal fabric called Thinsulate. Cotton flannel and lamb's wool are other common interlinings.

Why not mix things up a bit? I repeated a companion fabric, which is visible at the rolled-up cuffs, on the upper corners of the patch pockets. I also split the sleeve pattern and inserted a diagonal block of the collar fabric. When you split a pattern, don't forget to add seam allowances to either side of the split.

Pattern Pretest

A jacket takes one or two days to make, and satin brocade is expensive. Before cutting into the fabric, test the pattern in a scrap fabric. Old sheets make great pretest fabric. Forget about constructing the collar, facings, and cuffs. Just cut two fronts, a back, and one sleeve.

In 30 minutes, you'll know whether the pattern is a keeper and what alterations are necessary. While I don't particularly enjoy making pretests, I've never regretted doing it. More than once, a pattern has hit the trashcan while my expensive fabric was still intact.

How I Made This Jacket

You can make a jacket like mine using the step-by-step instructions in the following features:

Pattern Pretest (at right)
Jacket Structure (see p. 176)
Flannel Underlining (see p. 190)
Bagged Patch Pocket (see p. 191)
Hong Kong Facing (see p. 204)

Interlining

Interlining adds warmth to a garment. If you're interlining with cotton flannelette, don't forget to preshrink. For jacket fronts, fuse interfacing to the underlining layer. Place an interlining shape on the wrong side of the corresponding garment piece. Join the pieces with a row of pins from top to bottom. Fold the joined pieces in half along the pins with the fashion fabric on the outside. About ¼ in. to ½ in. (6mm to 1.3cm) of the underlining slides out, beyond the edges of the fashion fabric. Pin around the raw edges of the interlining and fashion fabric while still rolled.

Open up the garment piece. It curls a little toward the interlining, which gives you some turn of cloth. The outside (fashion-fabric) layer must be larger so that it can wrap smoothly around the interlining and your body. Hand-baste the interlining and fashion fabric together 1 in. (2.5cm) from the raw edges. Cut away any interlining that extends beyond the garment layer. Plan to line your jacket to cover the layer of interlining.

Machine Adjustments

Your usual machine settings for garment assembly need to be adjusted for interlined garment pieces. The layers make your seams thicker, so lengthen your stitch to 3.5mm (8 spi). Switch to an even-feed foot so that the top and bottom layers move together through the machine. Since interlining also takes up a bit of room inside the garment, sew the side seams at ⅜ in. (1cm) rather than ⅝ in. (15mm) to compensate.

CLASSIC CHANEL

Gabrielle ("Coco") Chanel is responsible for a wide variety of innovative styles. Yet for most women, the name Chanel conjures up the image of a simple, collarless cardigan with knit or braided trim. You can create a garment that has the same spirit and detailing as the chic numbers that came out of Chanel's studio back in the 1920s.

The original Chanel jacket was worn like a sweater. It was soft and comfortable—not overly structured—and was originally underlined with men's undershirting.

There are many suitable Chanel-inspired jacket patterns available. Look for a simple, collarless, cardigan style with small shoulders and high armholes like the one below.

Certain details make a garment extra special. This is one of them. A bit of weight was added to the hem to make smooth, straight vertical seams and to control the fullness. You can duplicate the effect with drapery weights inside the hem, but adding chain is more in the spirit of Chanel (see the jacket above).

The key elements of the Chanel look are the trim, the underlining and lining, and the weighted hem. The construction process is quite basic.

Trim and Fabric

Don't purchase your fabric until you visit a well-stocked notions department to see what's available in knit and braided trims. It's often easier to find the trim first, then select appropriate fabric.

Look for an interesting, pliable flat trim. Flexibility is extremely important if the jacket's front edges are curved. A trim designed to wrap to the wrong side of a garment works well on sweaters, but isn't suitable for Chanel-inspired creations. Choose a knit or braided trim that's finished along the lengthwise edges, since both sides will be visible on the finished jacket. Take samples of your trims along when you go fabric shopping. Look for bouclés and loosely woven tweeds that capture the mood of the Chanel jacket.

Underlining

A loosely woven fabric needs underlining to support the line of the jacket and the pocket detailing. Prewashed batiste Pima cotton, lawn, lightweight silk broadcloth, and silk organza are excellent underlining fabrics. For a crisper look, or to give support to a loosely woven fabric, underline the entire jacket with Fusi-Knit interfacing.

Chanel jackets don't have facings, but the underlining still needs extra support along the front edge and the neck. Use the facing patterns to cut interfacing shapes to fuse to the underlining.

Lining Insertion

Make sure that the lining isn't too skimpy. Allow enough back width for a 2-in. (5cm) wide pleat at center back. Cut the lining to the finished length of the body and sleeves. This will allow for a take-up tuck. A Chanel jacket lining comes right to the neckline and front edges, so facings are eliminated.

After the lining is attached at the neckline and front edges with right sides together, trim the seam, then press and pound it flat. Make 1½-in. (3.8cm) hems at the bottom of the sleeves and jacket. Attach the lining to the top of the hem allowance. Insert small shoulder pads.

Trim Application

Now it's time for the crowning touch. Measure the perimeter of the edge where you want to apply the trim. Measure the sleeve, multiply it by 2, and add it to the perimeter length. Cut a piece of trim to this final measurement plus 4 in. The trim goes around the perimeter of the jacket and the sleeves.

Mitering ribbon or braid is a simple process that follows the same basic assembly explained in "Mitered Hem with Walking Ease" on p. 105. Start the trim at an inconspicuous place like a side seam, turning under ¼ in. (6mm) to hide the raw edge of the trim. Pin the trim to the garment.

At the corner, hand-miter the trim by folding under one edge. This creates a diagonal fold across the corner. Pin the trim in place. Trim is mitered by hand on an authentic Chanel jacket. In addition, the corners are trimmed so that it's possible to make alterations. Hand-sew the trim to the jacket, mitering the corners. Hold the lining in place with hidden hand picking on the underside.

SATURDAY MORNING

You've spent an entire week slaving away, and now it's time to do some chores before relaxing for the weekend. But who says you have to do your running around wearing sweats? Instead, pull a casual jacket over jeans or a comfy T-shirt dress and head out the door. You have warmth, comfort, and style in one easy piece. What a great addition to a wardrobe. I bet you could even get away with this look in the office on "casual" Fridays.

Several design elements enhance the relaxed effect of this jacket. The fabric is loosely woven, so it hangs with a sweaterlike softness. Light interfacing and minimal lining keep the look unstructured. In addition, the jacket is slightly longer than the traditional business jacket, and the back is elasticized.

The same fabric I used for lining the fronts is used for several structural and detail treatments on the jacket, such as triangular patches that strengthen the front carriers for the self-fabric belt. I also added strips to the bottom of the sleeves for the rolled-back cuff.

Support Up Front

I fell in love with the loose weave of the hand-woven fabric in this jacket, but I also realized that its relaxed drape called for special treatment. Without reinforcement, the fronts would soon droop. To prevent this, I fused the wrong side of the fronts to Fusi-Knit. To hide the support, I lined the fronts with medium-weight linen. Another layer of the fashion fabric would be too heavy.

Collar Contrast

The contrasting fabric used in this jacket is an excellent match because it is the selvage of the fashion fabric. I was thrilled to discover that this hand-woven fabric had a totally different appearance on the densely woven selvage. Here was the contrast I needed. Although the selvage is wide, it's too skimpy for the depth of the collar and the pocket welt. Don't let a problem like this discourage you. Simply use some of the fashion fabric above the selvage.

On the collar, a bit of fashion fabric is visible near the neckline seam, as well as in the seam allowance. The reverse is true for the pocket welts—the fashion fabric is at the top opening and wraps to the inside. Contrast adds interest and makes the piece unique instead of just a line-for-line version of the pattern.

How I Made This Jacket

You can make a jacket like mine using the step-by-step instructions in the following features:

West Coast Hong Kong Finish (see p. 85)
Mandarin Collar (see p. 147)
Fronts-Only Half-Lining (see p. 201)
Turned-Back Cuff (see p. 210)

ANATOMY *of a Jacket*

Tailoring a jacket or coat is time-consuming, so it's wise to think through the steps before you begin. Although the word *tailoring* can be intimidating, the process of creating a jacket is quite simple when you take it one step at a time. Your tailored jacket can be as detailed or as streamlined as you desire. This garment was made from Vogue 7022 to which I added a collar.

Once you have the fabric and you've pretreated it to prevent shrinkage, you're ready for the nuts and bolts. The following steps offer a summary of the process. For additional guidance, refer to "Master Construction Methods" on p. 172.

1 Pretest the pattern in a scrap fabric that has a weight and drape similar to your fashion fabric. Carefully analyze the fit and the locations of buttons and pockets to determine the necessary alterations. If you shorten the jacket the pockets will need to be moved up, but never above the high hip.

TIP Leftover drapery and upholstery fabrics are great for jacket pretests.

2 Test your interfacing on a fabric scrap. If the fabric becomes too stiff, plan to fuse the interfacing to the underlining or use a sew-in interfacing. Interface the fronts, facings, sleeve caps, both collar pieces, and hem.

3 Cut the optional underlining from a natural fiber that breathes. Cotton batiste, lawn, or Pima cotton are good choices. Use a fabric-marking pen to transfer all pattern markings to the underlining. Baste the underlining to the garment pieces.

4 **Now cut out and prepare the lining** using Bemberg rayon (Ambiance), China silk, or silk crepe de Chine. Acetate ravels and discolors, and polyester is too hot. Don't forget to allow a center-back pleat in the lining. If you plan to line only the fronts, the assembly process differs from the norm. (See "Fronts-Only Half-Lining" on p. 201.)

5 **Construct the pockets** on the garment front. Keep in mind that the pocket in your jacket pattern is only one option. This is a place to express your creativity.

TIP **Keep a file of your favorite pocket patterns.**

6 **Your buttonhole** depends on the fashion fabric and the capabilities of your machine. Does it make reliable buttonholes even as fabric layers and depth increase? If not, bound buttonholes are a good alternative. (Make them before joining the front to the facing.) Another option is attaching a front placket with built-in vertical buttonholes. If you prefer one large button, consider a button loop.

7 **Stabilize the neckline or lapel roll line** with Stay Tape, twill tape, or a ¼-in. (6mm) wide strip of preshrunk selvage cut from fabric yardage. If you made pattern alterations, you may need to ease the back shoulders.

8 **Join the garment pieces,** pressing each seam as it's sewn. If seam imprint appears to be a problem, moisten the underside and press lightly with an iron, using a seam stick. If possible, use silk thread for a wool jacket so that the seams are nearly invisible.

9 **After you insert the sleeves,** trim the underarm seam allowances to ¼ in. (6mm) between the notches to eliminate bulk.

10 **The shape of the shoulder pads** is very important. I prefer a dolman pad even with set-in sleeve styles because it produces a softer shoulder shape. Contour the shoulder pads with hand stitches, shaping them over a tailor's ham. Using your machine to shape the pads flattens them too much for a jacket. Insert the shoulder pads into the jacket.

11 **Insert the lining and attach it** to the garment at the underarm side seam by sewing in the well of the seam. This anchors the lining inside the jacket. Another option is attaching the lining to the fashion fabric at the underarm by machine-tacking a 1-in. (2.5cm) long piece of narrow twill tape to the seam allowances.

12 **Couture finishing is optional.** Hand- or machine-sew narrow, flat braid to the seamline joining the lining to the front and back facings. To help the garment hang closer to the body, weight your hem with a narrow gold chain at the top of the hem allowance, underneath the lining take-up tuck.

Master Construction Methods

Once you realize it's possible to make numerous changes while a garment is in progress, you're on the road to fewer failures and styling that's perfect for you.

As you plan your new jacket, look beyond the style lines and detailing on your pattern. There's so much you can do to improve the quality of and add a creative touch to your finished jacket. With only a few simple steps you can shape the lapel's roll line, armhole, and hem. You can reshape the front opening, add some fun pockets, and even tackle a plaid.

Before you get started on your project, take the time to review the techniques on the following pages. You'll find some all-time favorites, plus some exciting new ideas. If you consider pattern changes a part of the creative process, you'll resent the pattern less and enjoy the results more.

PERFECT PLAIDS

Ever wonder why the top collar on a plaid jacket is usually made in a contrasting fabric? Many sewers and industry experts believe that plaids on a lapel can't be matched and that contrast is the only solution. But this isn't true, says Terry Fox, a sewing personality on British television. She showed me a fabulous technique for matching plaids while we were sharing a ride to the airport.

Here is proof that you can, indeed, make a perfect match on a plaid collar. One of the keys to this technique is cutting all pattern pieces through a single layer of fabric. This way you don't have to spend time lining up the little squares on doubled yardage, a method that is never foolproof. This technique works on both even and uneven plaids.

1 Plan your layout to cut each pattern piece from a single layer of fabric. For a "Cut 2" pattern piece, you'll cut one garment piece from the fashion fabric and then set aside the pattern piece.

2 Cut out one front pattern piece. If the plaid has a prominent stripe, position this at center front. In the subsequent steps, you need to match the plaids at the seamlines, not the cutting lines.

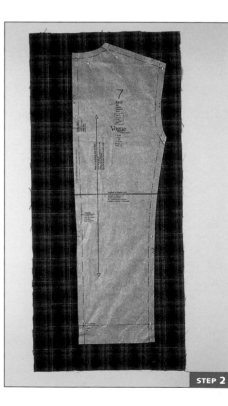

STEP 2

3 Use your newly cut garment piece as the pattern for the second shape. Flip over the first garment piece and place it on the yardage. Turning it over ensures that you end up with right and left sides.

4 Match the plaid on the cut garment piece to the plaid on the fabric. Make sure that the two fronts have a continuous plaid design when the front is buttoned.

5 As you work through the subsequent steps, cut all of the fabric pieces by using the first, flipped garment piece as a guide for the second.

6 Chalk-mark notches on the front fabric pieces. Write the name of each garment piece on a separate piece of tape and stick it on the wrong side of the fabric pieces to prevent mix-ups during assembly.

7 On the yardage, lay out the back pattern piece—still using a single layer of fabric—so that the plaid matches the front pattern piece at the side seam and the shoulder seam.

8 The shoulder seam won't match if the back is cut on a fabric fold, but this match isn't really necessary. To change a back pattern so that it isn't cut on the fold, add a ⅝-in. (15mm) paper extension for a seam allowance at center back.

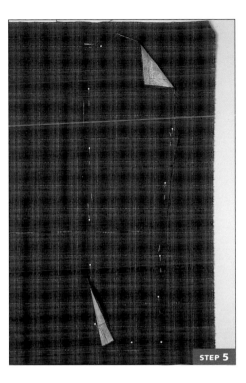

STEP 5

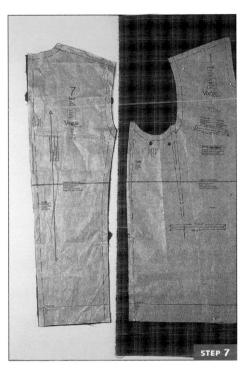

STEP 7

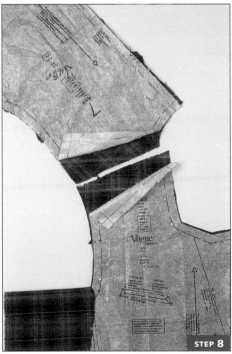

STEP 8

STEP 6

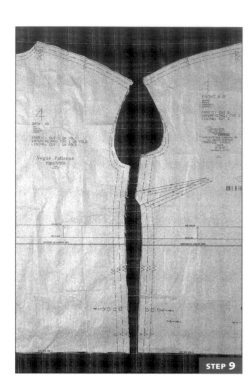

STEP 9

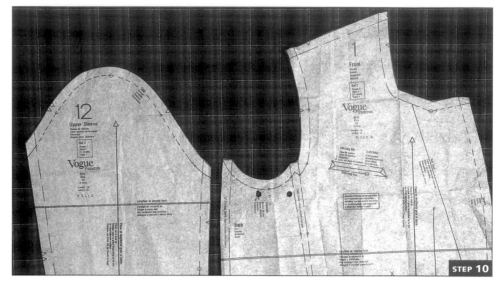

STEP 10

9 Match the plaid on the back piece to the front piece from the hem to the side dart.

10 Cut out the sleeve by matching the sleeve front to the front armhole from the notch to the underarm. If this is done correctly, the plaid on the sleeve will automatically match the plaid on the jacket from the armhole to the sleeve hem. Remember to match the sleeve seams on a two-piece sleeve.

[TIP] It isn't possible to match the sleeve cap to the armhole above the front notch because sleeve ease distorts the plaid. However, matching the sleeve from the armhole down is important so that the plaid is continuous when the arms hang to the sides.

11 Using the fronts as guides, cut mirror images for the front facings.

12 Split the undercollar pattern at center back and add a ⅝-in. (15mm) seam allowance. The undercollar on a plaid doesn't need to match the other pattern pieces. Cut it on the bias so that the plaid makes a chevron design along the center-back seamline.

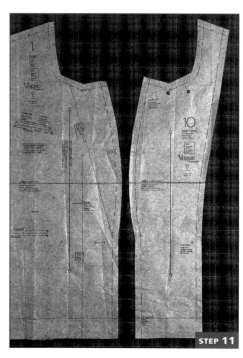

STEP 11

STEP 12

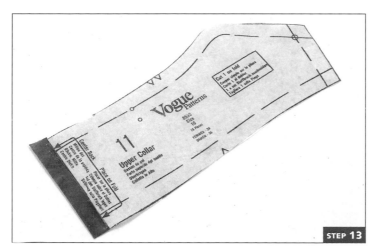

STEP 13

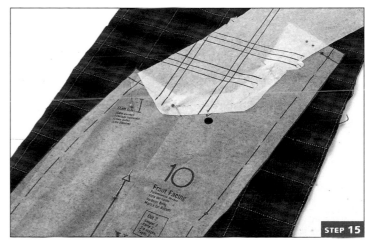

STEP 15

13 You must create a center-back seam on the upper collar for both sides to match at the lapel. This is a small price to pay for a flawlessly matched plaid collar. Cut through the upper collar pattern at center back and add a ⅜ in. (15mm) seam allowance at center back on both halves.

14 Cut the upper collar from Trace and Drape. Fold under the seam allowances. Place the upper collar on the front facing so that the dots for the lapel joint match.

15 Draw pencil lines on pattern tracing paper to continue the plaid design on the front facing. Use the paper template to cut the upper collar by matching the lines on the template with the fashion fabric.

TIP To prevent the top plaid on an unstable fabric from shifting as you sew, hold the seams together with double-sided basting tape. Sew with an even-feed foot for additional security against shifting fabric.

TRICK of the TRADE

A PERFECT PAIR OF PATCHES

The plaid on patch pockets must match the jacket fronts. The best way to get a perfect match is to start with a template.

Cut the pocket pattern from pattern-tracing fabric (or paper). Fold under the seam allowances and hems. Place the pattern-tracing fabric pocket on the front at the indicated pocket position. Draw the lines of the plaid front on the pattern-tracing fabric. Now cut the pocket pieces from the plaid fabric yardage, using the pattern-tracing fabric as the pattern and matching the plaid lines.

16 You can make welt pockets either in contrasting fabric or in plaid fabric with the pattern piece positioned on the bias. Cut the welt interfacing on the straight grain so that the fabric welt doesn't stretch during construction.

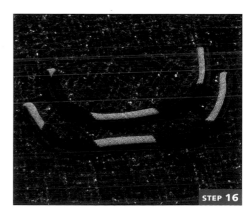

STEP 16

JACKET STRUCTURE

More than any other type of garment, a jacket needs a good understructure to maintain its shape. Choosing the right interfacing for the fabric and style determines your success. There's no need to be intimidated. My step-by-step process walks you through the selection of suitable interfacing, locations for application, and pretreating. My recommendations are based on years of experimentation, as well as on my examination of designer jacket interiors.

For a soft, sweaterlike jacket, use Fusi-Knit and keep the interfacing application to a minimum. For example, apply interfacing to the front but not the side front, as in the photo above.

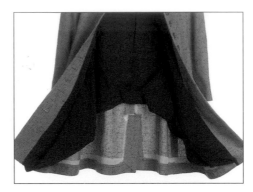

A jacket with lots of detailing—piping at the front opening, upper welt pockets, and hip patch pockets, for example—needs a crisp interfacing for a tailored effect. Choose Armo Weft or Suit Shape and interface the entire front. Of course, all styling details, like collars and pockets, must be interfaced regardless of fabric type. The details need support to maintain their shape.

Minimum structure results in a jacket that's almost like a blouse. In this case, apply interfacing only to the facing and behind the pockets. If the jacket has quite a bit of detailing but you want a softer hand, Textured Weft on the front—but not the side front—is your best bet.

INTERFACING CHOICES

There are many types of interfacing, so I'll recommend my favorites. Whatever your fashion fabric or intended use, you're sure to find a suitable product. (See "Interfacing Favorites" on p. 8.) If your local store has a limited selection, don't give up. Some manufacturers, such as HTC Inc., will give you the names of local retailers that carry their products. (See Resources on p. 226.)

Don't overlook mail order and online vendors. (See Resources for names and addresses.) Once you find an interfacing you like, consider buying it in bulk. A local retailer may be willing to offer you a good discount if you buy an entire bolt.

Take the time to find the right interfacing for your jacket. Don't compromise, because the results of using the wrong product are painfully obvious. HTC Handler offers a test fuse kit.

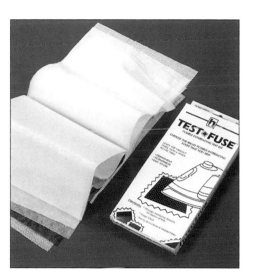

never use fusibles on wool crepe, silk crepe de Chine, charmeuse, chiffon, or georgette.)

3 The weight of the interfacing, fiber, type of resin (glue), and the way the resin is applied greatly affect the hand of the fashion fabric. It's very important to test your fusible before applying it to expensive jacket fabric.

4 It's perfectly acceptable to fuse the interfacing to an underlining. Since the underlining is basted to the garment pieces, you don't have to worry about the fusible ruining the drape of the fashion fabric or creating a bond that weakens over the years.

5 A sew-in interfacing may be the best option if you're not happy with the results of your fusible test. Stacey Dura Press, silk organza, and hair canvas offer different degrees of crispness. You might want to hand-baste a piece to a collar to test the effect.

1 Decide whether you want your jacket to be crisp or softly tailored. (See "Interfacing Ideas" on p. 9 for descriptions of my favorite products and where I like to place them in garments.)

2 Fuse a piece of interfacing to a scrap of your fashion fabric. You'll immediately know whether you can use a fusible on the material. If the fabric becomes stiff, a fusible won't work. (I

STEP 4

TRICK
of the TRADE

SEW-IN SUBSTITUTES

Nontusible interfacings are hard to find. An alternative is to underline the jacket with lawn, batiste, or Pima cotton, then fuse the interfacing to the underlining. In a pinch, an old all-cotton pillowcase or sheet makes a great underlining.

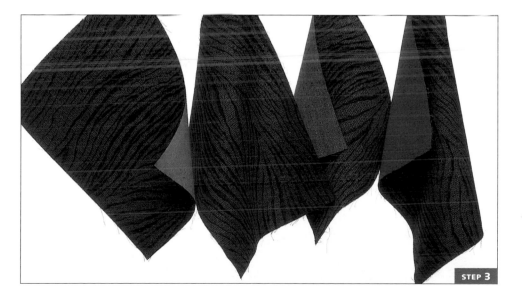
STEP 3

INTERFACE LIKE THE PROS

A great way to find out the secrets of jacket interfacing is to dissect ready-to-wear jackets. This isn't as expensive as you might think. Top-quality resale shops are perfect for research material. The jackets don't have to fit, and you don't have to worry about damaging them.

By taking jackets apart, I've discovered that the interfacing application isn't very complex. While there are some exceptions, almost all fronts, facings, upper and undercollars, and hems are fused to interfacing. The entire jacket, including the sleeves, is usually fused when made from a lightweight fabric.

Through my speaking engagements and newspaper column, I have the opportunity to tour garment factories and talk with industry experts. This has taught me a great deal about interfacing.

About half of all ready-to-wear jackets have the quiet, soft support of Fusi-Knit. The interiors of 20 percent are fused with Textured Weft, which is slightly

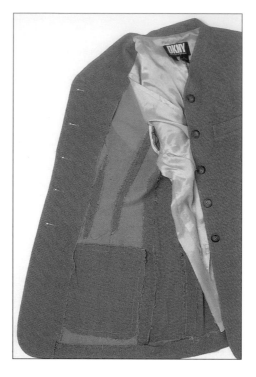

crisper than Fusi-Knit but still soft and pliable. Another 20 percent have a firmer, tailored effect because they are interfaced with Armo Weft or Suit Shape. The remaining ready-to-wear garments are fused with products that are difficult for home sewers to find.

Wouldn't it be great to be able to buy fusible organza interfacing? It would work so well for rayon crepes and silk dupioni! And what about fusible knitted wool for a tailored topcoat?

Here's a surprise. This rather expensive jacket, a top-of-the-line ready-to-wear item (see the photo above left), doesn't have any interfacing. It's a cardigan-style garment of medium-weight fabric, so the designer may have decided that interfacing would interfere with the casual drape. It's interesting that even such a relaxed garment has easing at the underarm. It's stayed with twill tape. A strip of fabric joins the underarm to the lining to prevent slippage.

Can you see the edge of the lightweight interfacing that's applied to the front facing (see the photo above right)? It's a sew-in that keeps the front edge crisp and supports the buttonholes. The heavier sew-in interfacing is an

TRICK of the TRADE

A CUT ABOVE

Look carefully at the interior of the designer jackets in the photographs on these pages. When I started taking the garments apart, I discovered that all of the darts were cut open before they were pressed. This eliminates bulk and helps the jacket shape to the body.

TRICK
of the TRADE
GRAINLINE DECISION

Before you cut interfacing on grain, consider the alternative. Fusi-Knit, for example, can be cut on the straight grain because it's so flexible. Woven fusible interfacings, on the other hand, drape better if they're cut on the bias.

upper-chest shield that extends around the entire underarm. A rectangle of fusible is applied to the pocket opening. Use the nonstretch direction of the interfacing, placed parallel to the pocket opening.

The jacket in the bottom photo on the facing page is closer to a traditional tailored style, so it needs more support. The entire front—but not the side front—is interfaced. There's also a small upper-chest shield and firm support at the hem.

The entire front of the herringbone wool jacket above is fused. The firm interfacing adds structure to the tailored style.

FUSIBLE INTERFACING PREPARATION

Fusibles straight off the bolt shrink when they're applied to fabric: The size of both the interfacing and the fashion fabric are reduced by the steam and heat of the iron. The effect may not be substantial, but in many cases it's sufficient to make an interfaced jacket front shorter. You'll notice the difference when you sew the fronts to the back at the side seams.

You can avoid this problem by preshrinking the interfacing in a basin of hot water. The collar shown below is smaller than the pattern because the interfacing wasn't preshrunk.

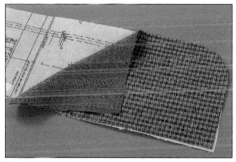

1 Soak the interfacing in a basin of hot water for 15 minutes.

2 Squeeze out the water and hang the interfacing over a shower rod to dry. Make sure that the yardage is flat and smooth, since you can't press out the wrinkles.

3 Apply the interfacing to the garment pieces with block fusing or by extending the garment piece. Instructions for both methods follow.

Block Fusing

Block fusing is the best way to obtain accurate garment shapes. However, it takes longer because you have to cut out the piece twice: once before it's fused and again afterward.

1 Pick out the pattern pieces that you plan to interface. Cut them from the fashion fabric and interfacing 1 in. (2.5cm) outside the cutting lines. Each piece ends up a little longer and wider than the corresponding pattern piece.

2 Fuse the interfacing to the wrong side of the corresponding garment pieces. Cut the exact pattern shape from each interfaced fabric shape.

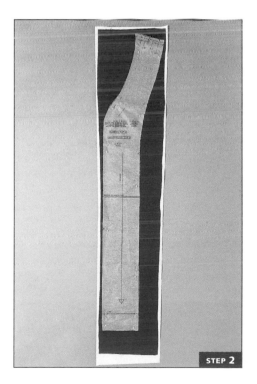

STEP 2

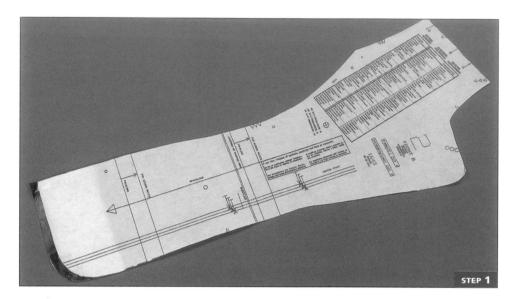

Garment Piece Extensions

In this alternative to block fusing, you lengthen the fabric and the interfacing shapes. This prevents the interfaced pieces from ending up shorter than the corresponding fashion-fabric pieces.

1 Pick out the pattern pieces you plan to interface. Tape a ½-in. (1.3cm) long pattern paper extension to the bottom of each of the selected pattern pieces. Lengthen the corresponding interfacing pattern pieces the same way.

2 Using the lengthened pattern pieces, cut the garment shapes from the fashion fabric and the interfacing. Fuse the interfacing to the wrong side of the fabric and construct the jacket.

3 In most instances, the fusing probably shortened the garment pieces by about ½ in. (1.3cm), so they're now exactly the correct length. If the fusing didn't shrink this much, cut off the extra fabric at the bottom of the fused pieces.

TRICK
of the TRADE

REDESIGNING A FRONT

If you'd like to create something unique from a favorite collarless jacket or vest pattern, redesigning the front edge is the way to go. As long as you keep the back neck the same and begin redesigning at the shoulder seam, virtually any shape is possible.

Place your jacket front on a piece of paper. Start your design work just beyond the shoulder seamline. Draw the new front on the paper, past the front edge of the pattern piece. Keep in mind that ⅝-in. (15mm) seam allowances will eat into the new design, so you need to slightly exaggerate the shape.

Trace the remaining front shape onto the pattern and cut your new front from the paper. Trim ⅝ in. (15mm) from the front edge of the paper so that you can

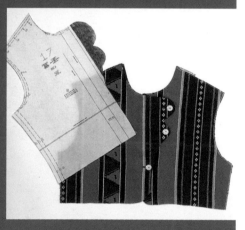

see the shape and position of the finished edge. Place the paper front on your body and refine your design. Once you're satisfied, use your new piece as the front and front facing pattern.

BUTTONHOLE PLACKET

This is the ultimate solution for people who have a buttonhole-making phobia or a sewing machine that makes less-than-perfect buttonholes. The button-hole placket is also ideal for making openings in velvet or when using very large buttons. I especially like this treatment for fabrics that have a loose weave or that ravel easily. It's also great for coats, jackets, or shirts, with or without a collar. However, the front edge must be straight rather than shaped.

Merely add a placket to the right front, with gaps in the seamline acting as vertical buttonholes. To close your garment, insert the buttons through the gaps. You end up with a clean, professional look without visible stitching. The finished buttonholes have more strength than the machine-stitched variety.

The following instructions explain how to adapt front pattern pieces with fold-back (cut-on) facings. You can easily adjust the steps for a pattern that has a sew-on facing.

1 This step is optional, but it may help you avoid a costly mistake. If your front pattern piece is "Cut 2," make two tracings so that you have separate left and right fronts.

2 If your right front pattern has a cut-on facing (it's part of the front pattern piece and is folded back to make the facing), cut it off along the foldline.

3 If your pattern has separate pattern pieces (one for the front and one for the facing), cut off the seam allowance on the long front edge of both pieces. The goal is to create a separate facing and eliminate any seam allowances on the joining edges of the front and facing.

4 Cut the left front from the fashion fabric. Because this pattern piece doesn't need buttonhole openings, it hasn't been altered.

5 Prepare the left front by folding back the cut-on facing and pressing along the foldline. For separate pieces, seam the left front and left front facing right sides together.

6 Cut all of the remaining pattern pieces from the fashion fabric. Interface them as desired.

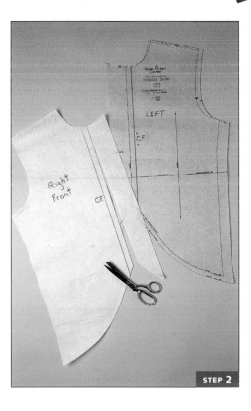

STEP 2

7 Cut a separate buttonhole placket from your fashion fabric. Make it 3⅛ in. (7.9cm) wide and the length of the garment front. The grainline runs along the length of this fabric strip. Interface the buttonhole placket.

[TIP] You can cut your buttonhole placket from a contrasting fabric for a snazzier effect.

8 On the buttonhole placket, mark the position of the first button 1 in. (2.5cm) from the neckline's raw fabric edge on the wrong side of the placket. This line indicates the beginning of the buttonhole opening. Extend the mark across the entire width of the placket.

9 Draw a second line under the first. This indicates the bottom of the buttonhole opening.

10 Measure and mark equally spaced buttonhole positions down the entire buttonhole placket. It's very important that all of the buttonhole openings are marked before you start any sewing.

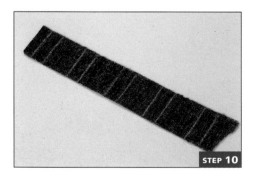

STEP 10

11 Pin the buttonhole placket to the right front with right sides together. Join the pieces by sewing between the markings for the buttonhole openings. Use ⅝-in. (15mm) seam allowances and reduce the stitch length for ½ in. (1.3cm) near the openings. The gaps between the stitching lines are the openings for the buttonholes.

12 Press the seam allowances open.

13 With right sides together, join the remaining vertical edge of the buttonhole placket to the front edge of the right front facing. As in the previous step, sew between the marks in order to leave openings for the buttonholes. Press the seam allowances open.

STEP 13

14 Imagine there's a vertical foldline in the center of the buttonhole placket. Fold the facing to the wrong side of the right front along the middle of the placket. Align the buttonhole openings.

STEP 14

15 With right sides together, seam the bottom of the placket together, then baste the facing and placket to the front along the neck so that it's easier to insert the collar.

16 Align the buttonholes by pinning along the seamline through all layers. Hand-sew the buttonhole openings together so that they work as a unit. Now stitch in the well of the seam between each buttonhole. Sewing by hand is more accurate on difficult fabrics.

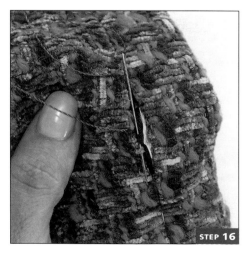

STEP 16

PROFESSIONAL PRINCESS SEAMS

When good fit is important, look for a jacket pattern with princess seams. This jacket was made from Vogue 7022. In the patternmaking process, the dart that's used to shape the front is shifted into the curved seamline—and then removed. To create bust shaping, the side front is cut longer than the front, then eased to fit. So when you sew a princess seam, you're faced with the task of smoothly joining the pieces.

That's not the end of the challenge, however, because the easing involves joining two opposite curves: The side front has an outer curve while the front has an inner curve. Here are some tips to help you make a great looking jacket with princess seams.

1 It's easier to join the front and side front if you clip the seam allowances on the front's inner curve before you sew the seam. Run a line of staystitching ½ in. (1.3cm) from the raw edge along the curved portion of the garment piece.

2 Make ⅜-in. to ½-in. (1cm to 1.3cm) deep snips into the seam allowance at 1-in. (2.5cm) intervals. With every snip, cut up to the staystitching 1/16 in. to ⅛ in. (1.6mm to 3mm). You've made enough snips when you can open the edge to a straight line.

STEP **2**

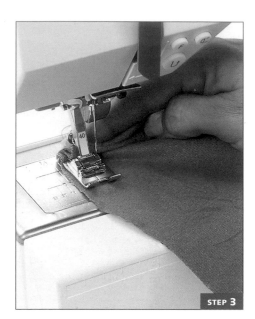

STEP 3

4 Lightly press the curve over a tailor's ham to eliminate a gathered look.

5 With the clipped front on top, start pinning it to the side front with right sides facing. Match the notches. If the side front's eased curve is too small, snip through one or more easestitches to release a bit of fabric.

6 Sew the pieces together at ⅝ in. (15mm) with the clipped front on top. Press the seam allowances toward the front and topstitch, if desired.

STEP 6

3 Since the pattern instructs you to ease, make the outer curve of the side front a bit shorter before joining the garment pieces. Sew close to the seamline at the curve on the side front only, pressing your finger against the back of the presser foot as you stitch to draw in some of the excess ease. You may need to lengthen the machine stitch on heavier fabrics.

TRICK
of the TRADE

MAKE A MATCH

Have you ever wondered why jacket fronts end up shorter than the back? Several factors can cause this. Since few sewers bother to pretreat their interfacing, it shrinks slightly as it's applied. This draws up the fashion fabric. To avoid this, preshrink the interfacing or cut the jacket-front interfacing on the bias.

Even with this precaution, some shrinkage still occurs. Compensate by cutting the front facing, fronts, and corresponding interfacing pieces ½ in. (1.3cm) longer than the pieces that won't be interfaced. Switch to a longer stitch length when it's time to join the front to the facing. A 2.5mm (10 spi) stitch, while perfectly suitable for side seams on other garments, shortens considerably when it has to travel through the multiple fabric layers. If a seam is piped, the additional thickness requires an almost-basting-length stitch.

NECKLINE SHAPING

A jacket neckline must *always* be stabilized with twill tape or Stay Tape. This simple measure prevents the neck from stretching while on a hanger and shapes the neckline so that it conforms to your body. No more gaposis! Your jacket will conform smoothly to the upper chest if you apply a strip of stabilizer at the neckline.

This is one of the first things you need to do to your garment pieces. In fact, it's best to cut the stabilizing strips to the neckline length before you take the pattern off the fabric. This saves time because you don't have to search for the pattern piece later, when you're ready to cut the stabilizer to fit. In an unstable fabric, a garment piece can start losing its shape as soon as the pattern piece is removed.

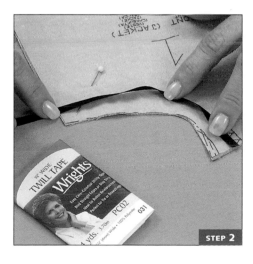

1 Cut the garment pieces from the fashion fabric. With the pattern pieces still pinned to the garment shapes, cut the stabilizers for the back and front neckline.

2 The exact length of each strip needs to be measured ½ in. (1.3cm) from the cutting lines on a V neck or along the roll line if the jacket has a lapel. Simply hand-walk the stabilizer along the pattern neckline. For stability, include stabilizer in seam allowances if the area is not interfaced.

[TIP] You can stabilize with straight-grain fusible or sew-in tape. The least expensive alternative is cutting a ¼-in. (6mm) wide strip of woven selvage from lining fabric. Make sure that it's preshrunk and tightly woven. Don't use nylon seam stabilizer because it stretches.

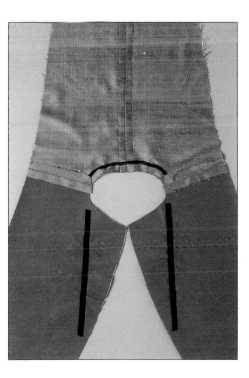

STEP 2

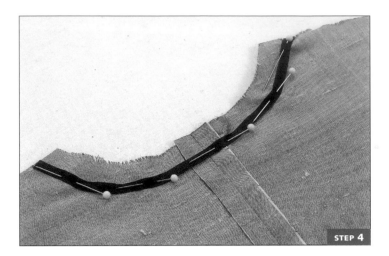

STEP 4

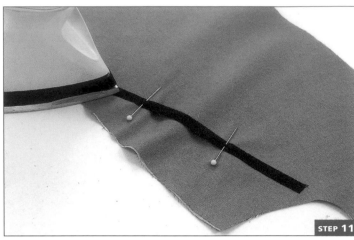

STEP 11

3 Apply the neck stabilizer to the wrong side of the back garment piece. The strip travels across the back neck from shoulder to shoulder so that the entire edge retains its shape.

4 Pin one end of the back neck stabilizer ½ in. (1.3cm) from the raw edge of the back neckline, at the shoulder. Continue pinning it around the neckline to the opposite shoulder.

5 You may need to fiddle a bit with unstable and loosely woven fabrics, easing the neckline to fit the stabilizer's length. For really stretchy fabric, try crowding and staystitching ½ in. (1.3cm) from the raw edge before applying the stabilizer if the neck seems stretched.

6 Straight-stitch (or fuse) the stabilizer to the back neckline as pinned.

7 Attaching the stabilizer to the front neckline is the fun part. Cut ¼ in. to ½ in. (6mm to 1.3cm) off each front neckline stabilizer. Work on one side at a time.

8 Pin the start of a stabilizer strip to the neckline at the shoulder seam, centered ½ in. (1.3cm) from the neckline's raw edge.

9 Pin the opposite end of same stabilizer strip to the bottom of the front neckline on a V neck or the bottom of the roll line on a lapel. Use this shorter stabilizer strip to draw in the neckline ¼ in. to ½ in. (6mm to 1.3cm).

[TIP] **The bigger your bust, the more shaping you need. Those of you who wear DD cups can cut the stabilizer strip shorter but must extend the easing section the whole length of the roll line.**

10 Now for the 3-D effect. Although the stabilizer is slightly shorter, the fabric will ease to fit during the fusing or sewing. Ease the front neck to fit the slightly shorter stabilizer. You need most of your shaping in the middle third of the neckline.

Pin the stabilizer to the upper and lower thirds of the neckline at a 1:1 ratio. The unpinned portion of the stabilizer is ¼ in. to ½ in. (6mm to 1.3cm) shorter than the corresponding area of the neckline.

11 Place the work on your sewing-machine bed with the garment neckline against the feed dogs. Sew through the center of the stabilizer, letting the feed dogs draw in the excess fabric in the middle third of the neckline.

12 It's tough easing ½ in. (1.3cm) in linen or other firm fabric. In this case, extend your easing section a bit farther than the middle third in both directions.

[TIP] **Fusible, straight-grain stabilizer is the fastest and easiest way to stabilize a neckline. Rather than easing the tape to fit the neckline at the machine, let the tape do the easing at the iron. Simply place the iron on the middle section of the neckline, and the fusible will draw in the fabric to fit. Make sure you use a straight-grain, not a bias, fusible stabilizer.**

ROLL-LINE MEMORY

Isn't it worth 15 minutes of your time to guarantee a neckline that hugs your body and always looks symmetrical? Whether you're making a shawl collar or a tailored collar, this technique makes the lapel work as a single unit at the roll line.

The lapel or collar always looks fresh and rolls out at the same location. In fact, it's the perfect solution for a facing that slides out of position on an unlined jacket. Months after making your jacket, the lapels will look as great as they did just after construction if you build in roll-line memory.

1 Join the front, side front, and back garment pieces. Don't insert the sleeves or add the lining yet.

2 If the pattern doesn't indicate a roll line, make your own. Slip into your partially assembled jacket, and pin the front shut. Adjust the collar or lapels to your liking. Place a row of pins along the roll line on both jacket fronts.

3 Remove the jacket. Finger-press (or hand-baste, depending on the product) a ¼-in. (6mm) wide strip of fusible webbing along the wrong side of the fabric at the roll line. Finish the collar or lapel.

4 During the construction process, the webbing melts, fusing together the upper and undercollars or lapels at the roll line. Glued together, the upper and undercollar of the finished garment act as one unit and roll beautifully.

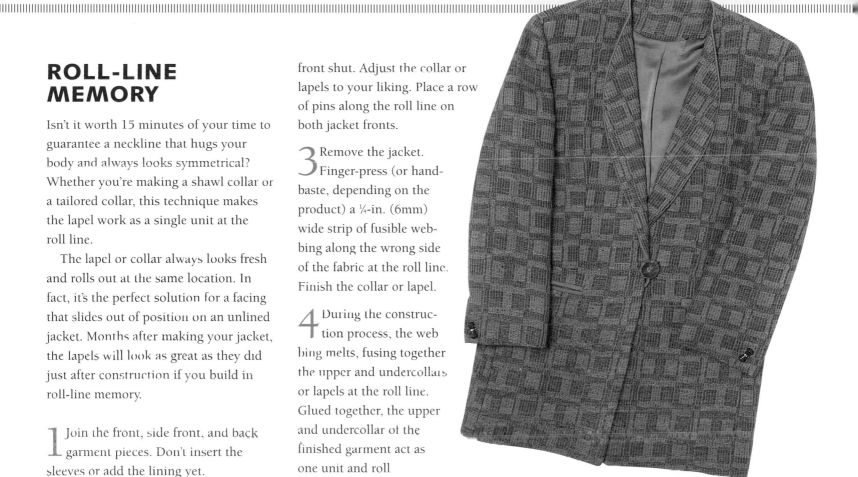

STEP 3

SHAPE-AND-STITCH LAPELS

Every season the fashion houses bring out some variation of the classic blazer with tailored lapels. Even if you don't normally wear blazers, mastering a lapel gives you options for both classic and trendy styles.

Lapel construction is one area of sewing where perfection and accuracy are required. This takes time. Sewing under deadline pressure seldom yields quality results. Set aside ample time when you won't be disturbed and follow my sewing procedure for a pattern with an upper and undercollar. The results are beautiful and well worth the effort. In this process, you never sew through more than two fabric layers at a time.

1 Cut out the garment pieces. Interface the fronts, facings, and both collar pieces. Staystitch the neckline and clip into the seam allowances at 1-in. (2.5cm) intervals.

[TIP] **Lapels need a crisper interfacing. I prefer Whisper Weft or Armo Weft for the facing and upper collar.**

2 On the jacket fronts, shape the roll line with twill tape. (See "Neckline Shaping" on p. 185.) Machine pad stitching can help the lapel roll correctly. No one will see the machine stitching on the finished jacket because it's on the underside of the lapel.

3 To do this, make diagonal lines of stitching parallel to the twill tape. Space the lines ¼ in. (6mm) apart, moving toward the point of the lapel. Stop ¾ in. (1.9cm) from the point so that the point won't be stretched. Shape the lapel over a tailor's ham.

[TIP] **Use the edge of your presser foot to space the lines of stitching.**

STEP 3

4 Pattern marking is very important. Sew tailor's tacks on the garment shapes for dots on the pattern pieces. This helps you accurately place stitching lines.

5 Join the back facings to the front facings at the shoulders. Sew the jacket fronts to the jacket backs at the shoulders. Press open the seam allowances.

6 Sew the front facings to the jacket fronts, stopping exactly at the large dot that indicates where the lapel joins the collar. Reduce the stitch length for ½ in. (1.3cm) as you get close to the dots.

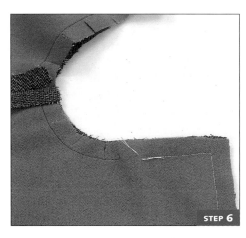
STEP 6

7 With right sides together and markings matched, pin the upper collar to the facing. Sew in one continuous seam between the large dots. Because both collars are interfaced, no stretching has occurred. Start and stop exactly at the dots—don't go one stitch farther.

8 Don't close the ends of the collar yet. (To help identify the upper collar in this photo, cream-colored interfacing is applied to the wrong side.)

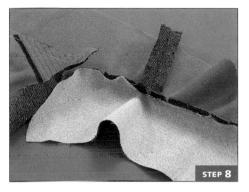

STEP 8

9 With right sides together and markings matched, pin the undercollar to the jacket. Sew them together between the large dots in one continuous seam. Once again, start and stop sewing exactly at the dots. The lapels now form a V.

10 To close the ends, match the upper and undercollars with rights sides together. Now match the jacket to the facing. Match the dots exactly.

TIP If the match points don't line up, fix the problem now. You probably sewed short of, or just past, one of the dots.

11 Sew from the outer edge of the facing and jacket to the center of the V and stop. Now sew from the outer edge of the upper and undercollar to the center of the V and stop.

TIP Because the seam isn't sewn continuously, there's a ⅛-in. (3mm) gap where the four seams join. This space helps you trim bulk, turn the work, and allows movement during later pressings.

12 Press open all of the seam allowances over a point presser and grade them to ¼ in. and ⅛ in. (3mm and 6mm). Make the seam allowances that are close to the outside of the facing wider from the roll line up.

13 On the jacket from the roll line down, reverse the process so that the wider seam allowance faces the outside of the jacket. The seam allowance that faces the top collar is the wider one.

14 Turn the collar and facing right side out. Hand-baste the edges for accurate pressing. Place the open seam allowances together at the neckline.

15 To anchor the seam allowances at the neckline, hand-sew them together invisibly, preferably with a stab stitch and doubled thread. Let the stitches sink into the well of the seam.

16 Pound the lapel flat with a tailor's clapper. Mold and steam-press the lapel and front facings on a tailor's ham. To eliminate stretching, pin the lapel to the ham, steam press, and let it dry completely before lifting.

STEP 9

STEP 10

FLANNEL UNDERLINING

Underlining is a wonderful way to give a jacket additional support, add depth, and hide hand stitching. It's a second layer of fabric cut exactly the same size as the garment piece. The matched shapes are basted together, then handled as a single layer during construction.

Batiste, lawn, and voile are excellent underlining fabrics for a soft look. Silk organza is the most common for a crisper effect. But my all-time favorite for jackets, coats, and some vests is lightweight flannel. It provides warmth without bulk and reduces wrinkling.

Underlining acts as a base for hand stitches, rendering all construction invisible. You can secure the hem allowances by stitching through just the underlining so that absolutely no hand stitches show on the exterior of the garment.

1 Preshrink the cotton flannel yardage in hot water and a hot dryer. This is mandatory because the fabric shrinks a lot.

2 Cut the garment pieces from your fashion fabric.

3 Fold up the jacket and sleeve hem allowances on the pattern pieces and cut the shapes from the cotton flannel. An underlined hem allowance is bulky, so cut the length of the underlining to end at the jacket's hemline.

4 Underlining isn't a substitute for interfacing. Cut a layer of fusible interfacing for the front, front facing, collar pieces, and upper third of the sleeve caps. Fuse the interfacing pieces to the smooth (nonfuzzy) side of the flannel pieces.

5 Place a garment (fashion-fabric) piece, wrong side up, on a table. Position the fuzzy side of the matching flannel piece against the wrong side of the garment piece. Hand-baste the layers together with a long stitch. It isn't necessary to baste along the hemline.

6 Assemble the garment, treating the underlining and the fashion fabric as one layer. The flannel underlining adds another layer of fabric, so lengthen your machine stitch to 3mm or 3.5mm (about 8 spi) to prevent the stitches from drawing up the seam.

7 Since the flannel takes up a bit of room, sew your side seams at ⅜ in. (1cm) to allow for the bulk. You may need to experiment with an underlined fabric scrap, lengthening your stitch to determine a suitable stitch length.

STEP 5

BAGGED PATCH POCKET

Try this easy way to make a lined patch pocket. It's fun because you sew around all of the edges, then pull the work right side out through a small opening.

What I like most about this method is that it's ideal for a great variety of patch pocket shapes. You don't have to worry about messing up the shape. This method also makes it easier to retain the

pocket's original shape. You won't end up with a mismatched set of pockets.

My technique for making a patch pocket isn't limited to a simple square or rectangular shape. Have some fun with your pockets: Notch the top, narrow the bottom width, or make the side lengths uneven or curved.

1 Cut the pocket from your fashion fabric. The finished pocket looks better when the lining doesn't peek out at the edges, so cut the lining on the bias to the same size and shape.

2 Trim 1/16 in. (1.6mm) off all of the edges of the lining piece. The feed dogs ease in the larger outer pocket to fit the lining. When relaxed, the seamline will roll slightly to the wrong side.

3 Interface the fabric pocket piece.

4 With the right sides together, pin the pocket and lining pieces together around all of the edges. Since the fabric pocket is slightly larger, stretch the edges of the lining so that the raw edges match. Pin from the lining side.

5 Sew down one side of the pocket using 5/8-in. (15mm) seam allowances and 1mm (18 spi) machine stitches. At the corner, pivot the work on an angle. Hand-turn the machine flywheel to make two diagonal stitches across the corner.

6 Pivot the work again to sew along the next side of the pocket. Sew around all of the edges in this manner. Don't worry about how you're going to turn the pocket right side out. Just sew entirely around your pocket.

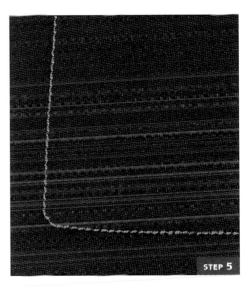

STEP 5

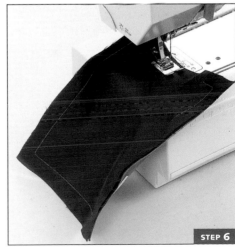

STEP 4

STEP 6

STEP 7

STEP 9

7 Before you turn the pocket right side out, press open the seam allowances by pressing the lining seam allowance against the pocket lining. Pressing in this manner makes it easier to get crisp edges and corners on the finished shape.

8 Trim all of the seam allowances to ¼ in. (6mm). Cut diagonally across the corner to within ⅛ in. (3mm) of the stitching.

9 Make a small, 2-in. (5cm) horizontal slash through the lining about 2 in. (5cm) from the bottom seamline. Pull the pocket right side out through the slash. Use a point turner on corners because scissor tips poke holes in the corners.

10 Place the pocket, fashion-fabric side up, on an ironing board. Press and pound the work flat with a tailor's clapper.

[TIP] If the seamline keeps rolling in, hand-baste the edges of the pocket before pressing them.

11 Flip the pocket, lining side up. Slip a small strip of fusible interfacing behind the slash so that it's inside the pocket layers. Make sure that the resin side is against the wrong side of the lining. Press.

[TIP] If you don't want to use fusible interfacing, simply close the slash with loose hand stitching.

12 Pin the pocket to the right side of the garment. Rather than bar-tacking the top of each side of the pocket, a small, straight-stitched triangle is strong and attractive.

Place the pocket and garment on the sewing-machine bed, with the needle ½ in. (1.3cm) down from the top at one side and ⅛ in. (3mm) from the side. Sew diagonally to the closest mark at the top of the pocket.

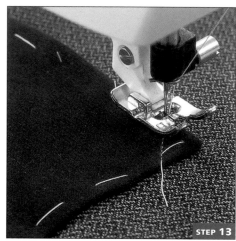

STEP 13

13 Pivot the work and sew across the top of the pocket for about ½ in. (1.3cm) from the mark to the closest side. Pivot and sew down the side, across the bottom, and back up the opposite side of the pocket. Repeat the stitched triangle at the opposite upper corner.

PAPER BAG POCKET

Looking for a pocket with pizzazz? This pocket is a two-in-one treatment with a great-looking flap and a second, hidden opening at the top. Don't worry about fussing with binding or lining the pocket; it's as simple as a basic patch pocket, but has a lot more punch.

The lining of the Paper Bag Pocket peeks out at the upper edge of the bag for a decorative effect. Use a contrasting fabric for the piping on the garment's upper collar and the pocket lining for maximum impact (see the photo below).

These instructions explain how to make a single pocket. You'll need two rectangles each of fashion fabric and lining to make a pocket for the left front and right front of your jacket. You'll make two little bags from the lining and fashion-fabric rectangles. A hole in the side of a lining seamline is used in a later step to turn the pocket right side out.

1 Cut two rectangles 8 in. wide and 20 in. long (20.3cm by 50.8cm), one from fashion fabric and another from a contrasting lining. (This pocket can be made any size. I cut larger pockets for men's jackets.)

2 Interface the wrong side of the fashion-fabric piece. Fold each piece in half with right sides together so that the dimensions are now 8 in. by 10 in. (20.3cm by 25.4cm).

3 With the fold at the bottom, sew both 10-in. (25.4cm) long sides of the fashion fabric rectangle using ½-in. (1.3cm) seam allowances.

4 Sew one 10-in. (25.4cm) long side of the folded lining rectangle. Sew the opposite long edge, leaving a 2-in. (5cm) long opening in the middle of the seamline.

5 Diagonally trim off the folded corners of the lining and fashion-fabric squares. Press all of the stitched seam allowances open by pressing one seam allowance back onto the pocket piece.

6 Turn the lining bag right side out. Slip it inside the garment fabric bag. Now the right sides of the lining and fashion fabric bags are together.

7 Pin the lining and fabric together at the top edge and sew them together with a ¼-in. (6mm) seam allowance. Sew with the most stable fabric (often the lining) on top.

8 Now it's time to use the hole that you left in your lining. Reach inside the pocket and pull the joined bags right side out through the opening in the lining seam.

9 Press and pound the edges flat. Machine- or hand-sew the opening in the lining closed. Push the pocket lining inside the garment fabric bag.

10 Press the pocket again, this time favoring the lining a bit so that it's visible for about ¼ in. (6mm) at the top of the pocket. Press down the top 2 in. (5cm) of the pocket to make a flap.

11 Position the pocket on the garment so that the fold for the pocket flap is at the pocket placement line on the garment. Pin the pocket, except for the flap, to the garment.

12 Topstitch the pocket to the garment, starting and ending at the fold for the pocket flap. Use 1.5mm (15 spi) stitches for the ½ in. (1.3cm) near the flap fold on both sides of the pocket.

13 Leave the top of the pocket free so that it can flop over to make a fun, loose flap.

STEP 12

SIDE-SEAM POCKET

A side seam is one of the easiest places to add a pocket to a coat or jacket. All you have to do is sew a teardrop-shaped pocket piece to each front and back at the side seam, then join the fronts to the backs. After you make a few seams, the entire process is finished!

Don't let the lack of a pocket pattern discourage you. You can make your own or borrow a pocket piece from another pattern in your stash—the shape is so common that you won't have difficulty finding one.

1 Find a teardrop-shaped pocket piece in an old pattern or, if you decide to draw your own, cut the shape approximately 6 in. wide and 8 in. long (15.2cm by 20.3cm).

[TIP] Think twice about making smaller pockets. The opening and bottom of the finished pocket bag must be wide enough for your hand.

2 Cut four pocket shapes from your fabric, placing the straight edge of the pocket on the straight of grain.

[TIP] Unless your fashion fabric is lightweight, use lining-weight fabric for the pocket pieces to reduce bulk. Lightweight flannel makes cozy pockets on a coat.

3 Decide where you want to place the pockets. Usually, the pocket opening is 4 in. (10.2cm) below the waist, but this is a matter of personal taste.

4 With right sides together, place one pocket piece against the front, with the widest part of the pocket at the bottom. Position the straight edge of the pocket even with the side seam allowance.

5 Although your garment pieces have ⅝-in. (15mm) seam allowances, attach the pockets with ¼-in. (6mm) seam allowances. This prevents the pocket bag from peeking out of the side seam in the finished garment.

6 Press the seam allowances toward the pocket.

[TIP] **Flatten the pocket by understitching the seam allowances to the pocket bag.**

7 Sew another pocket piece to the opposite front side seam. Make sure it's exactly the same distance below the waist as the attached pocket.

8 Now add pocket pieces to the back side seams, also sewn with right sides together and in corresponding locations.

9 Pin the front and back garment pieces together at the side seam with raw edges even. Start at the hem and sew up to the pocket. Continue the seamline 1½ in. (3.8cm) beyond the bottom of the pocket. Continuing the side seam into the top and bottom of the pocket keeps the pocket bag inside the finished garment.

10 Stop with the needle down, pivot the garment, and sew around the pinned pocket pieces. Stop at the side

seam, 1½ in. (3.8cm) from the top of the pocket. Pivot the work and sew the remainder of the side seam.

11 On the back seam allowance only, clip through the side seam allowances at the top and bottom of the pocket.

12 Press the side seam allowances open, the pocket bag seam allowances together, then press the pocket bag to the front of the garment. Because you clipped the back seam allowances, the pocket lies flat.

[TIP] **If you're using the in-seam pocket on a skirt or pants, include the top of the pocket in the waistband seam.**

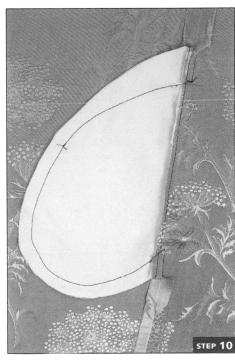

STEP 10

STEP 6

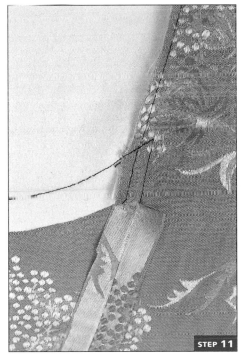

STEP 11

WELT POCKET WITH FLAP

A pocket opening hidden behind a flap is the most common treatment for coats and jackets. It's popular because the opening and flap lie flat against the body and can be set in straight across the jacket or at an angle.

I explain how to cut and sew the entire pocket in this feature. When it's time to make the flaps, try a creative approach. You can add multiple rows of piping, use a contrasting fabric, or make multiple rows of topstitching. This flap is inserted upside down in the lower portion of the opening.

Style Maker

COME ON, GET FLAPPY!

A pocket flap can be shaped or curved and is usually about 2 in. wide and 6 in. long (5cm by 15.2cm) on a woman's garment and 2 in. wide by 7 in. long (5cm by 17.8cm) on a man's garment. It's a good idea to keep to these dimensions for a functional pocket, but you can play around with the size for a decorative effect. At any size, you can reshape the loose edge with scallops or make the sides uneven in length for an asymmetrical look.

1 Cut a 2-in. (5cm) wide strip of interfacing that's 2 in. (5cm) longer than the pocket opening. This strip needs to be cut on the straight grain for maximum stability, and in the direction with the least stretch to prevent the pocket opening from drooping.

2 Fuse the strip to the wrong side of the jacket front at the pocket placement. You need to do this even if the jacket front is already interfaced.

3 Machine-baste the pocket placement using contrasting thread visible from the right and wrong sides of the garment.

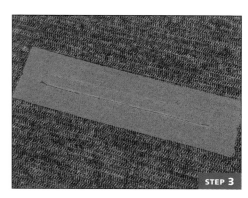

STEP 3

4 Cut the fashion-fabric pocket flap on the straight grain. Cut a piece of interfacing the same size as the flap. (The interfacing is always cut on the straight grain to prevent the flap from stretching during the insertion.) Interface the entire wrong side of the flap.

TIP Cut the flap on the bias if your fashion fabric is a plaid or stripe. This prevents matching problems and creates an interesting effect. The interfacing is still cut on the straight grain.

5 Fold the flap in half lengthwise. Make ⅛-in. (3mm) deep clips into the edge of the fabric at both ends of the fold.

6 Trim ⅛ in. (3mm) off the edges on one side of the fold. Place a pin on the untrimmed side so that you know it's the outside of the flap.

7 Fold the flap in half with right sides together and raw edges matching at both short ends. Sew the ends using ½-in. (1.3cm) seam allowances. Because the underside of the flap is smaller, the flap will bow when the ends are sewn.

STEP 7

8 Diagonally trim off the corners to eliminate bulk. Trim the seam allowances to ¼ in. (6mm) and press them open.

9 Turn the flap right side out and place it on your ironing board with the outside (the side with the pin in it) facing up. Remove the pin.

10 Cover the flap with a press cloth, and press and pound it flat with a tailor's clapper.

TIP To ensure that the pocket flaps are correctly shaped, hand-baste along the seamed edges before pressing.

11 With right sides together, place the raw edges of the flap at the placement line on the jacket front. The bulk of the flap goes above or below the placement line, depending on how you want your hand to enter the pocket.

12 With the flap below the placement line, your hand will enter from the top. If the flap turns down on the finished garment, so that you have to lift the flap to enter the pocket, position the bulk of the flap above the placement line.

13 Hand-baste the flap ¾ in. (1.9cm) away from the placement line.

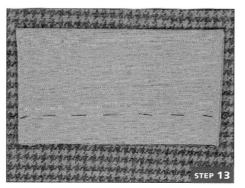
STEP 13

14 One rectangle of lining makes the entire pocket bag. Cut an 8-in.-wide by 12-in.-long (20.3cm by 30.5cm) piece of lining. Center the lining on top of the flap with the width going across the flap. Pin the edges of the lining to the jacket to keep them flat.

STEP 14

15 Turn the jacket front so that the wrong side is facing you. Set your machine for a 2mm (12 spi) stitch length.

16 Straight-stitch through the jacket, flap, and lining ¼ in. (6mm) away from the placement line on the same side that has the basting for the flap. Start and stop sewing exactly at the ends of the placement line. Don't backstitch.

TIP Don't stitch beyond the flap.

STEP 16

STEP 17

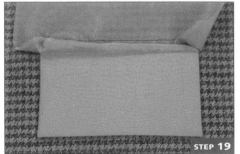
STEP 19

22 Place the jacket on a flat surface. Fold the upper half of the lining down to the lower half and pin them together around the edges.

23 Trim the bottom raw edges to match. Also trim the bottom edges if the lining hangs below the top of the hem allowance.

17 On the opposite side of the placement line, through the garment and the pocket lining only, sew a line of parallel stitching ¼ in. (6mm) away from the placement line.

To ensure that your pocket flap totally covers your pocket opening, start and end the stitching ¼ in. (6mm) short of the previous line of stitching.

18 Slash through the jacket and lining fabric between the two rows of stitching. About ½ in. (1.3cm) from each end, snip diagonally into the corners. Don't cut into the flap.

19 Push the lining through the slash to the wrong side of the jacket and leave the flap on the right side, over the opening. Make sure the lining doesn't show at the pocket opening from the right side of the garment. Pull both layers of the lining toward the hem.

20 Roll the jacket away from one end of the pocket to expose the cut triangles at the pocket opening.

21 Switch to a zipper foot so that you can sew close to the base of the triangles, attaching the triangles to the side of the pocket lining. The triangles are at a slight angle because one of the stitching lines is shorter.

24 Sew around the sides, anchoring the triangles to the lining and bottom of the lining to make the pocket bag. Don't sew through the jacket.

[TIP] Clip as close as possible to the stitching. If you don't go far enough, the finished pocket won't lie flat.

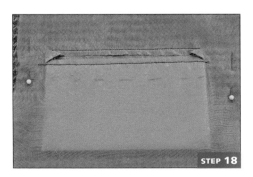
STEP 18

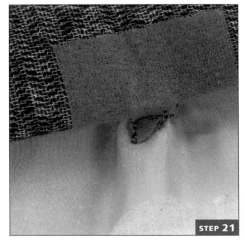
STEP 21

STEP 24

[TIP] Sew rounded corners at the bottom of the pocket so that lint doesn't collect in the corners of the finished pocket bag.

25 Press and pound the flap flat. If the flap extends up with the hand entering from the top of the flap, hand-sew the sides to the jacket. Sew from the wrong side of the jacket, using a cross-stitch and reinforcing the thread with beeswax for an easy, long-lasting attachment.

DECORATIVE PIPING FOR A WELT POCKET

Decorative piping can be just the right touch for a welt pocket. It's a particularly nice touch when other parts of the garment—the neckline or collar, for example—are also treated with piping. This jacket was made from Vogue 7022.

Unfortunately, there's a roadblock with this technique. Decorative piping often has a narrow lip that makes it difficult to attach to the pocket. I've solved this problem by sewing the piping to a 1 in. (2.5cm) wide bias strip of fabric before I start the welt pocket. Now I can proceed with a traditional welt pocket insertion, substituting lengths of decorative piping for the welts.

1 Cut a piece of decorative piping 1 in. (2.5cm) longer than the desired pocket opening. A standard pocket opening is 6 in. (15.2cm) in a woman's jacket and 7 in. (17.8cm) in a man's jacket.

2 Make a bias-cut extension for the piping with a 1-in. (2.5cm) wide strip of lightweight fabric that's color-matched with the decorative piping. Cut the extension to the same length as the piece of decorative piping.

3 Place the piping lengthwise down the middle of the fabric strip. Using a zipper foot, sew the piping to the strip. Use a straight stitch and sew as close as possible to the piping. Don't worry about the stitching on the piping, since it's hidden in subsequent steps.

4 Fold the bias strip in half lengthwise with the wrong sides together. Press it without flattening the piping.

5 Wrap a string around the piping to measure its circumference. Half of the circumference plus ⅛ in. (3mm) is the amount of room this side of the piping takes up in the pocket opening.

[TIP] Remember that you need two piping strips for each pocket. The decorative strips take up the space in the pocket opening.

6 The folded fabric strip may be too wide. Measure the

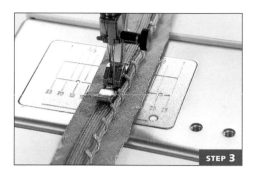

STEP 3

distance from the raw edge to the stitching line that joins it to the piping. This should equal half of the piping circumference plus ⅛in. (3mm).

7 Cut out the jacket front. Apply interfacing to the wrong side. At the pocket placement line, add another interfacing strip, 2 in. (5cm) wide and 2 in. (5cm) longer than the pocket opening. The nonstretch direction of the interfacing must be parallel to the opening. This prevents the pocket from gaping open later.

8 As with any welt pocket technique, it's a good idea to mark the exact position of the center of the pocket opening with basting in a contrasting-color thread. Mark the ends of the opening with 3-in. (7.6cm) long basting lines so that you can start and stop stitching in exactly the right location.

STEP 8

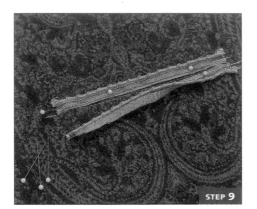
STEP 9

9 Place the clean side of the piping strip on the right side of the front at the pocket opening. Butt together the raw edges of the strips at the center of the pocket opening.

10 The seamlines that joined the piping to the fabric strips are just inside the top and bottom of the pocket opening. Let the ends of the strips extend ½ in. (1.3cm) past the left and right ends of the pocket opening.

11 Sew the piping in position using a zipper foot. Sew as close as possible to the piping using 1mm (18 spi) stitches.

12 Attach a lining by sewing a second line of stitching through the welts and the lining. Slash through the opening and turn the pieces to the wrong side of the fabric.

13 Complete the pocket by closing up the pocket bag and anchoring the loose ends of the piping in one stitching.

StyleMaker

ZIP TIP

Why not insert a zipper in your double-welt pocket? This treatment is very popular in ready-to-wear these days, and it's so easy to do. Pat Moyes explains the procedure in detail in her book *Just Pockets* (The Taunton Press, 1997), but here's a summary.

Make your welt pocket, but don't sew up the sides and bottom of the pocket bag on the wrong side of the garment. Baste the closed zipper to the underside of the welts with the slider on the side of the opening closest to center front. Sew the zipper to the welt by stitching in the well of the seamline from the outside of the garment. Now sew together the edges of the pocket bag.

FRONTS-ONLY HALF-LINING

Unlined blouses and jackets are easy to make, but they have a few drawbacks. With a sheer or white blouse, you reveal the edge of the facing and your undergarments. An unlined jacket lacks a nice finish on the inside and exposes construction details such as the inner workings and the edges of the facings.

The simplest way to hide details is to use a half-lining that covers only the garment fronts. This improves the interior without you having to add a complete lining. Cut an extra set of fronts from your fashion fabric or coordinating yardage. This gives the side seams a nice finish at the same time.

To prepare for this technique, buy a little extra fabric if you're using narrow yardage. An extra blouse or jacket length is sufficient. If your fabric is wide, you may not need any extra yardage at all. Assembly isn't complicated, although it doesn't follow the standard construction process for a blouse or jacket.

STEP 3

1 Cut out all of your garment pieces except the front facings. Now cut out an extra set of fronts from either your fashion fabric or a coordinating material. You now have four fronts rather than two. Interface one set of fronts (the front linings) and set them aside.

2 Stabilize the neck seamline of the back piece with staystitching and a length of narrow twill tape.

3 I know it seems out of order, but hem the back piece now. Fold up the hem allowance, use a Hong Kong finish on the raw edge, and hand-stitch the entire hem allowance in position. (See "West Coast Hong Kong Finish" on p. 86.)

4 Join the front and back at the shoulder seams. Baste the side seams with contrasting thread and try on the garment. When you're satisfied with the fit, permanently sew the side seams. Press all of the seam allowances toward the front. Make the collar and baste it to the garment.

5 Apply a Hong Kong finish to the bottom raw edge of the back facing.

6 With right sides together, sew the interfaced back facing to the second set of fronts (the lining pieces) at the shoulders. Press the seam allowances toward the front lining.

7 Place the front lining and back facing combination against the garment with the right sides together and the collar sandwiched inside.

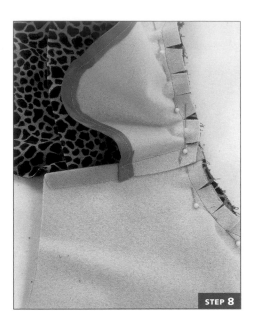

STEP 8

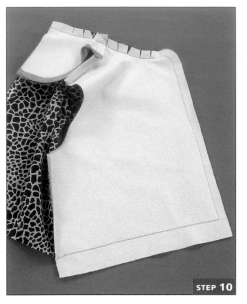

STEP 10

13 Sew another row of stitches on top of the original side seamline to join the lining front to the front and back. Now all of the raw edges are enclosed.

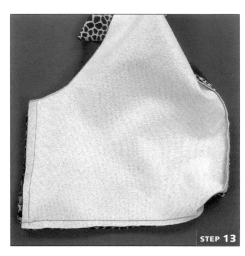

STEP 13

8 With the raw edges even, pin through all of the layers along the neck and front edge. Insert the pins from the lining side so that the interfacing makes it more stable.

9 Continue pinning the lining to the garment along the front and the hem. Because the back is already hemmed, your sewing line at the lower front edge is aligned with the hem crease on the back.

10 Insert the work under the presser foot, at one of the side seams. Start sewing the front and lining together along the bottom, up the front, around the neck, and continuing to the remaining side seam.

11 Press the seam allowances open. Trim and grade them. Turn the garment right side out.

[TIP] If you don't have a point presser, press both seam allowances to the fashion-fabric side of the corner, trim and grade, then turn the work right side out.

12 Bring the right side of the lining around so that the back is sandwiched between the front and the front lining. At the side seam, align the raw edges of the lining, front, and back.

[TIP] If the previous step is hard to visualize, you can also turn under the front seam allowance at the side seam on the lining and hand-stitch it to the side seam.

14 Turn the garment right side out at the shoulder. Repeat on the remaining side. Hand-sew the linings to the shoulder seams.

15 Insert the sleeves into the garment armholes, treating the lining and double front as a single layer. Cover the raw seam allowances with double-fold bias tape or a Hong Kong finish.

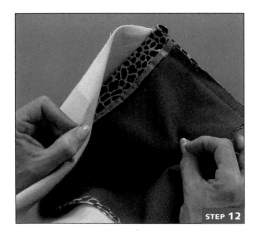

STEP 12

ATTACHING A FRONT FACING

If the front edges of your jacket flip out, the facing is fighting for the limelight. You can prevent this by joining the facing to the front edge of the jacket vertically—without stitching around the corner and into the hem.

I love using interesting fabrics for the facings on my garments. They're a fun surprise when the jacket is opened. I used a scarf to face this jacket. Notice that the very bottom of the inside edge of the facing isn't attached to the lining. This inch or so of raw fabric is bound with a Hong Kong finish. (See "Hong Kong Facing" on p. 204.)

Here's a construction method that keeps the fronts from flipping out.

1 Join the jacket fronts and back at the shoulders. Seam together the facing pieces at the shoulders.

2 With right sides together, pin the facing to the jacket up the front, around the back neck, and down the opposite front. The facing might be a little longer if you eased the neckline to prevent gaposis on a V-neckline jacket. (See "Neckline Shaping" on p. 185.) In this case, place the pins on the jacket side. When you sew, the feed dogs draw in the longer facing to fit.

3 Place the pinned pieces on the sewing-machine bed with the garment on top. Start stitching at the bottom of the facing—at the vertical seam, not along the horizontal edge (the hem).

4 Sew up the front of the facing, around the back neck, and down the remaining front. Slightly increase your stitch length to accommodate the extra layers and prevent the pieces from drawing up at the seamline.

5 Stop the seam at the bottom of the front. Don't sew the facing to the jacket front at the hem. Leave this unattached so that you can open it and apply stitching to prevent the facing from rolling out on the finished jacket.

6 Press the seam allowances open. Grade the facing seam allowance to ⅛ in. (3mm) and the garment seam allowance to ¼ in. (6mm).

7 Trim all of the seam allowances in the hem area to ¼ in. (6mm). Easestitch ¼ in. (6mm) from the raw edge around the entire jacket hem to draw in any fullness.

8 Press the hem allowance to the interior of the jacket. Marry the facing and the front near the seamline by sewing in the well for the depth of the hem allowance. This ensures that the finished jacket has a sharp lower corner.

9 Clip through the facing/front seam allowance immediately above the top of the hem allowance. Press the seam allowances above the hem allowance toward the facing.

10 Open out the facings and understitch the seam allowances to the facing. Press and pound the neckline flat.

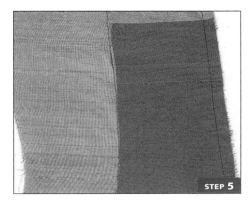

STEP 5

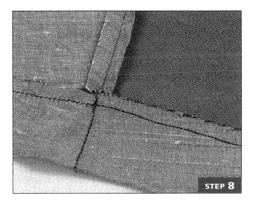

STEP 8

HONG KONG FACING

One of the more perplexing aspects of lining a jacket is figuring out what to do at the very bottom of the front facings. The last few inches aren't joined to the lining because the take-up tuck ends short of the bottom of the facing.

Your options are to serge the edge, leave the edge raw, or fold under the raw edge of the facing and hand-stitch it to the hem allowance. This gets bulky, so I prefer to apply a strip of lining for a beautiful, bulk-free solution. The Hong Kong technique is the perfect method.

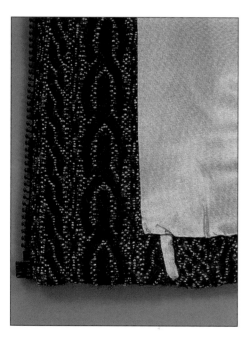

1 Attach the facing to the jacket. Turn up the jacket hem allowance and catchstitch it in place ¼ in. below the top of the hem edge.

2 Cut a 1½-in. (3.8cm) wide strip of lining fabric on the crossgrain. Make it 1 in. (2.5cm) longer than the area it needs to cover. This is usually 3 in. (7.6cm).

3 With right sides together, place the lining strip at the bottom of the facing. Let 1 in. (2.5cm) of the strip extend beyond the bottom of the facing.

4 Position the other end above the lowest point where the lining will be attached to the facing. Sew the lining strip to the facing with a ¼-in. (6mm) seam allowance.

5 Wrap the strip's extension around the bottom of the hemline. This finishes the bottom.

6 Wrap the loose, lengthwise raw edge of the lining strip to the wrong side of the facing, enclosing the seam allowances. Sew it in place by stitching in the well of the seam.

STEP 4

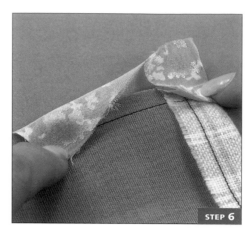

STEP 6

7 Fold the facing to the wrong side of the garment. Hand-tack the Hong Kong finish to the hem allowance.

8 Loosely catchstitch the facing to the jacket hem about ½ in. (1.3cm) above the hem edge so that the stitches are nearly invisible. The loose stitching allows some movement at the bottom front edge for pressing and ensures that the jacket front hangs smoothly.

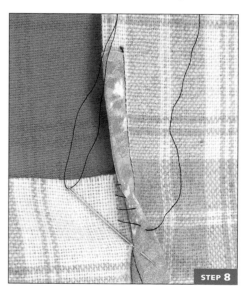

STEP 8

UPPER-COLLAR CONTOURING

You don't have to look like Arnold Schwarzenegger to have upper-back fit problems near the neck. Just a bit of muscle, perhaps from years of carrying babies, groceries, or a briefcase, is enough to make your jacket or coat collar ride too high on the neck—above the neckline seam—where the circumference is smaller.

There's no need to pull out the pattern paper and alteration tools for a muscular neck adjustment. Just reshape the upper collar when you cut out the collar pieces from the fabric. No alterations are necessary for the undercollar and the garment neckline. This technique isn't suitable if the upper collar is cut from a plaid or horizontal-striped fabric.

STEP 1

1 Lay out your fabric and pattern pieces. Place the upper-collar pattern on the fabric with the "Cut on fold" line on the fabric fold. At center back, pivot the lower edge ⅛ in. (3mm) away from the fabric fold. The upper edge at center back doesn't move.

2 Chalk-mark ¼ in. (6mm) below the lower neckline edge at center back on the upper collar. Using a French curve or hip curve, draw a gentle arc from the fabric fold, through the chalk mark, and tapering to the original

cutting line at the shoulder placement dot for the upper collar.

3 Because the upper collar is cut out slightly off grain, the extra give in the bias-cut edge helps the upper collar mold nicely to the rounded lower neck area.

4 Cut the undercollar on the bias so that it molds to fit the longer length of the upper collar. No adjustments are needed at the garment neck edge, which is staystitched before the collar is added.

TRICK of the TRADE

PRESSING ISSUE

Using a clapper when pressing open seam allowances from the wrong side of the garment leaves an imprint on the right side of the garment. To avoid this, press the seam allowances, wrong side up, over a rounded seam stick or a seam roll. A bead of water along the wrong side of the seam joint helps the seam allowances open up. Press with a dry iron. Don't move the fabric from the pressing surface until it's completely dry.

Flip the garment right side up on the seam roll. Spread a press cloth on top and lightly spray it with water. Press the seam allowance a second time, with a lighter touch, also with a dry iron. Again, let the fabric dry before removing it from the pressing surface. Otherwise, the pressed surface becomes puffy rather than flat.

If you've inadvertently created a shine on the fabric surface, you can remove it from natural fabrics but not from synthetics. The shine on synthetic fabric is caused by the fabric melting and is thus permanent. On a natural fiber such as wool, dampen the fabric surface and hold a dry iron ½ in. (1.3cm) above the surface to raise the fibers. Brush lightly with a soft brush.

UNDERARM SHAPING

Manufacturers of ready-to-wear have a neat trick to give a jacket extra shaping. A bit of ease is pulled in at the underarm after the sleeve is inserted. This reduces the armhole circumference just a bit, bringing it closer to your body. Now the jacket has a shapelier look and you have a wider range of movement when you wear it.

The idea is to bring the lower third of the armhole, between the front and back notches, closer to your body. A good

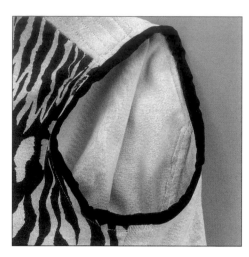

time to do this shaping is after the sleeve has been set in the armhole. Sleeves for coats and jackets are set in the round.

1 Adjust your machine to a 3mm or 3.5mm (about 8 spi) stitch length. Insert the lower armhole under the presser foot with the armhole notch directly under the needle and the bottom of the armhole closest to you. Lower the needle so that it's ½ in. (1.3cm) from the raw fabric edge.

2 Crowding is the easiest way to ease fabric. This method is used all the time by machine operators working on more expensive ready-to-wear.

Place your left index finger on top of the fabric, against the back of the presser foot. Sew the underarm from the front notch to the back notch. Continue holding your finger behind the presser foot so that fabric builds up as it's stitched.

3 When there's too much bulk, lift your finger to release the fabric and reposition it behind the presser foot.

STEP 4

4 Remove the armhole from the machine without pulling on the easing stitches. Check the new length against the pattern pieces from the front to the back notches. Your goal is to reduce the distance on the garment piece by ¼ in. to ½ in. (6mm to 1.3cm).

TRICK
of the TRADE
TOO MUCH CAP EASE

No matter how skilled you are at sewing, it's difficult to create a professional-looking garment if the sleeve cap is too big for the armhole. You end up with obvious puckers along the seamline.

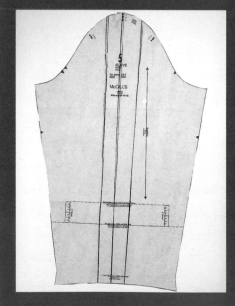

Unfortunately, many home-sewing patterns are drafted with too much ease in the cap. Most measure 1½ in. to 2 in. (3.8cm to 5cm) larger around the cap, from one underarm seam to the other, compared with the garment armhole. Ready-to-wear manufacturers use only ¾ in. (1.9cm) of ease in a typical jacket sleeve, or 1¼ in. (3.2cm) for a raised cap. I like to reduce excess ease by altering the sleeve pattern before cutting the garment pieces from the fashion fabric.

Do this by drawing three vertical lines from the sleeve cap to the hem, leaving a ¼-in. (6mm) hinge at the bottom sleeve edge. Cut the sleeve apart and overlap the pieces. To reduce the sleeve ease by ¾ in. (1.9cm), each cut overlaps by ⅛ in. (3mm), reducing the sleeve ease by ¼ in. (6mm) at each cut, for a total of ¾ in. (1.9cm) of reduced ease.

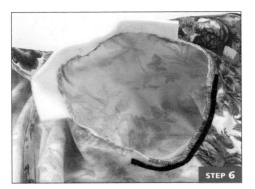

STEP 6

5 Snip through several stitches to release if you've eased too much, or make another line of easing to draw in more.

6 Stabilize the underarm by sewing a piece of twill tape on top of your easestitching. Place the stitching and tape directly on top of the easing, with the center of the tape ½ in. (1.3cm) from the raw edge.

7 Press over a tailor's ham to remove the puckers. Press the underarm flat with an up-and-down motion. Ease the remaining underarm in the same manner.

[TIP] **Reduce the width of the underarm seam allowances between the front and back notches to ¼ in. (6mm) to make your coat more comfortable.**

TRICK
of the TRADE

SLEEVE SUPPORT

Interfacing a sleeve cap improves its appearance, making it crisp enough to prevent the upper portion from collapsing. Place the top of the sleeve pattern on the crossgrain or bias of a piece of lightweight fusible interfacing. Cut the shape of the sleeve cap above the notches. Remove the pattern piece. Pink the lower edge of the interfacing shape to make the edge undetectable from the right side of the garment. Apply the interfacing to the wrong side of the sleeve before easing the cap.

SMOOTH SLEEVE CAPS IN DIFFICULT FABRIC

Some fabrics simply don't ease well, so getting a smooth, professional-looking sleeve cap is difficult. Whenever I encounter this situation, I stretch a strip of bias-cut hair canvas, mohair, or interfacing from the inside of an old tie while sewing it to the cap. The ease is pulled in when the strip returns to a relaxed state.

You'll be amazed at the amount of ease that can be drawn in with this method. The eased area won't have a single pucker. As an added bonus, you're building a sleeve head at the same time.

1 Measure the sleeve pattern piece from notch to notch over the sleeve cap. Cut a 2-in. (5cm) wide bias strip of hair canvas, mohair, or lamb's wool to this length.

2 For the best results, the sleeve cap must be eased in two steps. First, place the bias strip against the wrong side of the sleeve cap, on the wrong side of the sleeve. Line up the cut edge of the bias strip with the cut edge of the sleeve cap.

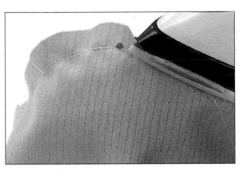

STEP 4

3 Start sewing the middle of the strip to the sleeve from the shoulder placement dot and down one side to the notch. Use a ½-in. (1.3cm) seam allowance.

4 Stretch the strip as you sew, working about 1 in. (2.5cm) ahead of the needle. Don't stretch the sleeve cap, just the strip.

5 Let the bias strip relax. As it returns to its unstretched state, it draws in one side of the sleeve cap.

6 Repeat Steps 2 through 5 for the remaining half of the cap, working from the top of the sleeve to the notch. Don't try to sew the entire cap in one continuous line of stitching. The ease must be worked from the top of the sleeve cap to the notch.

[TIP] **After completing the easing, insert the sleeve into the armhole. Leave the strip in the sleeve for extra lift at the cap.**

FEARLESS SLEEVE VENTS

A beautiful sleeve vent says "quality," especially when it's finished with real buttonholes. This coat was made from Burda 3647. I know more than a few women who are intimidated by sleeve vents on jackets, so I worked out a method that eases even the timid sewer through the entire process.

Start by measuring your arm to make sure that the sleeve pattern piece is the correct length. Don't cut out the vented sleeve from the fashion fabric yet. Since you can't change vented sleeves after constructing the vent, you're doomed to failure unless the length is adjusted before the sleeve is cut out. Once the sleeve pattern is adjusted, you can make the vent and insert the sleeve.

1 Measure your bent arm from the shoulder joint to just below the wrist bone. This is the finished length of your sleeve. Compare this to a pattern measurement from the seamline at the top of the cap to the hemline crease. The difference between these measurements determines how much you'll need to alter the sleeve length.

2 Fold up the hemline on the sleeve pattern. Fold the sleeve vent out of the way. Cut the pieces for one sleeve from scrap fabric. Join the seams and baste the sleeve into the jacket armhole.

3 Look at the sleeve in the mirror with your arm bent and then with it extended. A proper-fitting sleeve falls 1 in. (2.5cm) below the wrist bone when the arm is straight and relaxed. This may seem long, but it's the normal length for sleeves these days.

4 Still wearing the jacket, bend your elbow to determine whether the sleeve's elbow ease matches the shape of your bent arm. Now you know whether to adjust the sleeve above or below the elbow.

5 Adjust the sleeve patterns as needed and cut the sleeves from your fashion fabric. If the pattern vent has an angled corner for a miter, square it off when cutting out the pattern piece. The added thickness of the miter makes it hard to make buttonholes.

6 Interface the wrong side of the sleeve hem and the vent with fusible interfacing. If the jacket is unlined, serge or apply a Hong Kong finish to the bottom edge of the sleeve. If the jacket is lined, this step is unnecessary since the raw edges will be covered.

7 For the subsequent steps, construct one sleeve and repeat the process for the remaining sleeve.

STEP 8

8 With right sides together, join the under- and upper sleeves at the back seamline. Match the notches and stop sewing at the dot (transferred from the pattern) that indicates the beginning of the vent opening. It's easier to work flat, so don't stitch the other seam yet.

9 Fold the upper-sleeve hem allowance to the right side. Push the under-sleeve out of the way and sew the hem allowance on the end only to the upper sleeve. Press open the seam allowances and trim the hem to ¼ in. (6mm).

10 Turn the sleeve right side out and pound the vent and corner flat with a tailor's clapper. Now add the buttonholes.

11 The vent on the undersleeve still needs finishing. You could complete it in the same manner as the top vent by folding up the hem allowance and seaming it to the unstitched portion of the undersleeve, but I find this too bulky. It's also unnecessary because the undervent isn't as visible.

12 Instead, fold the hem allowance to the wrong side and join the raw edges with serging or a Hong Kong finish. Overlap the top vent and catch-stitch the undersleeve vent in place.

STEP 9

STEP 12

13 For a lined jacket, cut the lining to the finished sleeve length without a sleeve vent. (Since a sleeve vent is merely decorative and isn't buttoned or unbuttoned, the sleeve lining doesn't need one.) Simply fold the vents out of the way if your pattern doesn't have a separate sleeve lining pattern piece.

14 Join the lining pieces by sewing the lengthwise seams. Insert the lining into your jacket. Sew the bottom of the sleeve lining to the sleeve hem by hand, hiding the raw edges of the sleeve and the sleeve lining. Sew on buttons to complete the look.

STEP 14

TURNED-BACK CUFF

Ready-to-wear jackets often include an eye-catching turned-back cuff on the sleeves. This is a fabulous way to create a casual look for a one- or two-piece sleeve. The cuff is seamed to the bottom of the sleeve, creating an opportunity for creativity.

A turned-back sleeve cuff takes very little yardage, yet the finished effect is dynamic. If a fabric is very expensive and you can't justify the cost, why not buy a small piece for the cuffs? Check out your scraps for some interesting combinations, or buy an additional ½ yd. (0.5m) of coordinating fabric with this treatment in mind.

Whatever your choice, this detail doesn't need any pattern alterations. Simply cut off all but ⅝ in. (15mm) of the hem allowance, sew on the cuff, and you're in business. The following instructions explain how to make a single cuff. Repeat all of the steps for the second cuff.

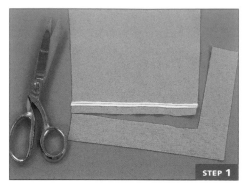
STEP 1

1 Cut the sleeve from your fashion fabric. Cut off the bottom of the sleeve just past the hemline, leaving only enough fabric below the hemline for a ⅝-in. (15mm) seam allowance. Later, the new cuff is seamed to the sleeve's hemline.

[TIP] **The circumference of the bottom of the sleeve has to remain constant. This means that you need to stabilize the raw edge of loosely woven or stretchy fabrics. On unstable fabric, machine-sew twill tape ¼ in. (6mm) to the wrong side of the sleeve ½ in. (1.3cm) from the lower raw edge.**

2 The cuff is attached in the round, so seam the sleeve and press the seam allowances open.

3 Make a pattern for your cuff by tracing the bottom 3½ in. (8.9cm) of the sleeve. If you're using a two-piece sleeve pattern, overlap the pieces at the back seamline and trace the shape.

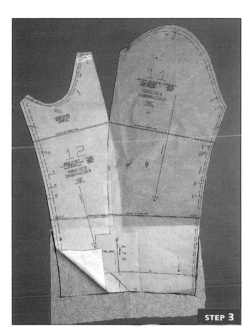

STEP 3

4 Cut four cuffs from fashion fabric—on the bias—to these dimensions. You need two cuff shapes for each sleeve. If your fabric is heavy, such as faux fur, use a lightweight fabric for the two (inner) cuff pieces.

[TIP] I prefer cutting the shape on the bias so that the finished cuff smoothly circles the sleeve. Napped fabric such as faux fur or velvet, however, is cut with the nap going down toward the bottom of the sleeve.

5 Cut a piece of medium-weight interfacing to the same size, also on the bias, and fuse or hand-baste it to the cuff. Join the short ends of all cuffs to form circles. Press the seam allowances open and trim them to ¼ in. (6mm). You now have identical cuff pieces.

6 Turn one set of cuffs right side out. Insert one of the wrong-side-out cuffs into each of the other cuffs. Sew the wide ends of the cuff together.

STEP 6

7 Trim the seam allowances to ¼ in. (6mm). Turn the cuffs so that the wrong sides face each other. Insert a rolled-up magazine or towel or a sleeve roll into the sleeve and press the cuff.

8 Insert a cuff into a sleeve so that the right side of the cuff (if you used a lighter fabric for the inside cuff) is against the wrong side of the sleeve.

9 Shift the garment pieces until the cuff seam is aligned with the sleeve's underarm seam. Sew the cuff to the sleeve as pinned.

STEP 9

10 Trim the seam allowances to ¼ in. (6mm). Serge or apply a Hong Kong finish to the raw edges. Turn the sleeve cuff to the outside of the sleeve. The seam is now hidden.

FACING FOR A HEM

It's imperative that the fashion fabric and lining of a loosely woven fabric hang free. This allows the fabrics to move and drape independently, which is essential for the coat or jacket to hang flawlessly.

In this situation, I like to attach a lining strip to the top of the hem allowance. This conceals the inner workings of the garment while providing a high-quality look. You can use the same application to hide interfacing, underlining, or the wrong side of the fabric where the lining isn't attached.

1 The first step is to make a crisp, smooth hem. Cut a strip of bias interfacing 1 in. (2.5cm) wider than the hem allowance. Make it the same length as the circumference of the jacket at the hem.

[TIP] A crisp, smooth hemline depends on interfacing. Fusi-Knit and Textured Weft are great if you can use a fusible. Otherwise, use sew-in organza or bias-cut hair canvas.

2 Sew a line of stitching near the bottom edge of the coat or jacket. As you stitch, hold your finger on top of the fabric behind the presser foot to slightly ease in the raw edge.

3 If the fabric is very thick, skip the easing and sew a deeper seam allowance in the hem, at about ⅞ in. (2.2cm) or whatever it takes to make the hemline lie smoothly.

4 Turn the hem allowance to the wrong side and press the foldline (hemline). Unfold the hem allowance. To reduce bulk, trim all of the seam allowances in the hem allowance to ¼ in. (6mm).

5 Place the interfacing strip at the bottom of the jacket, with one lengthwise edge positioned right on the crease. The width of the interfacing goes above the hem crease, not on the hem allowance.

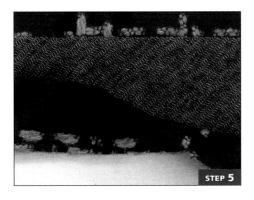

STEP 5

6 Fuse or hand-sew the top and bottom of the interfacing as positioned. A cross-stitch works well for sew-in interfacing.

7 Now for the lining strip that conceals the inner workings of the coat or jacket. Cut a 5-in. (12.7cm) wide piece of lining on the bias. Make the length equal to the circumference of the garment's hem.

8 With right sides together, pin the lining strip to the raw edge at the bottom of the garment. Slightly stretch the lining to fit the hem edge. This helps the lining fit smoothly inside the jacket when folded into position. Sew the strip to the hem with a ¼-in. (6mm) seam allowance.

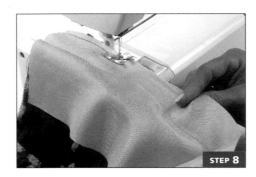

STEP 8

9 Fold up the hem allowance. Leave the lining strip hanging down, with the right side of the lining against the right side of the hem allowance. Sew the hem allowance to the coat ½ in. (1.3cm) below the raw edge of the hem allowance.

TIP Never take a stitch in the hem allowance and the garment at the same time. Take one stitch in the hem, move forward ¼ in. (6mm), and take one stitch in the garment. This type of stitching gives you the most invisible hem. Don't pull the thread too tight between the stitches, and knot the thread every 4 in. (10.2cm).

TRICK *of the* TRADE

HEAVY HEMS

If your fabric is heavy, hem the coat twice. Sew the first row of hand stitching halfway up the hem allowance and the second row near the top. This distributes the weight of the hem allowance and renders it far less visible.

10 Lift the lining strip above the hem allowance on the inside of the garment. Turn under the loose raw edge and hand-sew it to the garment the same way you attached the hem allowance to the jacket.

STEP 10

VISUAL GUIDE TO BAGGING A LINING

The method I describe on the next few pages is the only one used in the industry because it is fast, fast, fast. Fred Bloebaum, creator of La Fred patterns, showed me this wonderful technique.

The first portion of these instructions covers the preparation of the lining and jacket. The second half shows you—with step-by-step photographs—how to bag a lining the fast-and-easy way. Almost all of the seaming in this bagging technique is done by machine, thus bypassing the time-consuming hand method that most home sewers use.

Lining and Jacket Preparation

1 For the lining, fold up the hem allowance on the front, back, and sleeve pattern pieces. This way, the body and sleeves are cut to the finished length of the garment.

2 If you lengthen or shorten your jacket pattern before cutting, or decide to shorten the jacket after the first fitting, an identical adjustment must be made on the lining for it to hang properly. Sleeve adjustments also follow this rule.

3 On the lining, add a 1⅝-in. (4.2cm) wide extension down the length of the center back if the pattern piece was intended to be cut on a fabric fold. Now you have a center-back seam. If the pattern already has a center-back seam, merely widen the seam allowance.

4 Cut the front, back, and sleeve pattern pieces from the lining fabric. Remember that the back is no longer cut on the fabric fold.

5 With right sides together, sew the lining pieces together at center back, leaving a 6-in. (15.2cm) long opening in the middle of the seamline. When you're finished bagging the lining, the jacket is pulled right side out through this opening.

6 Also on the center back of the lining, sew a 1⅝-in. (4.1cm) seam allowance from the bottom edge to the waist and from the neck edge toward the waist for 4 in. (10.2cm). This leaves a pleat opening from waist to shoulder, where you need it.

7 Join all of the lining pieces at the seams and shoulders. Insert the sleeves in the lining.

TIP Switch to a 70/10 HJ needle for pucker-free seams in lining fabric.

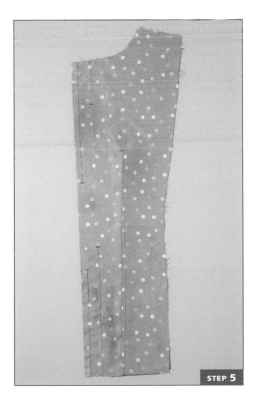

STEP 5

8 Completely construct the jacket, including adding facings, inserting shoulder pads, and hemming the bottom and sleeves of the jacket. Insert the pockets, make the buttonholes, and sew on the buttons.

9 Press the finished lining and the separate jacket because you won't be able to press open any of the seam allowances later.

10 Hand-stitch the hem allowance to the garment ½ in. (1.3cm) from the edge of the hem allowance so that you have enough fabric above the stitching to machine-sew the lining and garment together.

[TIP] Before beginning the lining process, interface hems on jacket and coat bottoms and sleeves. See Steps 5 and 6 in "Facing for a Hem" on p. 212. The result is crisper hems, which give the jacket or coat a more professional appearance.

Seams Easy Bagging

1 With right sides together, pin the lining and jacket along the fronts and neck facing, placing the pins on the facing side. Place the stable, interfaced side up when sewing. The bottom raw edge of the lining should match up with the hem crease at the bottom of the jacket.

2 Sew one continuous seam from the bottom of one front facing, up one side, around the neck, and back down the other side. Start and end this seam 1 in. (2.5cm) above the bottom edge of the lining. Press the seam allowances toward the lining.

STEP 2

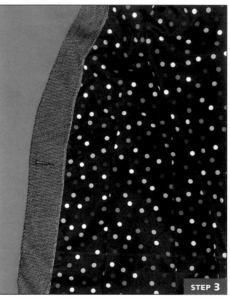

STEP 3

3 If desired, cover and decorate this seam by sewing on a narrow piece of flat braid or machine-sewing over the seam with decorative stitches.

[TIP] Piping is too bulky and makes an imprint during pressing.

4 Turn the garment right side out. Insert the sleeve linings into the sleeves of the garment. Try on the jacket.

5 Pin the garment and corresponding lining at the bottom of the sleeves. This step prevents the sleeve lining from twisting when you attach it.

STEP 5

6 Take off the jacket. Reach in from the open bottom edge between the garment and the lining. Turn one of the sleeves, including the lining, wrong side out by pulling it out between the bottom of the jacket and the lining. The garment sleeve will pull the jacket with it since they're pinned at the bottom edges of the sleeve at the seam joints.

7 Place the bottom edge of the sleeve lining onto the sleeve hem of the garment with raw edges even. Make sure that the sleeve seams are aligned (think of two elephants matching their trunks).

8 Sew the bottom of the sleeve lining to the fashion-fabric sleeve using a ¼-in. or ⅜-in. (6mm or 1cm) seam allowance.

STEP 8

9 Turn the seamed sleeve and lining right side out. Join the second sleeve and lining in the same manner. The lining is now attached to the jacket everywhere except at the bottom edge.

10 Spread the jacket on the table with the lining side down and the outside of the jacket facing you. Fold the sleeves into the middle, on top of the jacket.

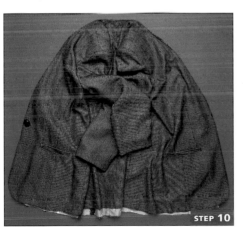

STEP 10

11 Turn the jacket back on itself by lifting up the hem of the jacket and bringing it toward the jacket's shoulders. Continue until the right side

of the jacket hem and the raw edge of the right side of the lining meet. The bulk of the jacket and sleeves are trapped inside this roll. Match the side seams on the jacket and the lining.

STEP 11

12 Sew the jacket hem to the bottom edge of the lining with a continuous ¼-in. to ⅜-in. (6mm to 1cm) seam allowance. Start at one side of a facing and stitch across the hem to the opposite facing, sewing only the jacket hem. Start and stop stitching 1 in. (2.5cm) before the ends of the lining.

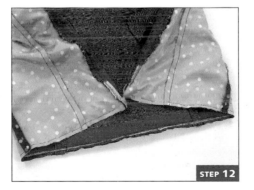

STEP 12

13 To turn the jacket right side out, reach in through the 6-in. (15.2cm) opening at center back of the lining. Turn the jacket right side out.

14 Using a ⅝-in. (15mm) seam allowance, close the opening with hand or machine stitching and press the pleat to hide the sewing. Fold in and hand-sew the raw corners of the hem's lining. Press.

STEP 14

15 Align the jacket and lining at the underarm seams. From the outside of the jacket, sew in the well of the seam for 1 in. (2.5cm) at the side seams of both underarms.

⌈TIP⌉ Another option for securing the lining to the jacket is linking the underarms at the side seam with a 1-in. (2.5cm) long piece of twill tape.

STEP 15

BETTER BUTTONHOLES

Even experienced sewers admit that making machine buttonholes is like playing Russian roulette: The results can be unpredictable. There are tremendous differences in quality among machines. We debate the merits of computerized versus mechanical sewing machines, and some swear by the old buttonhole attachments we used years ago.

Regardless of the buttonholer you prefer, I have numerous tips to give you more control over the end results. If funky-looking buttonholes ruin your beautifully constructed garments, you can dramatically improve your results. Using water-soluble stabilizers and learning to work with the feed dogs on your machine will increase your chances of success.

1 Determining the correct buttonhole size is tricky with domed and three-dimensional buttons. To determine the exact size of the buttonhole, wrap a piece of ribbon or Stay Tape around the button. Mark the point where the ends of the ribbon meet. Slide out the button and flatten the ribbon loop. Your buttonhole should be ⅛ in. (3mm) longer than this measurement.

2 There's an easy way to figure out the position of your buttons: Divide by the total number of spaces between the buttons, not the number of buttons. The number of spaces is always one less than the number of buttons. For example, to apply seven buttons over an 18-in. (45.7cm) area, use 3-in. (7.6cm) spaces. The formula is $18 \div 6 = 3$ ($45.7cm \div 6 = 7.6cm$).

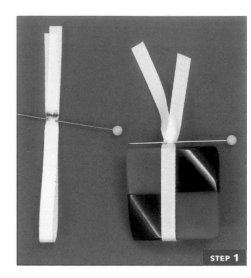

STEP 1

3 Cut a rectangle of fusible webbing slightly larger than the buttonhole area. Slip it between the facing and the garment at the buttonhole. Press to secure the layers.

4 Mark the beginning and end of the buttonhole on the garment with two parallel rows of hand or machine basting. Stitch from the neck to the hem, using a contrasting-color thread.

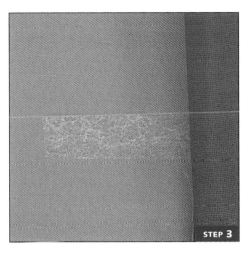

STEP 3

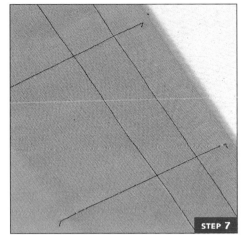

STEP 7

STEP 11

[TIP] Buttonholes are placed on the right front for women's garments and on the left front for men's garments.

5 Place the first basting line (marking the inner buttonhole edge) ¾ in. (1.9cm) from the finished edge of the garment. Space the second basting line the width of the buttonhole.

6 It's much easier to place buttonholes when the positions are basted on the garment front. The vertical basting lines also prevent the fabric layers from slipping during stitching.

7 At each buttonhole placement mark, baste horizontally from the garment edge to just past the inner (second) line of basting.

[TIP] Except in the case of shirts, buttonholes are horizontal to the garment.

8 Attach a buttonhole foot to your machine, preferably a foot that has two parallel grooves on the bottom. If your garment surface is uneven—or if there's a bulky seam—a sliding buttonhole foot is a better option.

9 Loosen the machine's top tension to produce a better-looking satin stitch on the right side of the garment. Place fine machine-embroidery thread in the bobbin and, if your fabric is lightweight, in the needle. Finer thread eliminates buildup on the underside of the buttonhole.

[TIP] I get the best results with a new 70/10 HJ needle. The point easily pierces multiple fabric layers without slowing down.

10 Draw buttonhole placement lines on a piece of water-soluble stabilizer. Place the stabilizer between the fabric and the buttonhole foot, aligning it with the basted placement lines. (You don't have to mark the stabilizer if you can see your basting through it.)

11 Insert another strip of stabilizer between the fabric and the feed dogs. It's important to use stabilizer both on top of and underneath your garment to keep the fabric moving smoothly during stitching and to prevent the buttonhole from stretching.

12 Starting buttonholes from the outside edge of the garment may prevent the buttonhole foot from lying flat. It's best to start the buttonhole away from the outside edge and work toward the finished edge of the garment. However, if you own a sewing machine that makes a buttonhole from front to back in a way that allows the buttonhole foot to remain flat, you can start at the garment edge.

[TIP] If your machine has an automatic tie-off feature, override this so that you decide where the buttonhole ends. The machine may slow down where it "thinks" the buttonhole should end, but keep your foot on the pedal until you reach the actual end of the buttonhole.

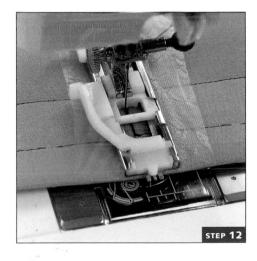

STEP 12

13 Position the buttonhole foot, step on the pedal, and let the machine do its thing. Any help from you will cause a gap between the stitches.

14 Cut the needle and bobbin threads of the completed buttonhole 3 in. (7.6cm) long. Tug the bobbin thread to pull the needle thread to the underside. Tie off the threads.

15 After cutting open the buttonhole, color the interfacing at the cut edges to match the fabric using a permanent felt-tipped pen. Dab No Fray or Fray Stoppa on the back of the buttonhole with a toothpick. This seals the color and prevents fraying.

TRICK
of the TRADE
WORD OF WARNING

If the area where you intend to place your buttonhole is so thick that you're having trouble sliding it under the buttonhole presser foot, the buttonhole will be a disaster. Avoid frustration by using an alternative closure such as decorative snaps, button loops, or frogs; or create an opening in a seam.

CORDED BUTTONHOLES

A reinforced buttonhole is the only way to go on a coat or jacket. The opening is more substantial and the cord helps the buttonhole maintain its shape.

In most cases, the corded buttonhole instructions that came with your machine explain how to use the buttonhole presser foot and adjust the machine settings. But there's much more you can do to make a gorgeous buttonhole. Placement, buttonhole positioning, directional stitching, and finishing greatly improve the quality of your corded buttonholes. The following instructions explain how to make a single corded buttonhole.

1 Cut two patches of water-soluble stabilizer 1 in. (2.5cm) longer and wider than the buttonhole. Place one stabilizer patch between the fabric and the buttonhole foot. Insert the second patch between the fabric and the feed dogs.

2 Position your buttonhole foot on the garment. Unless your sewing machine makes buttonholes going backward, you must sew toward the garment edge, not away from it. This ensures two perfectly spaced, parallel rows of stitches because the seam at the edge doesn't prop up the presser foot.

3 Stitching toward the garment edge also supports the stress point for a corded buttonhole. Take the first stitch by turning the handwheel. Lift up the presser foot. Loop the cord on the protrusion at the front of the foot and pull the ends of the cord to the back.

4 Lower the presser foot. Don't touch or pull the cord again. The grooves on the bottom of the buttonhole foot hold it in place.

STEP 4

5 Sew your buttonhole. Help the machine make the buttonhole—by pulling or pushing on the fabric—only if your fabric is very heavy. Because you're sewing toward the finished garment edge, the buttonhole foot is seated properly. The fabric feeds evenly under the needle and the rows are equally spaced.

6 When the buttonhole is completed, pull on the ends of the cord so that it's hidden under the stitches. Thread each end of the cord individually into a hand needle with a large eye, and pull the strand to the underside. Tie the ends in a square knot and cut off the excess. (The stabilizer was eliminated from the photo for better visibility.)

7 Pull off the stabilizer and press the stitching. Open the buttonhole, color the raw edges of the exposed interfacing with a matching permanent felt-tipped pen, and apply a liquid seam sealant to the underside of the button-hole and to the cord's knot.

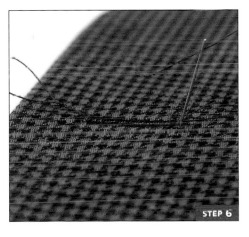

STEP 6

WEIGHTED HEM

Coco Chanel made this treatment famous in her chic jackets. Despite the passing years, a weighted hem is still considered a hallmark of a quality gar-ment. It's a final touch that makes a jacket look and feel expensive. Today, weighting chain is found only inside couture garments—and the clothes hanging in the closet of a savvy sewer.

The key to success is finding chain with enough weight but without the bulk that makes it visible from the exte-rior of the garment. Tailoring-supply companies carry this. (See Resources on p. 226.) Apply weighting chain by hand-sewing it to the seamline of the hem and the lining (see the photo below).

1 Completely assemble your jacket. Metal chain cuts through regular sewing thread, so use a single strand of upholstery thread or unwaxed dental floss in your hand-sewing needle. You can dip the dental floss in tea to darken it.

2 Position the jacket front so that the inside is facing you. Place one end of the chain at the inner edge of the front facing, near the top of the hem allowance.

3 Fold back the lining take-up tuck and position the chain on the seam-line joining the hem allowance to the lining. Hand-sew the start of the link to the jacket. Take a few stitches here to secure the ends.

STEP 3

4 Slide the needle along the underside of the seamline, bringing it out through the third link. Loop the thread over the top of the link and reinsert it into the seamline. Continue attaching the chain to the seamline every third or fourth link.

5 When you reach the facing on the opposite front, cut off the chain with wire cutters and secure the end with a few extra stitches.

PATTERN LIST

If you would like to sew your own version of a garment pictured in this book, the following is a list of the patterns that Sandra used. Patterns, like fashions, change frequently, and the original patterns are sometimes unavailable. In these cases, we have substituted similar patterns.

Vogue 7065 (see p. 24)

Vogue 7065 (see p. 28)

Vogue 7065 (see p. 25)

L. J. Designs 791 Short and Sassy (see p. 30)

Chapter 2

VESTS

Vest pattern from Sandra's book *No Time to Sew* (see p. 22)

Vogue 7065 without collar (see p. 26)

Betzina vest pattern from The Sewing Workshop Pattern Collection (see p. 31)

Betzina vest pattern from The Sewing Workshop Pattern Collection (see p. 23)

Vest pattern from Sandra's book *No Time to Sew* (see p. 27)

Discontinued Burda pattern, similar to Burda 2599 (see p. 33)

Vogue 7065
(see p. 36)

Discontinued
McCall's pattern,
similar to Stretch
& Sew 1515
(see p. 38)

Burda 3151
(see p. 44)

Chapter 3

PANTS

Vogue 7179
(see p. 48)

Vogue 7027
(see p. 50)

Vogue 7027
(see p, 51)

Vogue 7027
(see p. 52)

Vogue 7179
(see p. 53)

Discontinued Burda
pattern, pants
similar to
Vogue 7179
(see p. 55)

Burda 3193 with
zipper added to
pocket using
Sandra's technique
in this book
(see p. 67)

Discontinued
Shermane Fouche
pattern, similar to
Vogue 2333 with-
out belt loops and
widening legs
(see p. 69)

Burda 3204
(see p. 71)

Chapter 4

SKIRTS

Vogue 7087 View C
(Wrap top discontinued Burda, nothing similar)
(see p. 90)

Burda 3694
(see p. 94)

Vogue 7027
(see p. 75)

Vogue 9175 with top layer cut 6 in. shorter
(see p. 91)

Vogue 7025
(see p. 102)

Vogue 7027
(see p. 80)

Vogue 9541
(see p. 92)

Betzina skirt pattern from The Sewing Workshop Pattern Collection
(see p. 104)

La Fred Thalia Pants Pattern
(see p. 83)

See technique for tube skirt on p. 93

Burda 3694
(see p. 107)

Gored skirt pattern with godets added from Sandra's book *No Time to Sew*
(see p. 108)

Discontinued
Burda, nothing
similar
(see p. 110)

Gored skirt pattern
from Sandra's book
No Time to Sew
(see p. 114)

Vogue 9541
(see p. 120)

Vogue 7136
(see p. 121)

Chapter 5

DRESSES

Vogue 7024
extended 20 in.
in length
(see p. 124)

Vogue 7024
(see p. 124)

Burda 3118
(see p. 125)

Vogue 7055
(see p. 126)

Vogue 7055
(see p. 127)

Vogue 7055
(see p. 128)

Burda 3118
shortened for top
(see p. 130)

Vogue 7136
(see p. 132)

Burda 3101
(see p. 138)

Vogue 7024
(see p. 140)

D'Leas Jacket
D'Leas Fabric Affair
2719 E. 3rd Ave.
Denver, CO 80206
(303) 388-5665
(see p. 160)

Vogue 2188
(see p. 169)

Vogue 7263
(see p. 145)

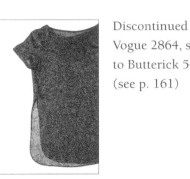

Discontinued
Vogue 2864, similar
to Butterick 5471
(see p. 161)

Vogue 7022
(see p. 170)

McCall's 7412
(see p. 147)

Chapter 6

JACKETS

Burda 3860
(see p. 171)

Haiku jacket
pattern from The
Sewing Workshop
Pattern Collection
(see p. 166)

Simplicity 7114
(see p. 149)

Burda 3120
(see p. 172)

Discontinued
Burda
(see p. 159)

Burda 2555
(see p. 167)

Vogue 2191 (runs
large, so check fit
before cutting)
(see p. 176)

Burda 2555 with collar added and shortened 5 in. (see p. 181)

Burda 2555 (see p. 188)

Burda 3647 (see p. 208)

Vogue 7022 (see p. 183)

Discontinued Burda, similar to Butterick 6208 (see p. 190)

Discontinued Burda, similar to Butterick 5764 (see p. 210)

Burda 2960 (see p. 185)

Burda 2555 (see p. 196)

Neue Mode 21386 (see p. 213)

Burda 3100 (see p. 187)

Vogue 7022 (see p. 199)

Vogue 7065 (see p. 216)

Burda 2846 (see p. 200)

AUTHOR

Power Sewing
95 Fifth Ave.
San Francisco, CA 94118
(415) 386-0440
(415) 386-0441 FAX
www.SandraBetzina.com
Free brochure available
Watch Sandra on HGTV and visit
with her at craftshop.com.

SMALL, INDEPENDENT PATTERN COMPANIES

Birch Street Clothing
PO Box 6901
1021 S. Claremont St.
San Mateo, CA 94403
(415) 578-9729
(800) 736-0854
www.birchstreetclothing.com

Clothing Designs by La Fred
4200 Park Blvd., Ste. 102
Oakland, CA 94602
(510) 893-6811
http://getcreativeshow.com/
la_fred.htm

Design & Sew Patterns
PO Box 5222
Salem, OR 97304
(503) 364-6285
www.designandsew.com

Diane Ericson/ReVisions
PO Box 7404
Carmel, CA 93921
(831) 659-1989
www.revisions-ericson.com

Great Copy Patterns
PO Box 85329
Racine, WI 53408-5329
(414) 632-2660

Kwik-Sew Patterns
3000 Washington Ave. N.
Minneapolis, MN 55411-1699
(612) 521-7651
(800) 328-3953
(888) 594-5739
www.kwiksew.com

L. J. Designs
PO Box 21116
Reno, NV 89515
(775) 853-2207

MacPhee Outerwear Workshop
Box 10, Site 16, RR 8
Edmonton, AB, T5L 4H8
Canada
(403) 976-3516

Park Bench Pattern Co.
PO Box 1089
Petaluma, CA 94953
(707) 781-9142
www.sewnet.com/parkbench

Patterns for everyBody
The Sewing Place
PO Box 111446
Campbell, CA 95011
(800) LVSEWERS
(800-587-3937)

The Sewing Workshop Pattern Collection
2010 Balboa St.
San Francisco, CA 94121
(415) 221-7397
(800) 466-1599
www.sewingworkshop.com

Silhouette Pattern Co.
Peggy Sagers
305 Spring Valley Village #326
Dallas, TX 75248
(972) 960-7373

Stretch & Sew
2035 S. El Camino Dr.
PO Box 25306
Tempe, AZ 85285
(602) 966-1462
(800) 547-7717
www.stretch-and-sew.com

MAJOR PATTERN COMPANIES

Burda Pattern Co.
PO Box 670628
Marietta, GA 30066
(770) 421-1234
(800) 241-6887

Butterick/Vogue Pattern Co.
161 Ave. of the Americas
New York, NY 10013
(212) 620-2601
(800) 766-2670
www.butterick.com
www.voguepatterns.com

The McCall Pattern Co.
11 Penn Plaza
New York, NY 10001
(212) 465-6800
(800) 782-0323
www.mccall.com

Simplicity Pattern Co.
2 Park Ave., 12th floor
New York, NY 10016
(212) 372-0500
(800) 334-3150
www.simplicitypatt.com

FURTHER INSTRUCTION

**Islander School
of Fashion, Inc.**
PO Box 66
Grants Pass, OR 97528
(541) 479-3906
www.Islandersewing.com

INDEX

OTHER THREADS BOOKS

Look for these and other Taunton Press titles at your local bookstore. You can order them direct by calling (800) 888-8286 or by visiting our website at www.taunton.com. Call for a free catalog.

- The Art of Fabric Collage
- Beyond the Pattern
- A Close-Knit Family
- Couture Sewing Techniques
- Distinctive Details
- Embellishments A to Z
- 50 Heirloom Buttons to Make
- Fabric Savvy
- Family Album
- Fine Embellishment Techniques
- Fine Machine Sewing
- Fit and Fabric
- Fitting Solutions
- Fitting Your Figure
- Great Quilting Techniques
- Great Sewn Clothes
- Hand-Manipulated Stitches for Machine Knitters
- Jackets, Coats and Suits
- The Jean Moss Book of World Knits
- Just Pockets
- Kaffe's Classics
- The Knit Hat Book
- Knitted Sweater Style
- Knitting Bazaar
- Knitting Counterpanes

- Knitting Emporium
- Knitting Lace
- Knitting Tips & Trade Secrets
- Linen and Cotton
- Mosaics
- Quilts and Quilting
- Ribbon Knits
- Ribbon Trims
- Rudgyard Story
- Scarves to Make
- Sew the New Fleece
- Sewing Basics
- Sewing for Plus Sizes
- The Sewing Machine Guide
- Sewing Tips & Trade Secrets
- Shirtmaking
- Techniques for Casual Clothes

Sewing Companion Library:
- Easy Guide to Serging Fine Fabrics
- Easy Guide to Sewing Blouses
- Easy Guide to Sewing Jackets
- Easy Guide to Sewing Linings
- Easy Guide to Sewing Pants
- Easy Guide to Sewing Skirts
- Easy Guide to Sewing Tops and T-Shirts